Reason or Rebellion?

Women's Fight for the Vote
in Devon

Pamela Vass

Pamela Vass,

Boundstone Books

First published in Great Britain in 2025 by Boundstone Books,
Tree Tops, Downs Lane, West Looe, Cornwall. PL13 2HX

ISBN: 978-0-9568709-7-1

Printed and bound in Great Britain by SRP, Exeter.

Dedication

In memory of my mother, a remarkable woman. Born into a world where women were still disenfranchised, at 99 she was the eldest person to vote at her local polling station, determined to exercise such a hard won right to the end.

Also by Pamela Vass

Fiction

Seeds of Doubt
Shadow Child

Non-Fiction

The Power of Three
Breaking The Mould
On Course for Recovery

Edited works

In My Own Words

For more information on Pamela Vass and her books see:
www.boundstonebooks.co.uk

Author's Note

In 2017 *Breaking The Mould, The Suffragette Story in North Devon* was published. It's a story I came across by accident when I stumbled on the remains of a grand mansion on Hollerday Hill in Lynton. It had been the pride and joy of Liberal MP Sir George Newnes, a great benefactor to the town. After his death it remained empty, until one night in August 1913 when the house was gutted by fire giving rise to persistent rumours. Was it an insurance scam? Or were suffragettes to blame?

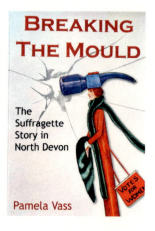

The question proved irresistible. Researching original documents, newspapers and reports between 1909 and 1913, I pieced together the events that led up to that fateful night. The story was told, or so I thought. But more themes were emerging.

There is much more to women's fight for the vote across Devon than previously told. The characters and events depicted in *Breaking The Mould* are included here but are now just part of a much wider story. Many Devon women chose a different path to make their voices heard, focusing on reason rather than rebellion.

The story also starts earlier, with the campaigning that swept the region during the 1870s and 1880s. Far from being an isolated outpost, Devon was in the sights of some of the most talented, outspoken, challenging and dedicated speakers of the time, women with the courage and character to flout convention and claim a political voice.

Wherever possible this story is told in the women's own words, taken from suffrage and regional newspapers of the day. Some passages are imagined and, while the text is not footnoted, all details are thoroughly researched from the sources listed in the appendix and reflect women's campaign for the vote across Devon, set against the background of the national story.

Acknowledgements

I am grateful to the following individuals and institutions for access to their archives, permission to include images, and for the knowledge they have so generously shared with me.

Ann Tanner at Sidmouth Museum, Margaret Atherton; Peter Christie; London Museum; Anne Corry, Gisela Aitken-Davies, Charles Payne; Mary Evans Picture library; Women's Library, LSE; British Library; North Devon Record Office; Westcountry Studies Library; Bideford & District Archive; Braunton Museum; Ilfracombe Museum; Gloucester Archive; The National Archives and The British Newspaper Archive. Also to John Derrick for his valuable historical insights and endless proof-reading.

My particular thanks go to Dr Julia Neville and all those who contributed to the Devon History Society Suffrage Activists Index. Although it hasn't been possible to include all the amazing women who campaigned across Devon, many of the women referenced there form part of this story. For further information see the Devon History Society index: https://www.devonhistorysociety.org.uk/devon-suffrage-activists-index/

Contents

This is "THE HOUSE" that man built,
And these are the Suffragettes of note
Determined to fight for their right to vote;
For they mean to be, each one an M. P.
And they'll keep their vow some fine day you'll see,
For the Suffragette is determined to get
Into "THE HOUSE" that man built.

Prologue
Ilfracombe, North Devon
January 1909

Marie is late. She hurries through streets unusually busy for a dark January night, not with couples out for an evening stroll or families returning home, but women, hundreds of them, streaming towards the Runnacleave Hotel. She's tempted to turn back. The hall might be full. No point squeezing herself in near the door where she'll not hear anything. Besides, there's more than enough to get on with at home.

'Marie.' A voice calls from behind. Marie hesitates, only to be buffeted by women pushing past. 'Glad I've caught up with you.' Annie Ball tucks her arm through Marie's. 'We can go in together, bit of Dutch courage.'

'I was just thinking… if it's going to be busy…'

'Brilliant isn't it? Not every day we get a militant here, so I'm not surprised. Come on.' There was no arguing with Annie Ball when she set her mind to something. Probably why she made such a good superintendent of the Nursing Homes in Ilfracombe and Barnstaple. She was made for business, as well as being an excellent nurse.

They hurry on, heads bent against the wind driving around Capstone Hill. It's the YMCA's first debate of the year and the organisers have lured Annie

Kenney, one of the new breed of militant suffragettes, to this rural outpost. The papers have christened her 'The Oldham Firebrand' for her fearless heckling of politicians and Parliament. Not to mention her orchestration of the mass marches and street protests that inevitably end in scuffles with the police and undignified arrests. It promises to be an interesting night.

They join the queue filtering through the conservatory entrance. 'Oh,' Marie exclaims, pointing to a notice displayed in the foyer. 'Miss Adela Pankhurst replaces Miss Annie Kenney for this evening's debate.'

'Would have been good to hear Miss Kenney but think about it, an actual Pankhurst, here in Ilfracombe!' Annie Ball is irrepressible. 'I mean, the Pankhursts are forever making headlines up country but can you ever remember one coming here?' She presses ahead into the cavernous hall that reeks of faded elegance. Mahogany panels frame enormous arched windows, obscured by folds of velvet drapes.

'But who is Adela Pankhurst?' Marie asks as Annie leads the way to seats near the front. 'I've heard of Christabel, even Sylvia, but Adela?'

Several men and one woman climb the wooden steps to the stage. 'That must be her,' Annie whispers.

It would be easy to be underwhelmed by Adela Pankhurst, barely five feet tall, slender and so nervous you'd think there was a price on her head. Nothing like the Amazon many might expect given press coverage of the Pankhursts.

The chairman steps forward. 'The question of woman suffrage is very much to the fore just now and demands serious consideration. Miss Adela Pankhurst will speak for the motion, Mr Blackmore against.'

Adela glances nervously round the hall then steps to the front of the stage. 'Ladies and gentlemen, I'm here to propose that the Parliamentary Franchise should be granted to women on the same terms as men.'

'The Parliamentary Franchise, that's the…' Marie whispers.

'The Vote, yes.'

'Men have won their liberty,' Adela continues. 'No taxes are imposed or laws made except by their direct representatives in the Commons. But women are excluded from such privilege. They also pay taxes but have no voice in how those taxes are spent.' Murmurs and mutterings follow every statement, with more than a little heckling from the men.

'The anti-suffragists say a woman's place is at home. They claim home would be neglected if women had Parliamentary duties. Well, women who have the municipal vote wash up, sew buttons on and cook dinner just as well.'

Laughter ripples across the hall - women's laughter.

'Criminals, lunatics, paupers - and women - have no vote. Is it not high time to lift us out of such company.' (Laughter and cheers.)

Mr Blackmore takes centre stage. 'The course proposed by Miss Pankhurst would lead to national disaster! Where is the evidence that the vote is wanted by more than a noisy handful of women? It is too great a sacrifice to gain the Parliamentary vote at the cost of our home life. Women are by nature unfitted for politics, their influence in the proper sphere will be greater without the franchise.'

The chairman has to shout over the bedlam. 'I would remind you,' he strains, 'that it is our tradition to give each speaker a fair hearing. I now open the debate to the floor.'

Arguments for and against rattle across the room until the chairman calls for the speakers to sum up. Adela stands. 'My opponents have made up their speeches before the meeting and have answered none of my arguments. (Laughter.) In Australia and New Zealand as soon as women had the vote men asked what they wanted.'

The news sinks in. Britain ruled the Empire yet two of her territories had already given women the vote! If there, why not here?

Adela continues. 'Women care for their children but no woman has a right to her child after it is seven years old. The law then recognises but one parent, the man! Let women have the vote to shape the law.' (Applause and cheers) Marie shudders. To have no say in her daughter's life. It was unthinkable.

'We'll move to a vote,' the chairman announces. 'Those for?' He pauses as tellers work their way down the rows. 'Those against?' Another rustling as arms are raised. But Marie's hands stay clenched in her lap. So much she has heard this evening has shocked and angered her, but to associate herself with women who commit criminal acts serious enough to put them in prison! It was a step too far - for now. She waits as the clerk hands the Chairman a piece of paper.

'On the Resolution that the Parliamentary Franchise be granted to women the voting is as follows.' He pauses for effect. 'For, 114. Against, 115.'

'You see the difference one vote can make,' Annie says.

Chapter One
Breaking The Mould
1866 - 1884

On that dark winter's night in rural Devon 'Votes for Women' became more than a slogan vaguely recognised from newspaper headlines. A woman had stepped onto a public stage, shocking in itself, and challenged her audience to wake up and embrace change. Not only that, but to publicly join her in that fight for change. It's a challenge we will explore but the story of votes for women actually started well before 1909, possibly much earlier than you might imagine.

A few well-placed women were able to vote as far back as the 1500s, although convention and propriety often deterred them. Unless involved with the Crown it was not seen as a woman's place to be involved in national politics, a theme that lingered on into the twentieth century. In 1832 this often contested arrangement was settled once and for all when a Reform Act was passed defining a voter as a male person. When Mary Smith from Leeds challenged this the only response was laughter in Parliament and a damning report in *The Times* which called her petition, 'simply absurd... in all affairs of civil rights, women are the gainers in their being administered solely by men.' You can imagine MPs shouting 'hear hear' as they passed laws reinforcing the principle that women needed men to manage their affairs for their own protection and benefit. Increasingly many women begged to differ. They needed the power to shape the laws that directly affected them. They needed the vote.

In 1866 Parliament was considering extending voting rights for men. In less than a month, 1,521 women from across the country had signed a petition demanding that at least some should be part of any Bill, including four from Devon: Catherine, Ada and MaryAnne Johnson from Honiton and Mary Caroline Cockrem from Torquay. Four women prepared to risk ridicule and derision to send out a powerful signal that it was increasingly unthinkable for women not to have a public voice on political issues. John Stuart Mill presented the petition to Parliament preparing the ground for when the Government introduced a new Reform Bill the following year. Mill then proposed an amendment in favour of female suffrage, replacing the word 'man' with 'person'. It was defeated by 196 votes to 73, with just two Devon MPs, the Hon George Denman (Tiverton) and Walter Morrison (Plymouth), voting in favour.

The franchise was extended, but only to more men. This was possibly the first time that the challenge ahead of them became clear for many women. They had to find a way of influencing, persuading, cajoling, forcing even, male MPs to publicly support votes for women.

Curiously, in November 1867 one woman did vote. Lily Maxwell from Manchester had a shop, so paid rates to the council. All men who paid rates were eligible to vote and somehow, in a by-election that year, Lily's name appeared on the list of electors. The returning officer had no choice but to hear her vote - 'hear' as votes were cast out loud at the time. She was clear she wanted to vote for Jacob Bright, a Liberal MP and supporter of women's suffrage. This emphatically contradicted a commonly held view that women had no political opinions. But women were still *persona non grata* when it came to voting. A court dismissed her claim, along with others who tried to exercise the same right. It ruled that, '...the word "man" included women when referring to the observance of laws and taxation [in other words, 'yes' when talking responsibilities] but included only male persons when referring to the Parliamentary franchise.' So, emphatically 'no' when it came to benefits.

It was time for the women to organise. In 1867 the National Society for Women's Suffrage was launched, bringing together societies that had already formed in London, Manchester, Edinburgh, Dublin, Bristol and Birmingham. The movement was gathering momentum. Women now spoke from public platforms, wrote pamphlets, lobbied MPs, organised petitions and sent speakers to all parts of the country, including Devon. It's easy to underestimate how significant this was. The lobbying, the public speaking, the drafting of political leaflets was definitely not considered acceptable, let alone ladylike. Women were turning expectations of what was considered appropriate behaviour upside down.

They were also doing this at a time when the only means of widespread communication was the written or spoken word. The expansion of the railways meant that women involved in the campaign could now travel the nation at speed and relatively cheaply. They were often met by enthusiastic crowds, happy to turn out to support, heckle, or simply enjoy this week's entertainment in the form of a new speaker at the local town hall. National and local newspapers covered speeches in detail, ensuring that an increasingly literate population were kept informed of this new movement, something that proved true even in rural Devon. All this activity was the precursor to three decades of campaigning that are often overlooked in the rush to get to the headline-grabbing events of the early 1900s. These earlier decades deliver an equally fascinating story.

In March 1870 a public meeting was organised at the Mechanics Institute in Plymouth. It was a response to what was already being seen as a growing movement to give women ratepayers the vote. Speakers included Mr Walter Morrison, Liberal MP for Plymouth and one of the two who had voted for John Stuart Mill's amendment. Among other justifications for giving women the vote, he thought it a scandal that they were so disadvantaged by laws that gave her no protection from a violent husband, or right to her own property.

After two and a half hours of wide-ranging debate, the motion, '...
that it is expedient to admit women to the franchise', was passed
unanimously. The procedure was then for the local MP, in this case
Mr Morrison, to present the petition to the Prime Minister. The more
petitions, the more pressure the women hoped to exert on the
government. So far so good. But two things leap out from this
gathering. On the positive side, men were actively lobbying for votes
for women but on the other hand, these were meetings exclusively
addressed by men still speaking *for* women. This was about to change.

In 1871 Mrs, or more accurately Madame, Jane Ronniger, arrived
in Devon, intent on drumming up support for a Suffrage Bill that was
coming before Parliament. As a French artist and performer she was
quite a draw and, according to John Stuart Mill, being pretty helped
with the male audiences. A reporter from the *Southern Times* wrote,
'She possesses a clear, sweet-toned voice and her enunciation,
although a trifle too rapid, is very distinct... Her musical voice fell
pleasantly on the ear...' Reporters often focused on the delivery of
women speakers. There were no microphones to ensure they could be
heard at the back of the hall or to help overcome noisy barracking.
The ability and confidence to own the stage and project their voice
was essential. Mrs Ronniger also demonstrated considerable stamina,
with a speaking programme covering six venues in Cornwall before
she arrived at Devonport on 27 February.

In her speech she was keen to clear up any misunderstandings
that might lead her audience to oppose votes for women. *The West
Briton* reported, 'The ideas as to what women's suffrage really meant
had been so vague and uncertain that for the movement to succeed it
had been found necessary for certain advocates to come forward... It
was not intended that a wife should have a vote. It was only proposed
that single women and widows who stood at the head of households
should have a vote... She had found that wherever these grounds had
been stated fairly all opposition rapidly disappeared.' Note her words.
This early movement wasn't about achieving votes for all women, but
exclusively for single and widowed, property-owning women. It was a
first step that was gaining support, demonstrated by figures Jane
Ronniger supplied. There had already been numerous Parliamentary
petitions in favour, with numbers signing increasing from 1,499 in

1866, to 134,539 in 1870. Generating more petitions was her aim on this speaking tour. Names that they would present to the government to convince them there was significant backing for women's suffrage across the country. She received what must have been welcome support from the Devonport audience. The Rev Binns commented, 'He did not believe domestic life would suffer by the suffrage being granted to women; on the contrary, he believed it would become richer and grander in every way by the fact.' The meeting was unanimous in passing a resolution supporting the current Suffrage Bill.

The next advocate to take up the baton in Devon was Millicent Fawcett, a remarkable lady. At 20 she was already giving suffrage talks, at 23 she published a textbook on the 'Political Economy for Beginners' and at 28, co-founded Newnham College for Women, Cambridge. In 1871 she was just 24 when she arrived to address meetings in Tavistock, Plymouth and Exeter. Tavistock New Hall was the venue for many public events. It was there that Millicent Fawcett delivered an impassioned speech demolishing the many reasons commonly given against women having the vote. For example; that women were already sufficiently represented by men; that women were intellectually inferior to men; or that if women had the vote they would want to enter the House of Commons where the intense excitement kindled by political strife would deteriorate their physical powers, and probably lead to insanity! Millicent also had a memorable repost to the objection that suffrage would destroy the harmony of the home. 'The harmony which depended on one note of the chord being dull, was not harmony at all.'

Feelings will surely have run high in the New Hall that evening, and later in drawing rooms across the town, as women read her speech printed in full in the *Tavistock Gazette*. The paper also covered national meetings, keeping women in this part of Devon well informed. They needed to be to counter the views of their local MP, Mr Russell. In 1870 he voted against women having the franchise on the grounds that, 'Women are too impulsive and too much guided by their feelings in their decision of political questions.' The women of Tavistock sent a very different message to Mr Russell with loud and prolonged applause after Millicent Fawcett's speech, and the meeting as a whole voted to support a Bill conferring the franchise on women.

The focus then shifted to the Mechanics Institute in Plymouth where Millicent delivered her lecture on 'Why women require the suffrage" to a packed audience, mainly of women. In her frequently applauded speech she suggested any apathy women felt over her campaign was because they were trained from infancy to believe that they had nothing to do with public affairs. If women had the vote more funds would be diverted to girls schools, colleges and universities. Medical degrees would be open to them. Women were already proving their competence beyond the sphere of the home with their election to school boards; why should they not have authority rather than servitude? Bizarrely, women sometimes benefited from the absurdities of the law as it stood. Millicent quoted the case of a Mrs Torpey who was acquitted of a charge of robbery because the law supposed that a married woman could not act independently of her husband.

Her next engagement was at the Royal Public Rooms in the County town of Exeter. She was accompanied by Lilias Ashworth, Hon. Secretary of the Bristol and West of England Society for Women's Suffrage, the sponsor of this West Country tour. There was immediate controversy when the Chair, Sir John Bowring, announced that the Mayor had been called on to preside but declined stating he had no sympathy with the objects of the meeting. Once the hisses had died down, Sir John ventured that maybe the Mayor was afraid of coming in contact with the eloquence of Mrs Fawcett. In her speech, reported in the *Western Times,* she used that skill to challenge some basic injustices. In her view, representation and taxation must go hand in hand; one class could never be represented by another and an unrepresented class was certain to suffer unjust and oppressive treatment from the hands of those who monopolised the business of making laws and administering them. She challenged a few often repeated clichés, including that women were angels, too good, gentle and pure to be burdened with the coarse, rough work of politics. Their exclusion from the political arena was, therefore, not to be considered a disability but a privilege. Such a privilege, Millicent countered, that the only other people who were permitted to share it were minors, lunatics, felons and idiots.

It was a detailed and well received speech from, as the paper declared, '…a young lady of prepossessing appearance; she has a clear, rich, voice, an excellent delivery, and her words were distinctly heard in all parts of the room.' She hoped that those electors of Exeter who agreed with votes for women would petition Parliament to abolish the measures which now stood in their way. She had obviously won her audience over. They were unanimous in agreeing a petition should be sent to both the House of Commons and the House of Lords.

The momentum continued throughout August 1871 with meetings in Torquay and Teignmouth chaired by Shaldon resident, Colonel Brine. He opened by commenting that, 'The subject was, he believed, a novelty in Teignmouth, and doubtless many were present from motives of curiosity, many more, he hoped, from a sincere desire to aid in a movement which was now becoming general throughout the country.' The speaker, Elizabeth Ramsay, from the Bristol Society, referred to the 619 national petitions, with 186,889 signatures in favour of giving women the vote, that had been sent to Parliament in that year alone. The Colonel's wife, Caroline Brine, already a signed-up supporter with the Manchester Suffrage Society, also gave a brief address, a taster for the more prominent speaking role she later took up. One comment, on the religious and social equality found in some ancient societies, clearly upset the Reverend Lyne who insisted that the Holy Scripture forbade women from speaking in public. After what was described as a 'warm discussion which threatened to wax into a hot theological argument', a gentleman on the platform came to Caroline's defence. 'Sir, my grandmother was a Quaker and spoke constant in church. I'm proud of my grandmother, and I am proud of her speeches; let anyone prove if he can, that she transgressed against the laws of God or man.'

While Torquay voted in favour of an extension of the franchise to women, the Teignmouth audience was more reticent. At the vote there were marginally more against than for, but this was on a sparse show of hands. Colonel Brine made two or three attempts to induce more to vote but the majority of the audience remained unmoved.

Caroline Brine was present two years later when Helena Downing, far right in this photo of the National Suffrage Societies lecturing staff, arrived in Teignmouth as part of a tour of Devon. She began on 16 September 1873 with a meeting in Lynton, then moved on to the Music Hall in Ilfracombe. Fashionable ladies visiting from up country were nothing new for these North Devon resorts, but fashionable ladies who raised a political voice on a public platform, that was very different.

Helena acquitted herself well though, reinforcing the messages already delivered by Jane Ronniger and Millicent Fawcett.

She began, as reported in the *North Devon Journal*, with the traditional view of womanhood. 'The ideal woman - such as men would wish to keep for ever - must be fair and gentle, sheltered from all the cares and storms of life in a father's house, which she never left until she entered that of her husband, to whom she looked thenceforward for guidance, wisdom and support.' Pleasant enough, she continued, 'But... everything that was pleasant was not right... it lessened the sense of responsibility in women... the inferior education given to women was another ground of injustice and inequality...[the vote] would materially help all those [unmarried] women dependent upon their own exertions for a living.'

She couldn't have wished for a more sympathetic review than that in the *North Devon Herald*. 'Miss Downing and her co-workers in this agitation may rest assured their zealous labours will not be in vain, and that the realisation of their aspirations is not far distant.' She moved on to Teignmouth and finally Dawlish, to an audience made up mostly of visitors. The *Women's Suffrage Journal* covered her essential message there. 'The advocates of women's suffrage asked simply that women who occupy houses and pay rates should be entitled in the same way as men are to vote for members of Parliament, and that the fundamental principle of the British Constitution that "taxation and representation go together" should not be ignored because it happens to be a woman and not a man who pays the taxes.'

The momentum in Devon continued into the autumn of 1873 with the arrival of American Suffragist, Mary Beedy. She was accompanied by Caroline Biggs, someone active in national suffrage groups and who had signed the 1866 petition. She was also editor of *The Englishwoman's Review*, a feminist periodical unique in recording the social and industrial work of women. Together, they embarked on a tour of the West Country, including Plymouth, Tavistock, Tiverton and Barnstaple, the first time suffrage speakers had reached this North Devon town. Until then the only information available may have been along the lines of a floridly anti-suffrage article in the *North Devon Journal* in 1871 about a Woman's Congress held in Cincinnati. 'Mrs Mary Wheaton M.D. has arisen and rides at full tilt at her sisters of the female Suffrage persuasion... women had no business to fly in the face of nature, and assume "a masculinity" not naturally belonging to her... woman's place was the hearth - man's the world. She denounced free lovers and suffragists as rebels; anathematised masculine women and effeminate men...' It was a view that would later resonate with those who became anti-suffragists.

Mary Beedy was clear. It was impossible for women to get justice from a Parliament that only represented men. On the topic of women's lack of education, she picked up Millicent Fawcett and Helena Downing's argument. 'Women could not do such good work as men because they were badly educated; and they were badly educated because there were no funds for their education; and they could not get the funds because they had so little influence with Members of Parliament.' Miss Beedy also had an answer to the perennial argument that women were intellectually inferior because their brains were smaller. A post-mortem revealing that a respected male historian's brain was smaller than average had been conveniently explained away by a physiologist. '...the fineness of the tissue and the multiplicity of folds made up for a lack weight.' If for a male, why not for a female? A view that generated loud cheers from the audience.

The following year Miss Beedy, accompanied by Lilias Ashworth, packed in two more tours, beginning in April at the Royal Public Rooms in Exeter. She eagerly embraced a challenge from Sir Henry James, Taunton MP and Solicitor General, who had declared that, '... when one half of the ladies of Taunton appealed to him to support female suffrage, he would do it; because he would then know that he was acting in accordance with the sympathies and feelings of the country.' Never one to shirk a challenge, Miss Beedy later presented him with a petition signed by 300 of the 562 eligible ladies, reminding him of his word.

In April 1881 Lilias made her third appearance at the Royal Public Rooms in Exeter. The *Express and Echo* recorded her disbelief that ten years had elapsed since the topic had first been brought before the women of Exeter. (When she visited with Millicent Fawcett) But, she stressed, times were changing and, 'Nothing proved more strongly the change that had taken place in public opinion than the fact that women were now considered to have the right to the widest and most unfettered intellectual training. The Universities of London and Cambridge had thrown open their doors to them.' Although they were still unable to graduate of course.

Jane Ronniger, Millicent Fawcett, Helena Downing, Lilias Ashworth, Mary Beedy and Caroline Biggs were all memorable speakers in their own way but none could match the inimitable, the unforgettable, the much travelled Miss Jessie Craigen. She was described by the writer Henry Hyndman as, '...ugly, self-taught, roughly attired, and uncouth in her ways. Yet all this was soon overlooked when once the lady began to speak... She came forward, dumped down on the table in front of me an umbrella, a neck wrapper and a shabby old bag. Then she turned round to face the audience. She was greeted with boisterous peals of laughter. No wonder! Such a figure of fun you never saw. It was Mrs. Gamp [The Dickens character] come again in the flesh – umbrella, corkscrew curls and all. There she stood with a battered bonnet on her straggling

grey hair, with a rough shawl pinned over her shoulders… In two minutes the whole audience was listening intently; within five she had them in fits of laughter, this time not at her but with her. A little later, tears were in every eye as she told some terribly touching story of domestic suffering, self-sacrifice, and misery.'

In October 1875 crowds turned out for Jessie's appearances at the Temperance Halls in Devonport and Exmouth, the Friar Hall in Exeter and the Town Hall in Bideford. Several bookings were by invitation of the Temperance Society and she often mixed and matched those talks with ones on Women's Rights. In Bideford she advertised a talk on 'Women's Suffrage' on the Friday evening and 'The Social Future Conditions of the Working Classes' for Saturday. But due to a 'misunderstanding' she was asked to change that to a teetotal talk. Whereupon half the audience left! Fortunately the Friday night audience remained in their seats to hear her passionate plea that the education of girls must be improved, that Universities should be opened to them, and that thousands of female lives might be spared if they had female practitioners of medicine.

The 1870s had opened the eyes of many Devon women to the new suffrage movement. Confirmation of its relevance to each and every one of them came just six years later with the arrival of Lydia Becker, a driving force in the Manchester Suffrage Society. Lydia firmly believed that, 'The shortest and most effective way, nay, the only way, of raising the position of women is to give them votes.' Lydia knew bold tactics were needed - women must have a voice, a public voice raised for a political cause. Visiting speakers were already addressing meetings but she needed local women prepared to step outside of any philanthropic role and advocate for political change. In 1882 Lydia, together with Helen Blackburn from the Bristol society, launched a series of Grand Demonstrations in key cities across the country, including Plymouth. It was audacious, it was shocking, and it was met with incredulity and indignation in this male-dominated society. How dare she challenge the facts as men perceived them - that a woman's place was in the home, that political agitation by women was not acceptable, that women should devote themselves to duties that their Maker designed them for?

An advert for the 1882 Plymouth Grand Demonstration in the *Woman's Suffrage Journal* gave local woman, Caroline Brine, second billing. Caroline had become well-known for chairing and speaking at meetings and acting as a focus for suffrage work. In 1886 she continued her particular brand of persuasion in a speech to the Teignmouth Working Men's Liberal Association. The *Women's Suffrage Journal* reported… 'Mrs. Brine advised working men not to imbibe their politics so much at the club or the public-house but to buy their daily paper and read it at their own firesides, and thus stimulate in their wives and daughters an intelligent interest in political subjects.'

Caroline would have felt pride at attending the Grand Demonstration, an event organised, addressed and almost solely attended by women, one that ranked with any male political rally. Such was the wider impact that a 78 year old Devon woman, Mrs Elizabeth McRobert from Ilfracombe, travelled all the way to Bristol to join 3,000 others at the Grand Demonstration there.

The Plymouth event inspired local women Margaret and Susan Bragg and Frances and Edith Latimer, all extensively involved with charitable organisations in Plymouth, to join the Bristol and West Suffrage Society. It was also the catalyst for Frances, with the Bragg sisters, to launch the Three Towns Women's Liberal Association - the three towns being Plymouth, East Stonehouse and Devonport, considered separate at this time. The first meeting in April 1884 was chaired by Isaac Latimer, Frances's father. He summed up the feeling of the meeting that women must get the vote before long and that educating women to use their rights wisely was the most important work the Liberal ladies could perform.

After a flurry of petitions in support of granting the franchise to women the news came: the Government proposed to introduce legislation to extend the right to vote, but only to more men. The 1884 Reform Act explicitly prohibited female enfranchisement by stating 'every man' possessed of the household qualification would be entitled to register to vote. An amendment to extend the Parliamentary Franchise to women was defeated by 271 votes to 135. To the thousands of women who had campaigned for the vote for over two decades it was a major blow. But it wasn't seen that way by all women.

John Bull: "**Very charming, I'm sure; but aren't you a little behind the times.**"

Printed and Published by the Artists' Suffrage League, 259, King's Road, Chelsea.

Chapter Two
A Unified Struggle?
1884 - 1897

From the perspective of the twenty-first century, the phrase 'Votes for Women' suggests a unified struggle for what was an obvious and justified reform. This was anything but the case at the time. Many women of a certain class were comfortable with the traditional view of a woman's role in society, particularly when the Married Women's Property Acts gave them control over their own assets. These instinctively conservative women found meaning and fulfilment in philanthropic activities and managing the home. They considered it entirely appropriate that military, international and Parliamentary matters were handled by men.

The Anti-Suffragists provided a natural home for these women, whether or not they actually joined or were simply part of the silent majority the leaders claimed to represent. While we might label their views as reactionary, this was the reality of the time. It was the foolish, misguided suffragists who, it seemed to many women, were out of step and deserving of ridicule, not those opposing reform.

Mary Augusta Ward, better known as Mrs Humphrey Ward, became the figurehead of the Anti-Suffrage campaign. She was well-educated, a prolific author, untiring in her efforts to improve women's education and a supporter of their growing involvement in local government. Yet all this, she insisted, was not only possible as unenfranchised citizens, but it was a status to be positively welcomed and defended, a challenging view from the modern perspective.

Westcountry women had the chance to become familiar with her views when reading the *Western Daily Mercury* of 31 May 1889. Under the heading 'A Counter Blast Against Women's Suffrage' the piece reported that, 'A formidable reaction against female suffrage has arisen in the ranks of the women themselves; and not only is an appeal against it signed by a considerable number of well-known women but women readers of *Nineteenth Century* [a highly regarded literary magazine] are invited to sign…'

Readers may have been influenced by an editorial suggesting that, 'Proposals for the extension of the suffrage to women are beset with grave practical difficulties.' One example given is, 'the probable enfranchisement of large numbers of women who lead immoral lives'. Controversial at best, but the editor continues, 'During the last half century all the principal injustices towards women had been amended by means of existing constitutional machinery.' [For example the Married Women's Property Act of 1870] It's an opinion that may have left many women open to the anti-suffrage point of view.

Mary Ward's 'Appeal Against Women's Suffrage', set out her deeply held belief that the women's campaign for the vote was wrong. 'While desiring the fullest possible development of the powers, energies, and education of women, we believe their work for the State, and their responsibilities towards it, must always differ essentially from those of men...' For Mary, there were specific areas of state that men were exclusively suited for - debate and legislation in Parliament, international relations, the military, finance, industry and commerce. Many women worked equally hard devoting themselves to philanthropic activities - to relieve the distress of the poor, of children, of the sick, so it's possible to argue a division of labour made absolute sense. But that's not the argument Mary Ward relied on. While welcoming women on School Boards, Boards of Guardians and other public bodies, she stated categorically that, '...we believe that the emancipating process has now reached the limits fixed by the physical constitution of women,' and that, '...the necessary and normal experience of women... does not and can never provide them with such materials for sound judgement as are open to men.' A contentious opinion now, but it was a view that commanded respect and considerable support at the time.

The 104 ladies who signed her Appeal included some well-known names, including Lady Randolph Churchill and, perhaps most significantly in the light of what was to come, Mrs H. H. Asquith. But attempting to gather wider support brought the anti-suffrage movement up against a dilemma. They claimed to speak for the silent majority, but how to prove this when by definition they objected to any involvement in national politics? The editor of *Nineteenth Century* issued a plea for these women to, '...do violence to their natural reticence, and signify publicly and unmistakably their condemnation of the scheme now threatened,' by signing and returning a statement of protest. The resulting petition against the extension of the Parliamentary vote to women gathered 1,200 signatures.

The Anti's insistence that fundamental differences between women and men made change untenable astonished the Suffragists. Lydia Becker responded, 'Most things worth doing in this world are beset with difficulties. The proposal to carry a railway over the Firth of Forth presented difficulties of a formidable nature, but these did not deter the engineers from undertaking the work.' Lydia claimed in the *Women's Suffrage Journal,* that the Anti-Suffrage Appeal was clearly, '...an indication of the strength of the movement in favour of the franchise, and of the apprehension of the opponents that the measure may soon become law.' This was possibly a rose-coloured assessment but she and Millicent Fawcett immediately launched a country-wide counter declaration in favour of Women's Suffrage. After just a few days the suffragist 'pro' lobby had accumulated over 1,500 signatures, later increasing to 2,538. Caroline Brine and Miss E Millett from Teignmouth and Frances Latimer, Miss Rooker and the Misses Bragg from Plymouth all signed. It was a stand echoed by Devonport Council who unanimously supported a petition in favour of extending the franchise to women. In May 1889 the Conservative Party of North Devon passed a similar resolution by an overwhelming majority.

Women's Liberal Associations [WLAs] also increasingly provided an arena for suffrage debates. The Three Towns WLA, which lapsed after 1884, re-formed in 1888 with Frances Latimer as President. She was a constant advocate for women's suffrage. In May 1891 she was given headline billing at a WLA county-wide event in Newton Abbot, with special excursions put on from Exeter, Plymouth and Teign Valley stations. Even North Devon delegates were catered for with a train from Barnstaple. The expansion of the railways at the same time as the emergence of the women's suffrage movement was crucial. It would have been impossible to campaign covering the distances that they did without the speed and frequency of the railway network.

Further debates hosted by WLAs, for example in Ilfracombe in 1891 and Barnstaple in 1899, helped to keep the subject of women's suffrage alive, but it seemed that some of the momentum had been lost. Suffragists were increasingly losing faith in petitions as a strategy, particularly when they patently failed to secure the vote for women in the 1884 Reform Act. According to Dr Margherita Rendel, in *The Campaign in Devon for Women's Suffrage,* between 1866 and 1884 there were 185 petitions, an average of 10 a year. But between 1885 and 1896 this dropped to only 42, an average of 3.5. By the mid 1890s even the most ardent suffragists were having to accept that most of their strategies, including petitions, were proving ineffective.

In May 1896 the Women's Franchise League summed up their frustration in their Annual Report. 'It is now recognised that no measure of reform has any chance of becoming law unless supported by the Government of the day. The Government of the day supports those measures which will increase its influence among the constituencies and win new adherents. The reforms which affect the position of women… are not of this nature, and therefore they are almost entirely neglected… For nearly thirty years we have petitioned and reasoned and expostulated; we have held thousands of public and drawing room meetings; we have circulated millions of pamphlets and leaflets; we have passed resolutions without number, declaring that we want the Suffrage… What response has there been to these appeals? None whatever… Year after year our friends in the House have presented our Bills but they tell us frankly, "There is not the slightest chance of success" for them.'

Just six months later, members of seventeen suffrage societies from across the UK also faced up to this difficult truth. At a gathering in Birmingham the speaker, Mrs Taylor, asked the question, '…with all these twenty-five years of work, Women's Suffrage is not yet won. How is this?' She supplied her own answer. 'You do not have the great mass of women with you. The majority of women do not really care about the Suffrage.' Raising awareness and encouraging involvement had to become a priority. There had been 309 suffrage meetings in the previous three years but there were counties, Devon included, where there had been none during that time. Mrs Taylor urged a systematic approach to reach what she described as 'those blank tracts of land'. Existing societies should cover specific areas, as the Bristol and West Suffrage Society had done in sponsoring the speakers who toured Devon in the 1870s.

To reenergise the campaign throughout the country Mrs Taylor strongly recommended the appointment of organisers who would systematically work these areas, avoiding large towns as much as possible. This seemed counter-intuitive but she argued her case. 'Any one woman's work is simply lost in a large town… But in a village the very appearance of a stranger is a novelty, and causes excitement. To call at a cottage and say a few words, and leave a leaflet or two, raises curiosity and causes much talk. And further, in almost every village there is at least one intelligent, open-minded woman, and this woman's name can be taken down and then, when Suffrage work of any sort is wanted, the Society knows whom to write to.' An apt approach for rural Devon.

One thing was key. Mrs Taylor concluded. 'I see no reason why at some future date the various Suffrage Societies… should not join and form themselves into one National Society for Women's Suffrage.' A year later, in November 1897, the same seventeen societies did exactly that, becoming the National Union of Women's Suffrage Societies [NUWSS]. Millicent Garrett Fawcett set the tone for this new, non-party organisation. She was passionate that they should rely on argument based on common sense and experience, campaigning for change through peaceful and legal means. They subsequently organised huge numbers of meetings, rallies and petitions, all demonstrating significant support for change.

It was only a matter of months since they had pulled out all the stops to try to persuade MPs to vote for a Private Member's Suffrage Bill proposed by the wonderfully named Mr Faithfull Begg. Charlotte Stopes, a scholar, author and campaigner for women's rights, reflected on their efforts in her article 'The Women's Suffrage Bill in the "Queens Year"'. She described how women deluged their own MPs with appointments, letters, enquiries and pamphlets in support of the Bill, capitalised on personal connections by writing to 'acquaintances in the House' and supported a campaign by suffrage societies to contact every MP. On the day of the first reading the men had to run the gauntlet, albeit a very refined and ladylike one, of a large number of women waiting in the Central Hall at the Houses of Parliament, determined to make their presence felt.

Despite the women's efforts, the Bill failed to make it onto the statute book. One Devon woman expressed her determination not to let this happen again in a letter to the *Western Morning News*. 'The most practical suggestion that can be made appears to me that every woman, who is in common justice entitled to vote, either as a ratepayer or owner of property, should, at the next election, whatever may be her political views, oppose as far as she can the return of any member who voted against the [Suffrage] Bill. If this is done the return of the Hon. Members for both Plymouth and Torquay… will be rendered very uncertain.' The writer possibly had Sir Edward

Clarke, Conservative MP for Plymouth and a known anti-suffragist, particularly in mind.

There had been some advances in women's involvement in local government. Between 1869 and 1894 women ratepayers had won the right to vote in local municipal elections, stand for School Boards and as Poor Law Guardians, and vote in local county and borough council elections. But many women agreed that debates, petitions and reasoning, tried now for over thirty years, were getting them absolutely nowhere when it came to the Parliamentary vote. No amount of polite lobbying had made the slightest difference. It was business as usual in the exclusively male House of Commons with MPs refusing to pass any Bills on Woman Suffrage. The time had come for new approaches.

"THIS IS OUR FIRST TASK"

Chapter Three
Liberal Momentums
1897 - 1906

There are pivotal moments in the story of women's fight for the vote in Devon, when significant figures emerged to drive the narrative forward. In the 1870s and 1880s it had been visiting speakers such as Jane Ronniger, Millicent Fawcett, Helena Downing, Mary Beedy, Jessie Craigen and Lydia Becker. After a lull in the 1890s, the focus shifted towards local women campaigning within Women's Liberal Associations [WLAs]. Frances Latimer and Caroline Brine were still active, alongside two others also making their mark - Alison Garland

from Plymouth and Mary Marrack from Tiverton. The Federation of
WLAs had been formed in 1887 to pressure the Liberal Party to
support women's issues. From the 1890s onwards a demand that the
organisation should campaign for women's suffrage became one of
their priorities.

Devon was increasingly well represented.
In 1892 alone, branches of the Association
formed in Devonport, Stonehouse, Tavistock,
Brentor and Marytavy, Dawlish, Teignmouth,
Exmouth, Exeter, Barnstaple, Bideford and
Great Torrington. This expansion in
membership was largely due to the passion of
Alison Garland, based in Plymouth but
influential across the county. She was a
dynamic public speaker, not afraid to step into
the limelight - literally. In 1892 the *Western Morning News* reported that,
'Under the auspices of the Women's Liberal Association, a lecture on
"Ireland", illustrated by limelight views [similar to magic lantern
slides], was given by Miss Alison Garland.' She was obviously unafraid
of technology. Limelight is a dazzling white light produced by
projectors fed by oxygen and hydrogen tanks, possibility not
something that would pass modern day heath and safety
requirements.

Alison initially earned her living as a music teacher, later adding
art and writing to her many talents. She was also one of those creative
women able to take her audience by surprise. In her play *The Better
Half*, women held the power in Parliament and men campaigned for
the vote. In the 1890s she focused on her career as a professional
lecturer, covering a fascinating range of subjects. Near the top of the
list was a cause dear to her heart, women's suffrage. In 1896 it was a
topic she took countrywide as part of a lecture campaign coordinated
by the Central National Society for Women's Suffrage. The *Women's
Signal* reported 'an excellent address' that she gave in November
where she shared both women's successes and their setbacks. 'The
subject was anything but a novel one; on the contrary, some
apparently seem to have got tired of the question. As they looked
back to the time, 30 years ago, when John Stuart Mill first brought up

the Bill, they could remember how the pulpit, the public, the platform and the Press were against them. There had, however, been a distinct advance since then, although it was difficult to get many at their meetings.'

Alison Garland spoke as a member of the Union of Practical Suffragists, a group within the WLA lobbying to withdraw support from any MP voting against Women's Suffrage, an echo of Frances Latimer's proposal. Significantly, in 1901 the *Western Morning News* reported Alison's view, '...that the parliamentary franchise should be simplified and the principle of one person one vote carried out... She knew of no good reason against placing women on an equal footing with men in the matter of representation.' At a meeting held in Exeter in May, Liberal men actually proposed a change in the legislation to 'one-man one vote' as long as they met a residency qualification. Alison must have been persuasive. In this male-dominated meeting her motion that women should be included was passed, although the vote was tight with 52 for, 48 against.

One person one vote, or universal suffrage, was a controversial view. It would have led to a majority of women electors, completely unacceptable to many. Thirty years earlier Jane Ronniger had pressed for the vote solely for single or widowed women householders in an attempt to defuse opposition. The NUWSS included married women but also demanded the vote, '...on the same terms as it is or may be granted to men', a proposal they judged more likely to gain support.

Alison Garland put her finger on one of the main reservations amongst male MPs. 'No doubt what influenced Liberals most in their decision not to place women's suffrage on their programme was their doubt whether the women's vote would benefit their party.' This echoed the commonly held belief that the middle and upper class women in line to get the vote were more likely to keep the Conservatives in government. Debate over the role party politics played in the fight for the vote was to become a constant theme, but for the moment the Liberals provided the backdrop for Alison Garland's campaign. As a member of the Executive Committee of the Devon Federation she was able to raise the issue at meetings across the county throughout the early years of the new century.

Someone equally dedicated, though perhaps more steeped in protocol, was Mary Marrack from Tiverton WLA. For two years running she and Alison Garland had something of a spat at the Devon Union of WLAs annual meetings. In 1898 Alison moved that, 'This Union re-affirms its adherence to the principle of Women's Suffrage, that men and women should be treated equally and that only Liberal candidates supporting women's suffrage should get assistance from Liberal women at elections.' Mary objected, insisting that the last part was omitted. As members of a Liberal Association she considered they were bound to support their candidates. In an attempt to resolve the impasse, Frances Latimer, presiding, suggested a compromise. "…that only such Liberal candidates as will not vote or speak against Women's Suffrage should receive the support of Women's Liberal Associations.' But, as the *Western Times* commented, by this point many ladies were leaving and in the confusion there was no official announcement that the compromise had passed.

A year later in Torquay, it was a case of déjà vu. A reporter from the *Exeter and Plymouth Gazette* captured the moment when a similar resolution was moved. 'This meeting keenly feels the necessity for the inclusion of Women's Suffrage in any measure of electoral reform which the Liberal party may adopt and urges Women's Liberal Associations to show their earnest convictions of the same by only working for candidates who will, at least, not oppose women's political enfranchisement.' Mary Marrack immediately proposed an amendment that the resolution should end after the word, 'adopt' to avoid women's suffrage becoming a test question for candidates. According to the *Western Times* she then condemned Liberal women who, because a candidate did not agree with them on one point, would throw over all the others, '…like a naughty child, who said, "If you will not play when I play you shall not play at all."'

Mary was supported by Caroline Brine but opposed by Ethel Phear from Exmouth, someone who was to become increasingly significant in the suffrage story in Devon. Mrs Balgarnie, who proposed the motion, ridiculed Mrs Marrack's amendment as 'feeble'. However, after a show of hands it seemed to have been carried. However, Alison Garland, as President, repeated the vote, thinking some women might have misunderstood what they were voting for.

The amendment was carried again but Alison still wasn't satisfied, insisting tellers undertook a proper count. Through her persistence the initial result was overturned. Mary's amendment was defeated by 45 votes to 38, leaving the original motion to be carried unaltered.

Despite this difference of opinion, there was no doubting Mary Marrack's overall support of women's suffrage. In 1902 she was elected President of the Devon Federation of WLAs and took full advantage of her public platform to champion the franchise for women. In Torrington the *North Devon Journal* quoted her as having, '...given many cogent reasons why the franchise should be extended to women'. On a Devon Federation picnic in Exmouth she spoke of women's suffrage as a wrong to be righted. In Bideford she shared her view that women's suffrage should be foremost. 'Above everything else they must work for their political emancipation'. In Exeter she contrasted the UK with New Zealand where every woman over 21 had been able to vote since 1893.

The following year, in Cullompton, Mary reiterated the aims of the organisation under her leadership. Namely, '...to help forward the Liberal cause by all legitimate means and to work hard to influence public opinion in favour of women's suffrage.' She continued to work hard herself, both publicly and behind the scenes. Towards the end of 1903 she wrote to all Liberals contesting seats in Devon at the next election, asking them if they would support women's suffrage. Four of the five new candidates agreed they would. Mr Mallet, however, standing in Plymouth, declined. Mary expressed the hope that Plymouth women would convince him otherwise.

Others kept women's suffrage on the agenda, but often with increasing frustration. Anne Martin, a member of Bristol WLA, was the speaker in Bideford in July 1903. The *Western Times* covered her comment that women's suffrage was, '... looked upon rather as a bore, but if men were tired of hearing resolutions on that topic how much more tired must women be.' She urged support for the resolution, 'That this meeting declares its determination to press forward the question of women's enfranchisement... and urges upon the members of the affiliated Associations to use all their influence... to secure the selection of candidates for Parliament favourable to women's suffrage.'

She graphically described the rank and file of the Liberal party as favouring the women's franchise but, '…the leaders were like people standing on the edge of a cold bath, and were afraid to take the plunge, but it was their [the women's] part and business to give them the push into it.' It was a reluctance Frances Latimer was all too aware of. In 1897 she had discovered a notice was being circulated by some Liberals who dreaded the extension of good old Liberal principles to the female half of the country, effectively sabotaging support.

Frances also had an original way of keeping women's suffrage a live topic. In March 1900 readers may well have looked twice at an advertisement in the *Torquay Times* for 'A Women's Parliament' where, 'The Hon. Member for Plymouth (Miss Latimer) will move the third reading of the "Parliamentary Franchise (Extension to Women) Bill 1900."' This she did, in a 'staid, unemotional manner', demonstrating that to keep the franchise from woman was lowering their dignity. Her remarks were met with undisguised approval from the majority of the Hon. Members, (other women). The wider public, forming the Gallery, played their part in keeping the performance authentic with cries of "shame", applause or laughter. At the conclusion of a lively debate the Speaker (Mrs Layland-Barratt) announced a majority of 27 for and 2 against.

Sisters Ethel and Winifred Phear, from the coastal town of Exmouth in East Devon, were also playing their part. As president and vice-president of their WLA, they made a rather specific request of Mary Marrack at their annual meeting in March 1903. According to the *Exeter and Plymouth Gazette*, they asked that she confine her remarks, '…entirely to the question of the female franchise.' Six months later, Ethel, Winifred and another Exmouth resident, Adelaide Montgomery, took the significant step of testing support for a local women's suffrage society outside of the Liberal Party platform. On Saturday 8 October 1903 a notice appeared in the *Exmouth Journal*.

'WOMEN'S SUFFRAGE. It is hoped, should sufficient support be given, to hold a Meeting in EXMOUTH this autumn to further the above cause. Will any, of either sex,

who are interested in this matter kindly communicate with
Mrs Montgomery, 9 Hartley Road, as soon as possible.'

They formed a small, strictly non-party, group with a committee
consisting of Adelaide Montgomery as secretary, alongside either
Ethel or Winifred Phear. Why non-party? Were they disillusioned with
the Women Liberal's stance, perhaps thinking they were not going far
enough? After all, Ethel had opposed Mary Marrack's watering down
of the motion at the WLA meeting in Torquay. Whatever the reason,
they now looked to another source for support.

The NUWSS had fulfilled their ambitious commitment to
support the campaign in Devon by providing speakers for meetings
organised by fledgling groups. After forming the Women's Suffrage
Group in Exmouth, Ethel Phear now turned to them for her next
undertaking. For this she joined forces with Amy Montague from
Crediton, someone who was to become a core presence in the fight
for the vote in Devon. On Monday, 31 November Amy was at the
Barnfield Hall in Exeter to welcome Mrs Francis, Executive
Committee Member of the NUWSS, to speak on 'Why women want
the vote'. The *Western Times* reported a small attendance,
disappointing for Amy, but the advice Mrs Francis offered on the
formation and working of branch societies for the promotion of the
Women's Suffrage movement was timely.

The following evening it was Ethel Phear's turn to preside at a
second meeting held in the Town Hall at Crediton. In her
introduction, Ethel made a strong plea for the extension of the
franchise to women. After Mrs Francis repeated her address of the
previous evening, Amy stood to close the meeting. Significantly, given
that she had just declined an offer to be president of the newly
formed WLA in Crediton, she emphasised that the question was, '...
not a Party one as yet and it had ceased to be a joke. It had become a
question simply of right and wrong.' The *Exeter and Plymouth Gazette*
reported a small attendance, the *Western Times* a very fair attendance
and the *Women's Suffrage Record*, '...a large audience of working men
and women.' It all depends on your perspective.

Over a year later, in March 1905, the Exmouth group arranged
for another visit from Anne Martin, this time apparently speaking

outside of her WLA role. The *Exmouth Journal* reported her core message. 'Women's suffrage was by no means a party political movement but arose from a feeling among women that if they were expected to contribute towards taxation and permitted to compete in labour with men they should have, through the Parliamentary vote, a voice in the making of the laws which they were to observe.' However, the group were struggling to generate interest, attracting what the local papers variously described as a small, meagre or sparse attendance. Adelaide Montgomery did her best to engage the support of the local council but her proposal was laughed out and a reply sent that the Council could not do anything. It must have been disheartening for the Phear sisters, Adelaide Montgomery and all those who had hoped to stir the Exmouth community into action in support of women's suffrage.

But there was a new optimism within the Devon Union of WLAs, where Frances Latimer, Ethel Phear, Alison Garland, Caroline Brine and Mary Marrack all remained active. In

February 1906 the *Western Morning News* reported a comment made by Anne Martin in a speech at Barnstaple that, '…there never was a Cabinet so favourable to women's suffrage as the present one.' This followed the Liberal's win at a recent election, prompting fresh hopes that success was close. After all, the new Liberal Prime Minister, Sir Henry Campbell-Bannerman had promised to support a Women's Suffrage Bill if elected.

On 19 May women from the Devon Union travelled to London to join almost 500 men and women from other Liberal Associations, suffrage societies, Trade Unions, Temperance organisations and philanthropic bodies from across the country. They were all eager to capitalise on the Prime Minster's agreement to receive a deputation. It was their opportunity to ensure that he made good on his promise.

The actual outcome was to be very different.

The *Exeter and Plymouth Gazette* reported, '…The Prime Minister flattered them. He told them they were as well qualified as men for the many duties of citizenship - in fact they were better qualified…

Having raised the hopes of the deputation to the seventh heaven, the Prime Minister proceeded to lower them to the realms of despair...' He concluded, '...seeing there were differences of opinion it would never do for him to make a definitive statement or give a promise.' This was a complete turnaround from his pre-election promise and, according to the paper, demonstrated his complete inability to lead, putting party convenience before principle. The women were devastated and at two subsequent meetings in London voiced their anger and disappointment at the new government.

At the 1906 annual meeting of the Devon Union of WLAs, Alison Garland, with perhaps more diplomacy than Campbell-Bannerman deserved, moved that, 'This meeting keenly regrets that differences of opinion in the Cabinet prevent legislation in favour of Women's Suffrage with which the Prime Minister expressed sympathy to the deputation on 19 May.' Regret was tempered with a new frustration though. For possibly the first time, Alison Garland expressed her irritation that forty years of peaceful campaigning was in danger of being undermined by a new breed of suffragists, the Suffragettes.

They were initially treated with curiosity and ridicule by the press - until April 1906. In what the *Western Mail* described as, 'An extraordinary and unparalleled scene,' suffragettes crowded into the Ladies Gallery in the House of Commons and interrupted a suffrage debate. The Gallery, according to Charlotte Stopes in her article on

women's suffrage, was a, '…badly lit, badly ventilated, uncomfortable space for three dozen women behind a screen [the Grille] like a hareem, with great placards of "Silence" and "No demonstrations allowed here".' Ignoring these warnings, the women thrust flags through the Grille shouting 'Vote, Vote' and 'Justice for Women', causing such a commotion the police were called to clear the gallery.

These disruptive tactics were becoming commonplace but at the time this carefully planned and executed demonstration in Parliament caused absolute astonishment. The comment was made on the floor of the House, 'Can there be any better argument [against women's suffrage] … than the scene we just witnessed?' The *North Devon Journal* reported Alison Garland's response. 'How unfair it was for [politicians] to be making light of this question because a handful of socialist women were moving in ways of which they did not approve. These women were in earnest but were quite mistaken in their methods…'

But this was only the beginning. The tactics of these 'mistaken women' were to become much more controversial amongst law-abiding suffragists, politicians and the public alike over the next eight years.

Annie Kenney and Christabel Pankhurst

Chapter Four
Deeds Not Words
1903 - 1908

The Suffragettes were the inspiration of
Emmeline Pankhurst who, in 1903, lost patience
with the polite lobbying of the NUWSS and
decided to launch a new organisation, the
Women's Social and Political Union (WSPU).
She had campaigning in her blood. As a child
she was bathed in arguments for women's
suffrage from her feminist mother and her
equally pro-suffrage father. Her husband was

also a keen advocate of women's rights, he had drafted the first Women's Suffrage Bill in 1870. For years she worked within the law-abiding NUWSS but by 1903 it was obvious to Emmeline, as to others, that the polite approach was failing. It was time to honour her family heritage and take centre stage. During a speech in Plymouth she said, 'In spite of the overwhelming demand which women have shown for the possession of the Parliamentary vote, in spite of the fact that every consideration of justice points to their right to possess it, the franchise has not been conceded, and in consequence women have found it necessary to take more vigorous measures.' For Emmeline and her daughters, Christabel, Sylvia and Adela, this meant breaking away from the NUWSS to form the WSPU, a new group with a new slogan: Deeds not Words. Out with polite petitions. In with direct action.

The WSPU grew rapidly, appointing regional organisers with the courage, eloquence and ability to galvanise crowds. The person destined to lead the campaign in the West Country had all of those qualities and more. She was Annie Kenney, the Oldham firebrand. Annie began her working life aged ten in a cotton mill. The noise, dirt and drudgery subdued many, but Annie was a fighter. Fascinated by politics she joined the local branch of the Independent Labour Party where she heard Christabel speak on women's rights. Annie fell under Christabel's spell, surrendering herself to the cause. She spoke of the militant movement as, '…more like a religious revival than a political movement. It stirred the emotions, it aroused passions, it awakened the human chord which responds to the battle-call of freedom...' She offered loyalty and unselfish devotion, both to the cause and to Christabel.

Sylvia Pankhurst described Annie as, '... eager and impulsive in manner, with a thin, haggard face, and restless knotted hands, from one of which a finger had been torn by the machinery it was her work to attend. Her abundant, loosely dressed golden hair was the most youthful looking thing about her... The wild, distraught expression, apt to occasion solicitude, was found on better acquaintance to be less common than a bubbling merriment, in which the crow's feet wrinkled quaintly about a pair of twinkling, bright blue eyes.'

Annie admitted suffragettes developed a different set of values to other women. 'The changed life into which most of us entered was a revolution in itself. No home life, no-one to say what we should do or what we should not do, no family ties, we were free and alone in a great brilliant city, scores of young women scarcely out of their teens met together in a revolutionary movement, outlaws or breakers of laws, independent of everything and everybody, fearless and self-confident.' That fearlessness was on show on 13 October 1905 when Annie and Christabel joined the crowds at Manchester's Free Trade Hall determined to heckle Sir Edward Grey, a potential cabinet minister. They thrust a banner into the air. 'Votes for Women' it proclaimed. Annie called, 'If you are elected, will you do your best to make Woman Suffrage a Government Measure?' She was ignored. She stood again, but was immediately pulled down by men in the crowd. Christabel repeated the question, unleashing a hubbub of cries from 'shut up' to 'let the lady speak.'

Eventually they were dragged from the meeting. During the scuffle a policeman accused them of kicking and spitting which, of course, they did. It was a deliberate ploy to get arrested. They were charged with assault and appeared in court. But far from being cowed, they were triumphant. Christabel had declared war. They refused to pay any fines and were sentenced to three days imprisonment. It was unprecedented. For the first time in Britain, women had used violence in an attempt to win the vote. The *Daily Mail* labelled this new breed of Suffragists 'Suffragettes', intended as an insult but adopted with glee by the WSPU

For Annie, it was a turning point. She took to the public platform, commanding crowds with her powerful voice and expressive language. Their movement would have to break through the old guard's rock-solid belief that a woman's place was in the home, but she was convinced that the WSPU would triumph. The Suffragettes were now grabbing the headlines with tactics derided by many, prompting correspondents on both sides of the argument to debate the pros and cons in the papers. In April 1906 a poem appeared in the *Western Evening Herald:*

> O' lovely Woman, why do you
> Dement yourself like this?
> Why stretch to strident politics
> A mouth that's built to kiss?

> We love you when you smile or coo,
> And even when you pout;
> We do not love you half so well
> When you begin to shout.

> We love you young, old, coy or prim,
> Condone your cigarettes;
> But spare our feelings, do not all
> Be shrieking Suffragettes.

The rhyme continues in a similar vein, suffice to say kitchens are mentioned. A couple of weeks later the *Royal Cornwall Gazette* published a response from a Miss Bowen. Her letter concluded, '…let Westcountry women be found intelligent enough to know that they have wrongs, and courageous enough to fight for them. The Prime Minister counsels patience, but methinks the time has come in the history of the Women's Suffrage movement when a little impatience is permissible. The question is one on which all that can be said for and against has been said. So the time for argument has gone; the time for action has come.'

In the autumn of 1907, Devon experienced Annie Kenney's revolutionary zeal at first hand. She focused on Exeter initially, although credit for the work there has to go to Amy Montague. She was perhaps one of the first in Devon who, when faced with the dilemma about whether to stay with the law-abiding NUWSS or make the move to the militant WSPU, decided to change her allegiance. In November, Amy was back at the Barnfield Hall in Exeter but this time under the banner of the WSPU. In something of a coup, Christabel Pankhurst had been booked to speak. The reporter from the *Western Times* found her, '…a smart, vivacious young lady, of prepossessing appearance and exceedingly fluent of speech… She was subjected to considerable interruption from the back of the hall, but dealt with the witticisms of the crowd with admirable temper… one of a body of students… interrupted with a series of indescribable sounds resembling the nocturnal music usually rendered by belated cats, whereupon Miss Pankhurst remarked: "That individual is going to have a vote when he is old enough. It seems rather hard on sensible women, doesn't it now?"'

Amy Montague was a staunch ally when Emmeline Pankhurst identified the forthcoming Mid Devon by-election as a prime target for opposing Liberal candidates. It was an ambitious strategy. There had been seven elections in the constituency since 1885 with a Liberal returned each and every time, on the last occasion with a majority of 1,289. The Liberals were so confident of success they even produced a mourning card lamenting the suffragette's defeat.

In Fond and Loving Memory
OF THE
Tariff Reformers and Suffragettes
Who fell asleep at Mid Devon January 17th 1908

The Suffragettes and Tariff Reformers are now very sore,
And should see it's no use contesting Mid Devon any more;
And the Hooligans of Shaldon you can send over and tell,
That a strong and Buxton Liberal has broken their Bell.
R.I.P

The final line refers to the two candidates, Mr C.R. Buxton, Liberal, and Captain E.F. Morrison Bell, Conservative.

Mrs Pankhurst was undaunted. Members of the WSPU, who dared to stand up to the Liberal Government, were already being imprisoned. She would do her utmost to unseat every candidate that stood for the party to protest at this injustice. She was joined by Nellie Martel, (seated in the image below) believed to be with Mary Gawthorpe, although some sources have the lady standing as Edith

Splatt from Exeter. Nellie was unique as a WSPU speaker in being a woman who already possessed the parliamentary vote in her home country of Australia. Since 1895 women over 21 had not only been eligible to vote, but had the right to stand for Parliament. Yet in England the Liberal Government still resisted the women's claims, even for a much more limited franchise. Together with a team of national and local supporters, Mrs Pankhurst and Mrs Martel organised an exhausting programme of public meetings. Amy Montague frequently addressed these and even composed an anthem to compete with the Liberal's election songs.

They divided the constituency into eight districts, with one or two workers in charge of each. The plan was to hold six or more meetings a day across the area, from Teignmouth to Chagford, Bovey Tracey to Ashburton. The first, held on 3 January 1908 at the Alexandra Hall in Newton Abbot, was the exception to the rule. Most were held outdoors attracting crowds of up to 500. They not only had to contend with heavy snow and bitter winds but tempestuous locals. In her account of the 'Women's Militant Suffrage Movement', Sylvia Pankhurst tells us, *'The Daily News* hailed with enthusiasm the formation of what was known as the "League of Young Liberals" which was in reality a gang of young roughs whose first act was to push a policeman through the plate glass window of the shop which served as our Committee Rooms... Miss Mary Gawthorpe... was not only compelled to hear language from some of the Newton Abbot Liberal partisans that brought a flush to her face and tears into her eyes, but had to resist by force the efforts of one man to mount the waggon from which she and several other ladies were speaking...' Then again, according to Mrs Pankhurst, '...we were treated with much more consideration than either of the candidates, who, not infrequently, were howled down and put to flight. Often the air of their meetings was thick with decayed vegetables and dirty snowballs.'

Mrs Pankhurst's bravado in the face of local gangs was almost her undoing. When the surprise result was announced, that the Conservative, Captain Bell, had won by 559 votes, riots broke out across Newton Abbot. Barricading was torn down at the Conservative Club and every pane of glass smashed. The police urged Emmeline to leave town at once. She laughed at such an absurd warning - until confronted by a mob of young men, clay cutters, all wearing the Liberal red rosettes. A shower of rotten eggs and clay balls sent the women rushing into a grocer's shop. They tried to escape through the back but the gang outmanoeuvred them. Mrs Pankhurst recounted, 'They seized Mrs Martel first, and began beating her over the head with their fists, but the brave wife of the shopkeeper... flung open the door and rushed to our rescue... As I reached the threshold a staggering blow fell on the back of my head, rough hands grasped the collar of my coat, and I was flung violently to the ground.' The gang of youths closed in but fortunately scattered when the police arrived. Her immediate ordeal was over but her injuries plagued her for more than a year.

The WSPU women were an obvious target given their opposition to the Liberal candidate, but they weren't alone in having an impact in the Mid Devon constituency. Two ladies from the NUWSS had actually been first to arrive. Edith Palliser summed up why they were there in the *Women's Franchise*. 'In an election one meets the electors - the arbiters of our fate - face to face, when their interest is roused in political questions, and moreover when they are most fully conscious of their own importance, and, therefore, of the value of the franchise. Under no more favourable circumstances can your appeal be made... I earnestly urge all who have the success of our cause at heart to come to Newton Abbot and help us.'

Their first task was to find a base. 'There was a scarcity of rooms "to let" and the pouring rain and wind was not very helpful in the work of hunting for Committee Rooms. Headquarters were, however, found at 70B Queen Street, a main thoroughfare leading from the station through the centre of town. This room we hope to open on Monday, possibly before the Liberal and Conservative Committee Rooms put up their posters.' Contrary to the WSPU's blanket opposition of all Liberal candidates, Edith's next task was to interview both candidates to establish where they stood on women's suffrage. While both claimed to be in favour, Mr Buxton declined to put any statement in his election address and Captain Bell was not prepared to pledge himself to support a Bill. Basically neither warranted their support so the NUWSS ladies focused on propaganda work, appealing to the electors to press the urgency of the women's claims on both candidates.

Edith Palliser set up in the Market Place, speaking from a trolley loaned by a coal merchant. Within fifteen minutes the quiet and orderly crowd had grown to around 400 and stayed for over an hour. This began a programme of daily meetings, addressing audiences in the parish room at Newton Abbot and outdoor gatherings of railway men and brickworks labourers during their lunch break. The reception could be mixed. 'One gentleman present declared, after trying to interrupt the speaker several times and being called to order, that "if the lady was going to have all the say, he would go home." Another was kind enough to offer me his stockings to darn. But far more serious and practical questions were put, such as, "How can we help you?" "Do you want to go into Parliament?" "What good will the vote bring you?"'

Edith vividly described the scene at Ipplepen. 'The meeting was held in a large barn or workshop, and though the drive out there in an open conveyance was cold, we received such a warm welcome, that the cold was forgotten. The owner of the barn had kindly arranged a platform of an inverted packing case, and had covered it with carpet.

On this were placed two kitchen chairs, two oil lamps were nailed upon the wall behind the platform, and some candles were placed on brackets round the barn.' At the close of the meeting an audience member called for a show of hands from those who were for giving women the vote. The majority raised their hands with none opposed. 'An old farmer then asked for three cheers for the ladies, which was given with intense vigour.'

The Town Hall at Chudleigh, capacity 500, '...was full from end to end, the ante-room and the landing were packed with a surging and interested crowd... The meeting was most enthusiastic - several questions were put at the end which caused intense interest.' One man raised an issue often forgotten in accounts of women's fight for the vote. 'Do the ladies on the stage think that I, who am unmarried and thirty years of age, ought to help them to get a vote before I have one myself?' The audience laughed, but it was a serious point. Around 40% of men were still without the vote.

For local residents, it must have been interesting watching the WSPU and the NUWSS juggling their pitches to avoid a clash. Having both organisations in town could be confusing. Edith Palliser wrote in the *Women's Franchise*, 'At Bovey Tracey we met with a very stormy reception, the audience being under the impression that we were opposing the Liberal candidate. They began by singing songs, which lasted for ten minutes. Then ensued a perfect pandemonium of yells, laughter, and singing. Eventually, however, we succeeded, after patiently waiting for half an hour, to secure a hearing... A gentleman then rose... and was sorry for he was not aware that there were two organisations of women working in Mid-Devon. After that I invited questions, and several were asked, the audience by this time being entirely restored to good humour; many were somewhat shamefaced at the treatment meted out to us.'

They kept up a programme of daily meetings, many of them outdoors on very cold days, with the threat of worse receptions hanging over them. One stop was the tannery works at Newton Abbot where the men threatened to duck the ladies in the river. 'Undaunted, Mrs Cooper and Miss Tanner spoke for twenty minutes and managed to avoid a close encounter with the mill leat.'

Edith Palliser (left) and Selina Cooper (right)

This Mrs Cooper was probably Selina Cooper, born in Callington, Cornwall, but now living in Lancashire. In 1907 she became a full-time organiser with the NUWSS travelling the length and breadth of the country. An assignment close to home must have been very tempting. Their reception had been so positive that Edith Palliser was moved to comment, 'The last days of work in Mid-Devon give promise of a permanent organisation being formed in the constituency when the election is over and excitement has subsided.' It was to be a while before these hopes were realised.

The final, intriguing, word about the Mid-Devon elections has to go to a post in the *Women's Franchise* from the Men's League for Women's Suffrage. When speaking of another forthcoming election the writer commented, 'We want no catastrophe such as that which formed the crowning scandal of the Mid-Devon election.' We're left to speculate what that scandal was. Possibly the WSPU's opposition to the Liberal candidate? Deeds not words was a policy already causing concern even though the deeds in Devon had, so far at least, been moderate.

Chapter Five
Stepping onto the National Stage
Spring - Summer 1908

Despite their success at Newton Abbot, Emmeline Pankhurst must have felt it had all been for nothing. The Conservatives claimed they'd kept the Liberals out with their Tariff Reform policies, while the Liberals blamed their defeat on Conservative promises of more work and higher wages. However, the *Manchester Guardian* supported the suffragette's claim that they had overturned a Liberal majority of over a thousand. It was a result greeted with astonishment in Barnstaple, as the *North Devon Journal* reported. 'To Liberals in other parts of Devon the news came as a thunderbolt, and so wholly unexpected was it that many at Barnstaple... refused to credit the first telegrams and expressed the opinion that a practical joke was being played!'

The women's victory was also controversial in other circles. The Socialist magazine, *Justice*, commented, 'Toryism was victorious at the Mid Devon polls, and these two well-paid lady organisers [Mrs Pankhurst and Mrs Martel] had helped to win the Tory Victory.' Exasperated Liberal losers complained at the, '...lavish expenditure on the part of their adversaries... the ladies are carrying on their "family party" campaign on middle-class money and against the democratic tendencies of the nation and of the age.' Working class women were disillusioned over suffragettes accepting Savoy dinners from well-to-do Conservatives. To add insult to injury, the WSPU were lobbying for the vote on the same terms as men. Essentially this meant for middle and upper class, property-owning women, a long way from the universal suffrage aspirations of the working classes.

There was also division within the WSPU itself. As early as February 1907 seventy-seven members followed Teresa Billington-Grieg and Charlotte Despard to form a new organisation, the Women's Freedom League. The move was a reaction to Emmeline Pankhurst's increasingly autocratic control and support of violent protest. It was the first of several schisms within the WSPU, including, a few years later, within the Pankhurst family itself.

Interestingly, it was the working class Annie Kenney who returned to Devon in the spring of 1908 as part of what the WSPU described as 'a national propagandist campaign'. *Votes for Women* reported, 'Edinburgh, Aberdeen, Glasgow, Bristol, Exeter, Lancaster, Bedford Teignmouth being some of the towns worked up by the organisers and visited with great success by the speakers of the Union.' Annie was joined by her sister, Nell, who opened on 2 April with a dinner-hour talk at Keyham Gates in Devonport and an evening talk at Plymouth Co-operative Guild. The following day she was at Plymouth Market Place, the same time as Annie was speaking at the Assembly Rooms in Teignmouth. Annie then returned to the familiar venue of the Alexandra Hall in Newton Abbot on 4 April.

Both Annie and Nell's talks highlighted a major event being planned for Plymouth Guildhall on 15 April, Christabel Pankhurst's second visit to Devon. The *Western Evening Herald* was at the Guildhall to record her performance. 'Of course there is not the faintest trace of shyness left in her. Alert, ready for, even courting (if one may use the word) opposition and humorous, she spoke fluently and with admirable clearness. Here was quite another type of woman, as much at home on the platform as the average woman is in the drawing-room or kitchen. But one got used to her energy, which was natural and unaffected. With head up, she turned to this side, grasping the platform rail; then hearing a remark from the arcade to her right, she would swing round to face the opposition and with outstretched hand emphasise her point… She was most dreadfully severe, was this young woman, on Mr Asquith… He was called the Mrs Partington of the Twentieth Century. "Mr Asquith is a very hard man; he won't bend, but," said Miss Pankhurst, arms outstretched and palms touching, "but he'll break."' Christabel's talk was part of a hectic schedule. The previous day she had been in Dewsbury and the following morning was due to make the return 300 mile journey back to Manchester, leaving Annie Kenney to keep the momentum going.

In May, Annie teamed up with Amy Montague to launch a 'Votes for Women' tour of Exeter, Torquay, Paignton and Plymouth, sometimes against all odds. After a polite reception from a small audience at the Royal Public Rooms in Exeter, Annie faced 100 Liberals in Torquay who came to retaliate for mid-Devon. Annie reported in *Votes for Women*, 'The meeting was closed very early, because I felt it a waste of our precious time to try to argue with men who were so full of enmity about a defeat, but we had an idea. We cleared them out one door, and I had scouts getting women in at another, and we had a splendid meeting for women only.' A more positive meeting the following day, stewarded by men apologetic about the Liberals' behaviour, left Annie optimistic that she could leave the work in Torquay in the good hands two local ladies, one of whom was probably Frances Latimer.

When her father died, Frances moved from Plymouth to Torquay. Having lobbied for women's suffrage for twenty-five years, she had made up her mind about the new

MISS S. FRANCES LATIMER.
From a Photo. by Hawke, George Street, Plymouth.

suffragettes. She wrote in the *Torquay Times*, 'Not being of the patient Griselda type, I am of the opinion that fifty years of polite and peaceable demand on the part of women for political enfranchisement is time enough to test the inefficacy of such methods... Therefore we should be thankful to the brave and sturdy women who stand forth in unpleasant notoriety, and do not shirk contest, reproach or imprisonment to obtain justice for their sex... it is high time that those who desire emancipation should resent the insincerity, the flouting and the talking out of bills and similar self-interested ways of objecting legislators.'

Her defence of militancy made for an uncomfortable scene at the Women's Liberal Association AGM in Newton Abbot in 1909. The *Exeter and Plymouth Gazette* reported, 'Miss Latimer... urged that it was no slight matter for women to be hunger-struck and to be gagged and fed. [Already happening in Holloway prison] Miss Latimer's further remarks aroused so much opposition that she had to desist.' A motion condemning violence, but urging WLAs to do their utmost to further the cause of women's suffrage by every orderly and legitimate method, was carried with just one or two against.

Continuing her 'Votes for Women' tour in 1908 Annie Kenney spoke to crowded audiences in Plymouth. At the Unitarian Church, the Forrester's Hall and the Athenaeum she repeated her belief that taxation and the franchise should go hand in hand. The injustice of women paying taxes but having little say in how they were spent was to become a constant theme. According to Annie, forty years of quiet work had merely shown that the time had come when begging and praying must cease and women must demand their rights and adopt militant methods. The *Western Morning News* even reported the views of Mr Tombe, who presided at the Forester's Hall, that, '...the tactics of the Suffragettes were not violent enough. Nothing could be got from a capitalist Government except by violence,' a conspicuously socialist view in this gathering.

Moving on from a meeting at the dock gates in Devonport, Annie was enthusiastically cheered at Cattedown. After a rocky start at Torquay she had worked her way from outright abuse, through polite hearings and warm approval to keen interest and rousing cheers

- until she returned to Teignmouth. The *Post and Gazette* recorded a number of lads with bells and a large whistle who caused an intolerable din! And at Newton Abbot she only managed to sidestep a, '…disagreeable demonstration by an hostile crowd consisting chiefly of women and youths', by slipping out a side door.

On a positive note, Annie was able to announce a local branch of the WSPU had formed in Plymouth and about two hundred local women were expected to join a demonstration in Hyde Park. This wasn't the first time women had gathered in London. In February 1907 the NUWSS had organised a mass demonstration, known as the Mud March because of the appalling weather, to show support for a Suffrage Bill before Parliament. With 3,000 women participating it was the largest demonstration up to that time. A year later around 10,000 joined a second NUWSS procession through London. But both were to fade into relative insignificance after 21 June 1908.

The rally was stimulated by a challenge from the newly elected Liberal Prime Minister, Herbert Henry Asquith, to demonstrate that the campaign for women's votes was more than a flash in the pan. In *Votes for Women,* the WSPU paper, Emmeline Pankhurst spoke of her ambitions for the day. 'We intend to have not 10,000, but over 100,000 women present to claim their enfranchisement. It will be remembered that on the famous occasion in Hyde Park when the men pulled down the railings, 67,000 men demonstrated. [In July 1866 when they were fighting for the vote] Though Mr Gladstone [the Home Secretary] said that he did not expect women to show as large numbers as men have shown, we are confident of being able to double this figure.' Gladstone's remark was predictable. Like Asquith, he was also against women's suffrage.

Twenty-three year old Gwyneth Keys was a lynch pin of the newly formed WSPU Plymouth committee. She accompanied Annie on all her talks and worked on advertising events, identifying the Picture House at St James Hall as ideal given their publicity would be seen by thousands. They also planned to leaflet doctors, nurses, teachers, shop girls and all the political parties. Women went out at night to chalk pavements, advertising meetings at the Corn Exchange and Public Hall, in Stoke and Keyham and at Fore Street dock gates. Men and women came from miles around, 3,000 on one Thursday night alone. The polite and amiable crowd followed Annie to her car. She had to threaten to deliver another speech if they didn't leave! Of her time in Plymouth she concluded, 'If energy, time and enthusiasm will bring success, Plymouth women will see that failure is impossible… It was the last place Drake visited before he faced the enemy. It was the first place I got new recruits ready for Hyde Park.'

Gwyneth's views fluctuated over the years and deciding which organisation to actively support, the WSPU, the NUWSS… or both, became a running theme. And she wasn't alone. A couple of years later other Plymouth activists, including Edith Fewins and Marion Phillips, joined her in also signing up for the NUWSS. Then a little later they again became caught up with enthusiasm for the WSPU when a new organiser arrived. But this was all in the future. In the first week of June 1908 Annie showed remarkable fortitude by returning to Torquay and Paignton, fortunately to a much better reception. Fund-raising committees were formed and she reported, '…a magnificent meeting at the Public Hall in Paignton where they sold £2 15s [over £400 today] worth of tickets for Hyde Park.'

These weeks in Devon were fundamental in prompting women, many of them unaware of the activity in the last century, to become involved with women's suffrage. In Torquay, two nurses, Sister Marie and Sister Hollis, opened up their nursing home, Kent House, for a meeting. Annie commented, '…these ladies a week ago had never thought seriously about the vote and had only four days to work it up.' Multiply this gathering by all the events where tickets were sold and it makes for a significant deputation from Devon to Hyde Park.

With military efficiency, the WSPU chartered special trains to transport suffrage groups, professionals, academics, church members and more from across the country to join seven processions carrying 700 banners through London. The entire procession took over two hours to pass spectators lining the route in what *Votes for Women* proclaimed 'The Largest Political Demonstration in the History of the World.' The best way to capture the sheer excitement and atmosphere of the day is through the words of someone who simply signs herself 'Exonian,' thought to be Edith Splatt, a journalist who contributed articles for the *Express and Echo*. She was one of the small group of Exeter women who were also active for both the WSPU and

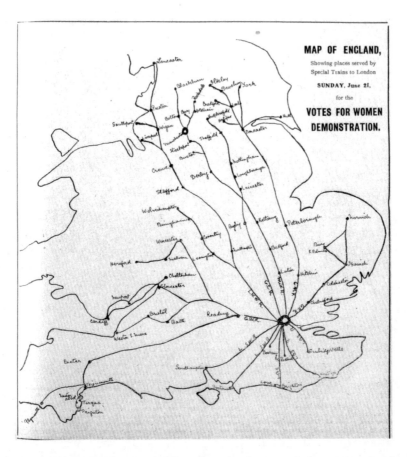

the NUWSS. In 1908 she takes us to the heart of the action in these excerpts from the *Western Times* on 23 June:

'It was absolutely unpremeditated, my visit to Hyde Park on Sunday. I went to St David's Station to see the Exeter section of militant suffragists off by the excursion that started at 9.55am and the infection of their enthusiasm carried me along too... They were a very small band who joined the train at Exeter. Mrs Montague, graceful in the white toilette which the leaders of the movement were to wear... was distinguished by a broad shoulder sash of white silk petersham, boldly bordered with purple and green and bearing in big purple letters, the legend, "Votes for Women." In addition she wore her speaker's badge, an artistic white moire ribbon depending from a green and purple bow, and having the word "Speaker" embroidered on it diagonally in purple between two bold green lines, and a laurel wreath in gold encircling the purple letters "N.W.S.P.U." With Mrs Montague were some half-dozen ladies, and two or three gentlemen, with "Votes for Women" cards in the hat bands of their straw hats. Just at ten o'clock the train steamed in with the band of delighted-looking enthusiasts on board who had come up from Plymouth, Paignton,

Torquay and Teignmouth, and places down the line... Greetings and a few "Votes for Women" shouts are exchanged as we join the crowd, and then we are off... We stop for a minute at Tiverton Junction, and not again until London is reached...

A small crowd greets us with cheers and shouts of "Votes for Women!" as we run into the terminus. The marshals take us in hand on alighting. Banners are produced, the standard-bearer steps proudly to the front and we are off. Outside the station the contingents from Bath and other Somerset and West-Country towns are awaiting us, formed up four deep, their banners all in the purple, white and green of the N.W.S.P.U. colours brilliant in the sunshine. Of those we have brought, Torquay and Paignton shows a man and woman clasping hands with the motto, "Justice and Equality." Plymouth's, borne on one side by a high school mistress in cap and gown, [most probably Eliza, known as Elsie, Aitken-Davies, seen here behind her sister] bearing the legend, "N.W.S.P.U. Votes for Women. The Ever Faithful City is represented by the big-emblazoned word "Exeter" alone. The well-known actress,

GREAT VOTES FOR WOMEN DEMONSTRATION IN HYDE PARK,
SUNDAY, JUNE 21, 1908.

and Devonian lady, Miss Marion Lind… officiates as one of our banner-bearers, and the steadying purple ribbons are held on the right by an authoress of high repute…

We are not used to processions - personally I have never even been a bridesmaid - so we experience some difficulty at first in keeping step and line, but the police are exceedingly kind and courteous, and we are anxious to do our best, so by the time the Victoria Gate is reached we are swinging along to the music of our bands in fine style. Crowds have lined the route down Westbourne Road, and all the way, but they are as nothing to the throng in the Park.

Here the remarks begin too. Devonians and lovers of the land of curds and cream evidently abound among the friendly onlookers. "Well done, Plymouth Argyle!" a group of working men shout as the Plymouth banner comes into view. "Up Devon!" "Good old Exeter!" we also hear, and then - we wince - for we are only 18 all told, and we make as brave a show as we can - we hear a contemptuous voice, in unmistakably Cockney accents, exclaim, "Exeter must be a small place." We hear some rough jeering and jesting of course. "What's the old man doing? Home washing the dinner-plates?" some of our middle-aged associates are asked, but the remarks are all taken in good part.'

The 'authoress of high repute' was probably Mary Willcocks. She was a prolific writer of romantic novels that reflected her feminist beliefs, focusing on strong, determined women struggling in a society that denied them their basic rights. Becoming an inaugural member of the Exeter NUWSS the following year was a natural fit for her. Given her reputation as a formidable lecturer and debater it's not surprising that she became a regular speaker at meetings across the county.

MISS M. P. WILLCOCKS.

Back in Hyde Park, Mary probably joined our Exonian catching snatches of the speeches, including that given by Amy Montague from platform 8, chaired by Christabel Pankhurst. Each speaker was listed in *Votes for Women*. 'Mrs Amy Montague, wife of Leopold Montague, J.P., of Crediton in Devon comes on her mother's side of old Huguenot stock, which had suffered for the cause of religious freedom. Her father was a Mutiny veteran, who fought at Delhi, and commanded a troop of irregular cavalry. She has travelled in Morocco, Holland, France, Italy and Norway. She has been an active woman Suffragist for several years.' Her place on the platform was probably arranged when Christabel visited Exeter the previous November.

There were around twenty of these raised platforms, surrounded by crowds eager to hear Keir Hardy, Bernard Shaw, Mrs H.G.Wells and Emmeline Pankhurst make the case for women's suffrage. As she later wrote in her autobiography, *My Own Story*, 'When I mounted my platform in Hyde Park, and surveyed the mighty throngs that waited there and the endless crowds that were still pouring into the park from all directions, I was filled with amazement not unmixed with awe. Never had I imagined that so many people could be gathered together to share in a political demonstration'.

It must have been well into the early hours before all the Devon women arrived home, women such as Barbara Hunt from Paignton, who shared her experiences in *Votes for Women:*

On Saturday evening, the 20th, our eyes were anxiously directed to the heavy sky. But on Sunday morning, all those who started from Paignton by the 8.10 train were exhilarated by an almost deliciously cool midsummer day.

Amid handkerchief waving and cheering, the members of this Union streamed out on their way to join the long-talked-of pageant of women in Hyde Park. Every face wore happy smiles, and conversation barely flagged until Paddington was in sight - with waiting friends and banners already unfurled. Very soon our order of march was complete, and we started off almost at a run, but only for a few yards. With many short waits we streamed along, feeling like soldiers in battle array. The fine marches that were played by the bands were fully appreciated by processionists and onlookers, who seemed to have thousands of eyes, most of them interested and animated. Some of the spectators lining the pavements and upon balconies unmistakably wore our very vivid colours. The banners, swelled out by the light breeze, were grand to behold. Our banner bearers, Miss Florence Hughes with martial dignity, and Miss Beard, splendidly gowned in beige shantung embroidered with cherries, nobly bore our standard presented and worked by Paignton ladies. When we arrived in the park there was, no longer any room to spread out our banner its full width, as crowds of interested and even enthusiastic people narrowed our path. Expressions of admiration were heard from many lips, and the men in our procession had to stand the fire of numberless jeers and witticisms, which they bore very good naturedly.

The references in both accounts that deserve a mention are to 'the men in our procession'. It was not simply Devon women who had signed up; many men supported the women's suffrage organisations too.

The Manchester Courier was fulsome in its praise. 'Only those determinedly deaf or who have just awakened to the fact that there is a woman's suffrage movement were to be found asking what it is that yesterday's Hyde Park demonstrators want. To have roused such sleepers is indeed a mighty success, and it may fairly be said to-day that the women agitators have effected the first part of their programme triumphantly.' But *The Times* offered a caveat, echoed in other newspapers. 'We can but offer a tribute of admiration to the wonderful skill in organisation displayed by those responsible for this remarkable demonstration... it would be idle to deny... that a great many women are, for the time, eagerly desirous of the franchise, though of course, 30,000 demonstrators and a crowd of a quarter of a million to watch them is no proof such as the Prime Minister required, to the effect that an overwhelming majority of the women of this country demanded the vote.'

After the excitement of what became known as Suffrage Sunday, the momentum continued in London. However things seemed to go quiet across Devon - apart from in the traditional autumn Carnivals. A suffragette choir performed at Crediton, a float at Topsham depicting 'Suffragettes in Downing Street' was declared a clever and original tableaux and at Chumleigh, Mr Webber's Suffragette float gained a consolation prize. At Appledore the *North Devon Journal* reported, 'Great amusement was caused by [locals taking the part of] Miss Pankhurst's party of Suffragettes who were making a deafening noise with a bell.' There was also a float on the 'Suffragettes at Bow Street' at Sidmouth that raised a laugh. By the summer of 1908, suffragette appearances in court were increasingly well-reported so the float, possibly created by the embryonic anti-suffragist group there, would have struck a chord with the crowd.

It was a topic for all ages. Mr W. B. Luke chose the suffragettes for his address to the girls at the Edgehill College Prize Day in Bideford. The *North Devon Herald* recorded he, '...bade them to be strong. That was one of the lessons which must be learned from the Suffragette movement. Whatever might be the development of that controversy it was certainly going to affect the future of the nation considerably, and girls would need to be no puny, ailing damsels with weak hearts, weak backs and weak minds, but strong in muscle, bone and sinew, and overflowing with healthy vitality, so that they might communicate some of it to the somewhat apathetic man.' One way or another the suffragette cause was resonating across Devon.

THE NEW MRS PARTINGTON (OF THE ANTI SUFFRAGE SOCIETY)
"SOMEHOW THE TIDE KEEPS RISING!"

Chapter Six
Holding Back the Tide
Autumn - Winter 1908

Through election campaigning and recruiting for the Hyde Park demonstration, both the suffragists and the suffragettes were having an impact in Devon. However, their determined response to Asquith's challenge, to prove that the majority of women wanted the vote, had brought feelings to a head amongst others who felt quite differently. Devon women now not only had to distinguish between the law-abiding suffragists and the militant suffragettes, but also those who believed women shouldn't have the vote at all, the anti-suffragists.

It was almost twenty years since Mary Ward had published her Appeal Against Women's Suffrage in the *Nineteenth Century*, and many supporters considered their views so widely accepted that any organised action was unnecessary. But the headline-grabbing tactics of the suffragettes had rattled and re-energised antis right across the country. So much so that in July 1908 they came together to launch

The Women's National Anti-Suffrage League. The first edition of the *Anti-Suffrage Review* in December announced:

> No moment could be more favourable for the appearance of our little journal. The recent performances of the Women's Social and Political Union; the attempt to 'rush' the House of Commons, with its accompaniments of riot and injury, and its sequel in a mock-heroic trial, and a mock-heroic imprisonment, which could be terminated at any moment by the will of the prisoners; the ludicrous, but none the less scandalous, attack by women of the same body on the decency and dignity of the House of Commons itself, have sent a shock wave of repulsion - a wave of angry laughter - through England, and are bringing recruits from all sides to the Anti-Suffrage League... the strong antipathy of our serious slow-moving middle class has been aroused; and no movement has ever yet been successful in England that had the feeling of our great middle class against it.

The 'rush' on the House of Commons had taken place on 13 October when members of the WSPU attempted to force their way inside, leading to the arrest of 24 women and 12 men. This attack on the dignity of the House of Commons was compounded when Muriel Matters, from the WFL, chained herself to the Grille in the Ladies Gallery. It was through acts like these that the anti-suffragists believed the suffragettes were destroying respect for women, both in the home and in their communities.

They took heart from Mary Ward's experiences in America where, according to the *Western Evening Herald*, '...she finds that after sixty years of agitation... the movement in the United States is now in the process of defeat and extinction at the hands of the women themselves. Wherever the suffrage movement became strong, an anti-suffrage movement was started, and it invariably conquered. In the middle of the last century four States granted the suffrage to women, but four years ago no fewer than thirteen States rejected Women Suffrage Bills.'

Significantly, alongside a few high profile men, the British organisation was largely fuelled by the initiative and hard work of women. They continued firmly to believe that philanthropic activity and voting in local or municipal elections gave women far more influence on domestic concerns than having the Parliamentary vote. It was inappropriate, their reasoning went, for women to have a voice in things that were not their natural concern, such as international matters or war. Men who had built up the State, and whose physical strength protected it, must govern it.

Up to this point, support for the anti-suffrage standpoint was so mainstream that a formal organisation hadn't been felt necessary. But groups now sprang up across the country, including in Devon. On 30 October the New London Hotel, Exeter, was the venue for the first Anti-Suffragist League meeting in the county. It was chaired by Lady Acland, Gertrude Acland that is, of Killerton House near Tiverton. She opened the meeting with a personal statement, covered by the *Exeter and Plymouth Gazette*. 'Lady Acland... had taken a very long time to decide whether to belong to the League or not... but she considered the present time to be a crisis, because the Prime Minister had challenged the women of England; the challenge must be accepted and they must range themselves on one side or the other... They could all be Suffragists if they believed the welfare and interests of women were bound up in the Parliamentary vote, but they did not believe it... In days gone by, women as a whole were not sufficiently considered. But times had changed, and many doors had opened and were still opening to women. They saw women inspectors, women guardians, co-opted members of Education Committees and they had votes for County and Borough Councils... Her Ladyship concluded by saying that she could not help thinking that if women turned their attention to getting women on these Boards which were open to them, and did their best to educate the rising generation, they would really be adding more to the happiness and welfare of mankind than by simply agitating... for the Parliamentary vote.'

Lady Acland then read a telegram from Countess Fortescue of Castle Hill in North Devon, wife of the Lord Lieutenant. 'My sympathies are now entirely with the objects of the meeting and I wish you every success.' Lady Fortescue had recently concluded that, '...now women have shown how totally unfit they are to take such heavy responsibilities on themselves, I feel it will be an evil day when they become voters…'

It was a very different stance to that taken by Lady Acland's niece through marriage, Eleanor Acland, who was already a committed suffragist. Over the coming years both she and her husband, Francis Dyke Acland, a Liberal MP, become steadfast advocates for the suffrage cause. Although based in London, she became increasingly active in the west country, later accepting a post as vice president of the South Western Federation of the NUWSS. Her pro-suffrage views must have made for some interesting conversations when they visited the family estate at Killerton. Although she and her aunt may have found some common ground in their condemnation of WSPU militancy. Eleanor often took to the papers to share her views and, in correspondence with Christabel Pankhurst in *Votes for Women,* she was adamant that militant tactics were harming the cause.

But Gertrude Acland remained resolutely anti-suffragist, happy to welcome Miss Mary Angela Dickens, the honorary secretary of the Anti-Suffrage League, to their Exeter meetings. In their *Review,* Mary, granddaughter of Charles Dickens, claimed that, 'The matter was urgent and unless action was taken the country might drift towards revolution… If women's suffrage was ever conceded the disasters which would ensue would lie… at the door of women's apathy and selfishness. To laugh at the Suffragists, or to ignore them, was a sorry jest. It would be playing into their hands and give over to them without a struggle that for which the Anti-Suffrage League should fight to the last.'

Miss Dickens made her views clear on the incident in Parliament when Muriel Matters chained herself to the Grille in the Ladies Gallery. 'Public patience is being sorely tried by these outbursts of feminine fanaticism,' she wrote in a letter to the *Western Times.* 'These Suffragists… have got out of their proper lines and must get back again.' Her words shed light on how differently she, and many others, viewed the growing campaign for the vote. 'The whole of the Suffragist propaganda,' she continued, 'was based on ignoring and defying the fundamental differences fixed by nature herself between man and woman. The claim of the Suffragists was therefore against nature - abnormal.' An extreme statement from our 21st century perspective but it's important to remember that at the time this was a socially conventional and completely acceptable view.

The autumn of 1908 saw a noticeable increase in anti-suffrage activity in South and East Devon. In September and October, Beatrice Hamilton Derry, from Mount Radford in Exeter, was busy sharing her views in the *Western Morning News*. 'I heard Annie Kenney speak, and all I could think of were the ravings of a delirious person, and several friends told me it made them ill to listen to her. They longed to say, "My good woman, do go and take a 'rest cure'. Prison is the very place for all such, but not the same prison as we give to our worst criminals."' It's easy to write this off as typical anti-suffrage hostility but Annie was in fact heading for a stay in a sanatorium within a few months, one reason why Adela replaced her for the meeting in Ilfracombe in the New Year.

Beatrice sent several letters to the paper, her views ranging from the credible to the extreme. On the question of 'no taxation without representation', she maintained that women were represented via the municipal vote, a fair point at the local level. Specifically of the suffragettes, she wrote, 'I often wonder that they are unable to see that nine tenths of what they write and speak, so far from being convincing, is positively damaging to their cause. It proves them only capable of drivelling sentimentality, and an utter inability to see things in their true light.' It may be difficult to empathise with these blunt, unequivocal remarks, but the suffragette's actions, if not their words, increasingly led others to a similar conclusion.

The *Western Morning News* printed a response from Gwyneth Keys, speaking for Plymouth NUWSS. 'For forty years there have been women's suffrage societies, doing their best in a quiet way to get the Parliamentary vote for women. Forty years is a sufficiently long time to test the efficacy of such methods, and their inadequacy is proved by the fact that until a few years ago - to be exact, until the WSPU started the present agitation - but few persons were aware of the existence of such societies, and even now, in the minds of most people, the question of woman's suffrage is solely connected with the names of Pankhurst and Kenney. Of the quiet labourers of forty years - to whom all honour is due - they know nothing. The present tactics have raised the question of votes for women from an academic dream to a question of practical politics.'

The antis were undeterred. At the beginning of November a branch of the Women's National Anti-Suffrage League was formed in Torquay. In an orderly meeting, Miss Harriet Mallock and Mary Dickens spoke on the arguments and objectives of the League and the necessity for organising an effective opposition. Mrs Ely, who was to become the Torquay contact for the anti-suffragists, spoke of her practical experience in America, '...which had there kept back the threatened concession of women's suffrage for forty years.'

By contrast, just three days later a WSPU meeting in Newton Abbot descended into chaos. The *Western Times* reported, 'There was a disgraceful scene at a meeting organised in support of the Women's Suffrage movement... at which addresses were to have been delivered by Miss Mills of Paignton and Miss Potter from Dartmouth. The audience was composed mostly of working women, and there was an indescribable scene from start to finish. The women in the body of the hall sang, jeered, shrieked, and rang bells, and would not allow the speakers to utter a single word.' When Constable Martin was called, the women claimed they were only doing what the suffragists themselves had done at Liberal meetings. Only a year before, local youths caused similar chaos during the Mid Devon by-election. But this time it was working women making their feelings plain. After an hour and a half the meeting was abandoned.

The following week, Miss Dickens was in Sidmouth where *The Sidmouth Herald* reported her plea for women to realise, '...the exceeding urgency, the intense importance of the point at issue.' She held passionately to her belief that the suffragists were completely mistaken and that the vigorous energy and ability with which they pressed their claim were the feverish manifestations of their denial of nature. In contrast she believed that the anti-suffragists possessed, '... No hysterical forces. No artificial stimulated powers. Simply the quiet resolution of normal women. A great power truly - one of the greatest in the world.'

Mary Dicken's definition of 'normal women' deserves exploration. The core membership of the Anti-Suffrage League was comprised of upper middle class and aristocratic ladies and their husbands. Their views stemmed from the exclusive world they inhabited. They tended to be women of traditional values and beliefs, while those in favour of suffrage were more aware that the world was changing and that they needed to be part of that change. Mary Dickens again disagreed. Anti-suffragist women were, '...first of all women of exceptional mental culture who have studied the subject in all its bearings, who are well informed on all the political, social and domestic problems involved, who are qualified on all counts to form an opinion, who have weighed and decided the question. In this little body of women beats the heart of the Anti-Suffrage movement. To them it owes its life.'

She challenged the suffragist's claim that possession of the vote would raise women's wages and improve working conditions. These, she argued, were reforms which would be, '...brought about much more easily through the woman's exercise of her rightful powers as councillor, as pleader, as moral influencer, than through the antagonistic enforcement of equal rights.' It was a well-received message and the motion to establish a Sidmouth branch of the Women's National Anti-Suffrage League was passed unanimously. It was a development supported by the *Sidmouth Herald* which published a statement of the objectives of the Anti-Suffrage League every week from the Christmas of 1908 through to the autumn of 1909, each concluding with the appeal, 'The Women's Suffrage movement must be defeated by women themselves. Women of England, we appeal to your patriotism and common sense.' It was a message that resonated with many Sidmouth residents. As well as regular meetings, they conducted a house-to-house canvass armed with petition forms, distributed by the League nationwide. There was a brief delay over the winter months due to sickness in the town, but the campaign was well under way again by the spring of 1909.

There's an irony to the establishment of an anti-suffrage group in Sidmouth. A lady called Mrs Partington, who had lived in a cottage located almost on the beach there, became immortalised in folklore through a speech given at Taunton in 1831 by the Rev Sydney Smith. The *North Devon Journal* published his words following the Lords' rejection of a Reform Bill intended to extended men's voting rights. 'The attempt of the Lords to stop the progress of reform reminds

COMING IN WITH THE TIDE

me very forcibly of the great storm at Sidmouth, and of the conduct
of the excellent Mrs Partington on that occasion. In the winter of
1824 there set in a great flood upon that town - the tide rose to an
incredible height, the waves rushed in upon the houses, and
everything was threatened with destruction. In the midst of this
sublime and terrible storm, Dame Partington, who lived upon the
beach, was seen at the door of her house, trundling her mop,
squeezing out the sea-water and vigorously pushing away the Atlantic
Ocean. The Atlantic was roused. Mrs Partington's spirit was up. But I
need not tell you that the contest was unequal. The Atlantic Ocean
beat Mrs Partington. She was excellent at a slop or a puddle; but she
should not have meddled with a tempest.'

As a result, the phrase 'Mrs Partington and her mop' became
shorthand right across the English speaking world for a person
engaged in an unequal and futile contest. It was an image
enthusiastically embraced by the suffrage movement to represent the
futility of the anti-suffragist stance. But it was a stance gaining a
significant hold, for the moment at least, in this corner of Devon.

Lady Acland kept the momentum going in Exeter, appealing
through the *Exeter Gazette* to, '…all patriotic women to join our
League, and to exert themselves to defeat the women's suffrage
movement.' She presided over a large and influential gathering in
Heavitree at the beginning of December where she invited all those
who disapproved of the present suffrage agitation to join them. They
were encouraged to support it by every means in their power, given
that the granting of the franchise to women would be revolutionary.

The revolution theme, introduced by Miss Dickens, was reinforced by other speakers. Women's suffrage would shake the whole fabric of society to its foundation, undermining the very basis of the Empire. An Anti-Suffrage branch soon formed in Exeter with its stated aim, 'To resist the proposal to admit women to the Parliamentary Franchise and to Parliament.' Anyone wanting further information was urged to contact Mrs Ely in Torquay, Mrs Reginald Yonge in Plympton or Miss Chalmers in Sidmouth.

In January 1909, the Men's League for Opposing Women Suffrage was formed, with Lord Cromer as President. Sir Thomas Acland, husband of Lady Gertrude and also present at the Exeter meeting, spoke of the dangerous consequences of women possessing the power to legislate, and that everyone who recognised the danger must oppose it. It was a view that attracted a significant following. A reporter from the *Gazette* was impressed with turnout at the meetings. 'Whatever may be the merits or demerits of this burning question, Miss Dickens is to be congratulated on securing so influential a backing for her cause in Exeter.'

THE ANTI-SUFFRAGE SOCIETY AS PORTRAIT-PAINTER

BRITANNIA UNSEXED

"THE A.S.S.—
This, my dear Mrs Britannia, is a true & authentic portrait of yourself if ever you get the vote."

Published by the Suffrage Atelier.

The anti-suffrage movement continued to gain ground across Devon. By the beginning of 1909 branches had formed in Sidmouth, Exeter, Torquay and the Three Towns and District, just four of 43 branches established countrywide. In February 1909 there was a meeting at the Bath Saloons in Torquay, a few days after Mrs Pankhurst had appeared there. According to the *Western Morning News* there was, '…a full attendance, chiefly of ladies, including a number of Suffragists, [including Frances Latimer] who at the back of the room, occasionally made their presence known by their demonstration of feelings (including a few hisses) and also by handing up written questions.' Professor Dicey, a member of the Anti-Suffrage League unable to be present, wrote, '…the granting of votes to women was, whilst appearing to be an extension of their rights, in reality the imposition upon them of duties which they were unable to perform,'

These harsh words would have raised the hackles of the suffragists in the hall. But the speaker, Admiral Freemantle, may have been more difficult to take issue with, initially at least. He invited the audience to consider a question at the core of government procedure; could suffragists argue fairly and justly and be reasonable to their opponents? He answered, 'Mrs Pankhurst had boasted that no member of the Government had been allowed to say a word in public for the last six months.' We should perhaps add, 'without interruption', but it supports his view that Mrs Pankhurst, '…would not listen to fair argument therefore was not fit to take part in discussion of any questions that Parliament was concerned with.'

He then repeated the anti-suffragist's conviction that any concession was a chink in the wall with universal suffrage, the vote for all men and women, bound to follow. 'Of the new voters… half would be women who had never thought of giving a vote before. Did they think this would be compatible with the safety of the country…? If the Anti-Suffragists were to avert this revolution and danger they must be energetic in defence of their view and show the shrieking Suffragettes that they had no claim to represent the women of England.' Frances Latimer attempted to open up a discussion about women and divorce proceedings but was closed down by the Chairman.

At Honiton Miss Chalmers, President of the East Devon branches of the Anti-Suffrage League, heralded their success in the *Exeter and Plymouth Gazette*. 'Although the League had been established in Sidmouth for only about five months, she thought it could be safely said that they had practically expelled the Suffragettes from the place, although at first they made a great deal of noise.' The *Sidmouth Herald* followed-up with a damning statement from Lady Arundel. 'When the question of granting the suffrage to women was first mooted she firmly believed that spinsters and widows who had a property qualification could in all justice claim a vote. But now when it was proposed to make it general she had altered her views and had become a member of the Anti-Suffrage League. The more she thought of it the more anti she became.'

This belief, that granting the vote to any women was a precursor to universal suffrage, was repeated time and time again by the antis. But both the NUWSS and the WSPU had always campaigned for the vote on the same terms as men. Given the property requirement this would have excluded most women, leaving them alongside the 40% of men still without the franchise. Regardless of this, the anti's message was gaining ground. The Sidmouth branch had already grown to over 200 members and associates.

The Honiton meeting was part of an April campaign that, according to the Anti-Suffrage League, had been, '...crowned with brilliant success.' The speaker, Mrs Archibald Colquohorn, confirmed, '...the intelligent and thoughtful people of the constituency are waking up to the importance and truth of the Anti-Suffrage cause.' Meetings at Budleigh Salterton and Exmouth followed, though only 30 attended there. Then it was back to a packed Barnfield Hall in Exeter - but not just full with anti-suffragists. The word was out and infiltrators from the NUWSS, including Selina Cooper, Jessie Montgomery, secretary of the newly-formed Exeter branch, and organiser, Margaret Robertson, stationed themselves in the front seats. Sir Thomas Acland launched into his speech, contending that, '...the interests of women had been, ought to be, and would be provided for from time-to-time as women decide by their male relations and companions.' [*Western Times*] Margaret Robertson raised questions but, like Frances Latimer in Torquay, was silenced and forced to resort to a letter in the paper with her challenges.

In Plymouth, the anti's cause had been taken up by Mrs Reginald Yonge from Sparkwell and the Mayoress, Mrs Spender. An initial meeting was held in November 1908 where a committee was formed with a view to creating a local branch. Six months later a notice appeared in the *Western Morning News*. 'Sir - May I... appeal for help to all ladies who are not in favour of the Parliamentary vote for women? The Prime Minister having asked all women of the United Kingdom to express their opinion about female suffrage, the "Women's

National Anti-Suffrage league" has undertaken to present a petition to Parliament, an instalment of which, numbering nearly 244,000 names, has already gone up.' Two hundred and forty-four thousand women, who under other circumstances wouldn't dream of making a political statement, felt strongly enough to publicly express their opposition to the suffrage campaign. There was also widespread support for their views amongst others not brave enough to add their names.

Prominent speakers in both the WSPU and the NUWSS attempted to define this surge in anti-suffragist sentiment as proof that they had recognised, and were reacting to, the growing strength of the suffragist movement. And they may have been right. Up to this point the antis had believed their stance to be so mainstream that no formal organisation was necessary. The appearance of branches of the Women's National Anti-Suffrage League in Devon reflected an acceptance that this was no longer true. They needed to become more visible. It was a demonstration of commitment from educated and often influential women that suffragists were keen to undermine. Propaganda was urgently needed to marginalise their views and counter a movement that was undeniably gathering momentum.

Chapter Seven
A Strenuous Campaign
Winter 1908 - Spring 1909

While the anti-suffragists thrived in East and South Devon there was a brief lull in WSPU activity county-wide, possibly due to Annie Kenney being called away to focus on events in Bristol. But their campaign was revitalised in November 1908 with the arrival of Elsie Howey. It was the WSPU's strategy to not only appoint regional coordinators such as Annie, but also paid local organisers who targeted areas to be developed with an exhaustive programme of public meetings, fund raising and street canvassing. They would stay for six weeks at a time, before leaving ongoing campaigning in the hands of local workers.

Elsie was one of those who responded to an appeal by Emmeline Pethick Lawrence in *Votes for Women* for, '…young women of private means or with parents able and willing to support them and give them freedom to choose their own vocation to come and give a year of their life to the cause.' The piece continued, 'Mrs. Howey and her two daughters have given generously of all that they have, but the best prized gift is the life-work of this noble girl who has undergone two periods of imprisonment for the sake of women less privileged and happily placed than herself. She is one of our most able and successful organisers, and takes all the duties and responsibilities of our chief officers.'

Elsie was an experienced activist. The prison sentences mentioned were for taking part in demonstrations outside the House of Commons and Herbert Asquith's home. Her task in Devon was less confrontational; preparing the ground for a significant meeting at Plymouth Guildhall on 27 November where Emmeline Pethick Lawrence was their headline speaker. Emmeline, and her husband Frederick, were key players in the WSPU. They made their London house available for the organisation's headquarters, no small feat given a staff of over 100. They also

financed and published *Votes for Women* and bailed many suffragettes facing prison. Hundreds of women had already taken to the streets in London, joining peaceful deputations to the Houses of Parliament to demand the vote. Many like Elsie were arrested and, if they refused to pay a fine, were sentenced to Holloway Prison. Emmeline and Elsie were well able to bring home the injustice of the women's treatment to a Devon audience.

Volunteers were recruited to distribute handbills and copies of *Votes for Women* outside theatres in the evenings. And there were plans to reinvigorate the campaign in Torquay, nominating the town as a regional centre. In the *Torquay Times* Annie Kenney highlighted the area as, '...a very promising place to obtain workers for this movement because she heard there were many more women in the town than men and that women either owned or occupied most of the houses. Did not those ladies, who paid rates and taxes, think that they should be entitled to express their opinion by the vote?' Of course, the answer from some may have been 'no', given that many were already supporting the anti-suffrage cause there.

Elsie focused on open-air meetings to drum up interest. There were the usual interruptions from youths but, with her powerful speaking voice and the set of steps she took everywhere to raise herself above the crowds, they didn't faze her. Plans were also underway to launch weekly 'At Homes' in the Masonic Hall at Paignton and to open shops as a base for spreading the word and fundraising. Their presence attracted comment from the *Western Evening Herald*. 'In Plymouth, the Suffragists are so bolstered as to open a propagandist department, in the front window of which, picture posters... are exhibited for the clarification of the man in the street. We think it was an unnecessary slight to group the ladies among the ineligibles represented in the Plymouth front window... Very few, indeed, would class even the Suffragettes among the lunatics.'

For three days Elsie and her volunteers drove round Plymouth in a decorated wagonette and held meetings to advertise the appearance of Emmeline Pethick Lawrence. Clara Mordan, a wealthy suffragette who had been the main funder of the 1908 procession, was the warm-up act. She had the crowd in fits of laughter with her characterisation of the modern suffragette, as reported in *Votes for Women*. 'For 40 years they had tried to promote their cause by being demurely, blushingly, retiringly feminine, and the only notice the public seemed to take of them was to give them the most singularly inappropriate nickname ever devised. They called them "The Shrieking Sisterhood." Why, exclaimed Miss Mordan, we would have shrunk into the ground rather than shriek, we were far too well behaved. We were the pink of propriety (laughter)… But some young suffragists said: "How long is this to go on?"'

She introduced Annie Kenney as one of those young suffragists, the young blood of the movement. 'If we don't get the vote we shall be more militant than ever before. We younger women are not going to grow grey in asking for the vote; we are going to grow grey in working for constructive reform as voters.' Emmeline Pethick Lawrence picked up the militancy baton, focusing on men's objections to their methods and how, '…men ought to be sorry they had made these methods necessary for women; that they had driven women to forego their most natural instincts, set aside the traditions and conventions in which they had been brought up, and expose themselves to abuse and violence, and suffering…' It was an inspirational speech that struck a chord with the audience gathered at Plymouth Guildhall that night. The meeting was declared a great success, not least because entry tickets raised £30 13s 6d, the equivalent of around £3,115 today.

But this meeting was only the beginning. Another was planned for 16 December at the Bath Saloons in Torquay with Sylvia Pankhurst. The publicity machine leapt into action again and the decorated wagonette took to the streets. Meetings were held on Paignton Green and at the Masonic Hall, where their branding campaign was on display with Christmas presents wrapped in the colours. For its time, the WSPU was uniquely effective in using art to create a corporate identity. Sylvia Pankhurst, amongst others, designed logos, flags and banners that made a WSPU gathering unmistakable.

The Bath Saloon was again the focus in February 1909 when *Votes for Women* advertised a meeting with Emmeline Pankhurst urging, 'If any readers of this paper have friends living in Devonshire, would they kindly write and advise them to seize the opportunity now before them to hear Mrs Pankhurst.' Women, including Amy Montague, walked the streets selling the paper, a shocking sight in itself. Respectable women acting as common street sellers! It was unheard of. Yet that's exactly what they did, tirelessly publicising meetings in Paignton, Totnes, Teignmouth and Dartmouth. 'Open air meetings are being held in all the surrounding districts and great numbers of handbills are being distributed. On Monday, Dartmouth was for the first time visited by workers of the WSPU when Miss Elsie Ball and Miss Mary Mills held a splendid open-air meeting. Over 400 people listened most attentively and a good collection was made.' Mary Mills, the WSPU organiser, was particularly active, campaigning alongside Amy Montague and Elsie Howey at numerous meetings across the South Hams.

Mrs Pankhurst's first engagement was to a packed house at the Bath Saloon in Torquay. Every detail was thought of, right down to her bouquet - themed in green, white and violet, the colours of the WSPU. Emmeline set out her stall with stunning eloquence. She defended the tactics of disrupting political meetings and accosting MPs that had made it impossible for any Cabinet Minister to address a public meeting without being surrounded by police - the very boast the anti-suffragists used to claim that she was not fit to take part in Parliamentary government. But most of all, it was a rallying call to action that rang round the Bath Saloon that night and again the following Wednesday at Plymouth Guildhall, the location for the 'Great Demonstration' almost thirty years previously. A generation had passed with so little to show for it. Was it any surprise that she challenged her audience to decide what part they were going to take in the struggle for the freedom of their sex? Ada Flatman is typical of those ladies who responded to the rallying cry. (Transcript from a 1946 BBC recording)

'Here I am, a very proud old militant suffragette. How did I become one? It was after attending a meeting in the Horticultural Hall, Westminster where Christabel Pankhurst was to be the speaker. There I saw a young girl in her early twenties giving out handbills at the door and speaking to people as they came in. She later went on to the platform and gave a fighting speech telling how constitutional suffrage had failed to capture the public attention and only militant suffragettes could break down the

press barrier. It thrilled me through and through and I knew I must
be one of that valiant band.'

The women's movement was on the one hand becoming more
established but at the same time, further
divisions were opening up. The militant
WSPU was making a significant impact in
Devon but hot on the suffragettes' heels
was Margaret Robertson, a regional
organiser with the suffragist NUWSS. In
the autumn of 1908 she stepped up
recruitment to meet both the growing
unease many women felt over the tactics
of the suffragettes and the re-emergence
of the anti-suffragist movement.

　　She initially focused on East Devon,
as reported in *The Western Times*. 'In connection with the National
Union of Women's Suffrage Society, a most successful meeting was
held in the Small Manor Hall, Sidmouth last evening. [26 November]
The Hall was not only packed to its utmost capacity, but the entrances
were thronged, and many were unable to gain admittance. Instead
also of brickbats or any other missiles, the crowd heartily
applauded...' Why Sidmouth? Perhaps because it was barely three
weeks since the antis had held their meeting in the town and there
was every prospect of them developing a significant following. In the
Women's Franchise Margaret commented, 'There is a great deal of
prejudice to surmount in this part of the country but the Anti-
Suffragists have done us some service by having been here already,
and left people saying, "Is *that* all they have to say?" '

　　The tone of the evening was set by Mr Roberts, in the chair, as
reported in the *Western Times*. 'While he was a sincere advocate of the
extension of the franchise to women (applause) he was not a
supporter of the militant section of the movement. He thought they
had done infinite harm to the cause they no doubt thought they were
advancing.' He then introduced Mrs Morgan Dockerell, an Irish
suffragist active in support of the cause internationally. Despite not
being local she had obviously caught up with the presence of the

antis in Sidmouth. 'Whenever women's progress came about, there was always the party with the mop, [a reference to Mrs Partington] No matter where the progress had been, they always had that party [the Antis] They had them in Sidmouth.' She obviously wasn't a fan and urged her audience, '...not to be put off with the absurdity and smallness of thinking that a woman wanting a vote was an unwomanly thing... As surely as they stood there they were going to get their votes - (applause).' At the close of the meeting around 40 ladies joined the society and a number remained behind with Margaret Robertson to discuss forming a temporary committee presided over by Mrs Kennet-Were. Other significant figures in Sidmouth included Mary and Annie Leigh Browne and Mary Stewart Kilgour, all committed suffragists who divided their time between London and their family home in this East Devon town. Annie first became involved with suffrage groups in London, but it was when she was elected President of the Devon Union of Women's Liberal Associations in 1906 that she developed a more direct connection with suffrage activities in Devon. They were to remain actively involved with the group for the next decade.

A second meeting, held in the Drill Hall the following evening, was also a success although, according to Margaret's report in the *Women's Franchise*, '...there was an element of flippant youth at the back and we only secured a few more members.' She was joined by local speaker and supporter, Edith Clarence from Coaxdon Hall, Axminster. For a week either side of these meetings they had opened a shop in Sidmouth to distribute literature and promotional post cards where Edith, later to become Hon. Secretary of the WSPU branch in Axminster, had been, '...indefatigable in carrying on the work.'

At the beginning of December Margaret moved on to Plymouth as, according to the *Western Morning News*, '...the NUWSS were unwilling to leave the advocacy of the cause locally to the more aggressive Women's Social and Political Union.' [The WSPU had formed a Three Towns branch the previous April] She settled herself into her accommodation at 12 Old Park Road and planned her campaign, starting with taking a shop for ten days. She promptly advertised in the *Women's Franchise* for help with the rent. It was a successful appeal. The person who stepped forward to cover the cost was none other than Evelina Haverfield from Dorset, someone who was to play a significant role in Devon.

Organising meetings caused Margaret Robertson some trepidation, as she recounted in the *Common Cause*. 'All those who have organised will know the despair which descends upon one when one receives yet another letter of polite regret from a potential supporter... Speakers too must be secured... Now to see the meetings are properly advertised. In Devonport the bulk of the men work in the Docks, so our easiest way of advertising is by a few thousand handbills given out day by day at different gates. I also post handbills to every schoolmistress and every clergyman in the place, about 60 in all... The Plymouth meeting we advertise by poster, handbills sent to every political, religious, and charitable association and distributed by sympathisers at every opportunity - by press advertisement and a characteristic Plymouth method - the triangular barrow wheeled about the streets which takes, on each side, three Artist's League posters and three posters of the meeting, the pictures proving an unfailing attraction.'

Despite the stress, her efforts paid off. Margaret reported in the *Women's Franchise*, 'Foundations have, I think, been laid for a strong society in Plymouth... a few open-air meetings led up to what the local press calls an "admirable meeting" in the Corn Exchange, presided over by Sir Charles Redford and addressed by Mrs Swiney,

Mrs Cooper [possibly Selina Cooper] and me. Forty-one members for the local branch are already secured, and there is every hope of a strong committee being formed after Christmas.'

December was also busy in Exeter. A meeting was held at 10 Baring Crescent Exeter by invitation of Miss Montgomery, someone already significant within Exeter. Jessie Montgomery was a founder and secretary of the university extension movement there, pivotal in establishing the Royal Albert Memorial Museum and untiring in her work to improve educational opportunities for girls. She had been a supporter of women's suffrage since 1897 and was prominent at the Hyde Park rally, so it's unsurprising that she took the initiative to launch the NUWSS in Exeter.

She hosted two meetings at her home in December 1908, both sufficiently supported for her to invite the great and the good of Exeter to the Barnfield Hall in February 1909 with a view to forming a branch. An audience of around 150 gathered to hear Eva Gore Booth, a keen advocate for working women. She pressed her audience to consider pay inequalities, the way that women's voices were overlooked in any industrial matters, and how they had no one to take their side in Parliament. This wider theme of women's social and working conditions was embraced by many in the NUWSS. Not appreciated at the time was how significant Eva's sister was to become. Constance Gore Booth, later known as the Countess Markievicz, became the first woman ever elected to Parliament, although, as she stood for Sinn Féin, she never took her seat.

Margaret Robertson pressed on with meetings at the Drill Hall in Tiverton. Lady Frances Balfour, the speaker, was the only member of the British aristocracy to have a leading role in the suffrage movement. On this visit, her first to Devon, she packed in four meetings, following Tiverton with Plymouth, Exeter and finally, Sidmouth on 26 February. She was a passionate advocate for women's rights. Together with Millicent Fawcett she had led the 'Mud March' in 1907 and served on the executive committee of the NUWSS from its inception in 1897. Lady Balfour accepted an invitation to become President of the newly-formed Sidmouth branch.

Margaret continued her 'strenuous campaign,' as she termed it, throughout February. 'Meetings have been organised in Plymouth,

Exeter, Sidmouth, Tiverton, Wellington, Hemyock, Devonport, Tavistock and Truro.' The challenge was to find local women with the passion and experience to take on the organisation of a new branch. In Plymouth she was fortunate in persuading two key figures to do just that. A flourishing Three Towns and District society was established in April 1909 with Clara Daymond as the Chair, a post she held until 1919. Clara was born and bred in Plymouth and was already dedicated to serving her community. She was an enthusiastic campaigner for the involvement of women in local politics through her work with the Women's Co-operative Guild, and outspoken in her support for women's suffrage. As someone who had declared she was not a suffragette, the NUWSS was a perfect fit.

Margaret Robertson also persuaded Dr Mabel Ramsay to take on the role of honorary secretary. Mabel Ramsay was a relatively new arrival in Plymouth. She had qualified and practiced as a doctor in Scotland and showed signs of already being prepared to pursue her own path, training as a gymnast to help with her orthopaedic studies.

She moved to Plymouth in 1908 to join her recently widowed mother, Annie Ramsay, at 4 Wentworth Villas, where she set up her medical practice. Until that point she hadn't been involved with the suffrage movement at all, but John Stuart Mill's book, *The Subjection of Women* changed her mind. When Margaret Robertson came along, Mabel embraced her request to help build the Three Towns branch of the NUWSS. Within a short time the branch had grown to over 100 members.

Mabel was to play a pivotal role in promoting the suffrage question, whether through organising numerous public meetings or as an accomplished and resourceful public speaker. When militancy created waves a couple of years later, every debating society but one in Plymouth refused to put Women's Suffrage into their programme. But she was up for the challenge delivering, '…a Suffrage pill well wrapped in jam in the form of a lecture on Florence Nightingale.'

Mabel also kept up a regular correspondence in the press, including the *Western Morning News*. She encouraged women to vote in municipal elections to, '...reap record attendance at the polling station... to refute the statement that women do not want the extension of the franchise...' She also made other appearances in the press. Having been given the stage as a judge for the Mayor of Plymouth's baby competition, she was quick to use it to highlight the achievements of the many women appointed as town Mayors.

MR. ASQUITH'S EASTER EGG.

Chapter Eight
Young Hot Bloods
Spring 1909

Meanwhile, Mrs Pankhurst and her WSPU followers continued to deliver fighting speeches across the country, building an impact way above their numbers. She launched a series of Women's Parliaments where the language rang with rebellion. Speeches would end, 'To arms! The call to battle has gone forth'. Many women responded, following their leader in public protests outside the House of Commons. It was an astonishing initiative that initially left the police wrong-footed. After all, convention dictated a deference to ladies –

but not these ladies. Police surrounded them on foot and horseback. Women were jeered at and, when they failed to see reason, physically assaulted. Instead of a hearing, women who went peacefully to the House of Commons risked being battered and abused. Elderly grandmothers were manhandled and publicly shamed in the streets with their underclothes pulled up over their heads. Those who wouldn't give up were hauled off to court and sentenced to weeks in Holloway, subjected to the worst possible conditions.

It was a massive wake-up call for Devon women such as Marie Newby, Edith Clarence and Amy Montague. It wasn't just criminals who were imprisoned but ordinary, respectable women who simply wanted to petition their elected - not by them of course - representatives in Parliament. How could that be a crime? Mrs Pankhurst wrote, 'Those women... were prepared to do something that women had never done before - fight for themselves. Women had always fought for men, and for their children. Now they were ready to fight for their own human rights. Our militant movement was established.'

In the spring of 1909 Elsie Howey decided that Plymouth needed a dedicated organiser. By the end of April Vera Wentworth was in place, working out of rooms at 11 Alfred St, The Hoe. Her arrival must have presented a challenge to the healthy NUWSS branch in Plymouth with women asking themselves, should they remain law-abiding suffragists or join the new suffragettes? Mrs Pankhurst's speeches in Torquay and Plymouth left no-one in any doubt about the WSPU's militant stance but these suffragettes were exciting, raising the profile of 'votes for women' in a new and dynamic way.

Vera, in particular, was a controversial figure. She was born Jessie Spink but changed her name shortly after joining the WSPU, possibly to protect her family's reputation. Like Annie Kenney, she was a member of a group within the WSPU called the 'Young Hot Bloods', women who were selected for 'danger duty', pledged to carry out acts that might result in a prison sentence. But for now Vera concentrated on recruiting local women as speakers for a packed programme of meetings. She organised weekly classes for promising local orators such as Eliza Aitken-Davies, who took second prize for the best maiden speech on Woman's Suffrage at a fete held in Mount Edgcumbe Park. Vera reported in *Votes for Women*, 'It is thought by most people in Plymouth that the competition was originally arranged to provide amusement for rowdy youths, who were expected to make fun of the subject. Instead, however, to everybody's surprise, not one competitor treated the subject with levity. Miss Millward took the first prize, Miss Davies the second...' However, for someone with Vera's reputation, spreading the WSPU message wasn't straight-forward; not because of any lack of interest in the cause, quite the opposite in fact. Prominent Plymouth families had supported women's suffrage since the 1860s and in 1873 an entirely male Plymouth Town Council voted to support a Women's Suffrage Bill before Parliament. But Vera provided fuel for women uncomfortable with increasing militancy.

Growing anti-suffrage feeling across Devon was summed up in a regular women's column in the *North Devon Herald*. 'For a short time the eccentric pranks of Mrs Pankhurst and Co. created some amusement; they have ceased to do so, and are now looked upon merely as a nuisance... The suffragette seems to me to express aggressiveness and all other unwomanly traits rolled into one... Fortunately there are few sympathisers with the suffragettes here in Barnstaple. I am acquainted with two or three who have the temerity to avow they want the vote, but in each case they are maiden ladies with insufficient work to occupy their time.'

Dissatisfaction with the suffragettes was also voiced in a debate in Barnstaple. Young Liberals were divided on whether the franchise should be extended to women, but united in a strong condemnation of the actions of the suffragettes. And five hundred women present at a Barnstaple WLA meeting unanimously supported a resolution presented by local woman, Kate James. 'This meeting, whilst earnestly desiring the vote for women, strongly condemns the action of the suffragettes in opposing the election of Liberals for the House of Commons... and believes this action is against the best interests of our country'.

It was against this backdrop that Adela Pankhurst had arrived in Ilfracombe in January 1909. It was the first time since the 1880s that women in North Devon had had the opportunity to make up their own minds about the suffrage campaign. And not only the women. At a second debate in Barnstaple, reported in the *North Devon Journal*, Mr Rowe was a convincing advocate for the women's cause, delivering a speech punctuated with positive arguments. 'Those who have to obey the laws should have a voice in making them... Taxation and representation should go hand in hand... Women share the responsibility of managing cities and boroughs, choosing Parliamentary representatives needs no greater wisdom... It's impossible for a council of wise men to legislate on questions concerning women without the assistance and guidance of that sex. How much longer can this absurd condition exist?'

How much longer indeed? It was a persuasive argument. Mr Rowe concluded, 'The spirit of justice and freedom will continue to triumph until the slavery of sex has followed that of caste, colour and race and woman, no longer the chattel of man, has taken her just place as his helpmate, companion, friend - with no rivalry between them...' He retired to thunderous applause.

Speaking against the motion, Mr Copp aired views the women were to hear time and time again. 'There is a danger the easy-going public will drift into female suffrage with the indifference born of familiarity. (Laughter)... Women have done admirable work on Local Government bodies because they are within their rightful province. The extension of the franchise would place a burden on them for which they have neither capacity nor leisure... Voters moved chiefly by sentiment would be a great menace to the equilibrium of national politics... It is desirable that women should devote themselves to work other than political, their mental and moral development fitting them for a better fate,' Mr Copp concluded to laughter and applause.

This was swiftly becoming a situation where men were again speaking for women. Then Kate James, stood. 'I would not like to go away thinking no woman was prepared to speak in favour of the extension of the Parliamentary Franchise to women. (Hear, hear)... It is time we had a right to vote.' (Cheers)

The Chairman moved to the vote. 'Those in favour of the Parliamentary Franchise being granted to women.' A forest of hands filled the room. Unlike the debate Marie and Ann had attended in Ilfracombe, the motion was passed by an overwhelming majority. The newspaper correspondent who believed there were few sympathisers with women's suffrage in Barnstaple had her answer. It would take enormous courage to break aside from convention, especially for women of position such as Marie Newby and Annie Ball, but the WSPU was about to offer an unusual inroad into activism.

'It made no difference you know, what happened at mid-Devon.' Annie Ball was poring over her copy of 'Votes for Women' together with Marie Newby, Margaret Eldridge and other members of their group. 'Asquith won't introduce a Suffrage Bill. Christabel is incensed. She and Mrs P. have called a war council.'

'They didn't call it that, surely,' Marie says.

'Sent shivers down my spine too. But Christabel says women are being defrauded, insulted, and dishonoured; that it's time to demand a Bill giving women taxpayers the vote. Why pay taxes if we have no say in how they are spent?'

'But if it means taking to the streets… to be locked up with common criminals! Look,' she points to the paper. 'It says the ladies who followed Mrs P. to protest outside Parliament were jeered at, manhandled, beaten and abused. Then forced to suffer the indignity of being brought before court. Fifty-nine arrests, and confined as ordinary, second class prisoners in Holloway.' She shudders.

'They somehow found the courage,' Annie says quietly. 'They are all respectable women like us who simply want to have a voice.'

'I know,' Marie sighs. 'I know we have to do something. But not that, not yet. What else can we do?'

Annie smiles. 'Sew. We look like a ladies' sewing circle and the WSPU is looking for contributions for a Great Exhibition. Apparently no-one is too poor, too old, too young or too frail to do something. So no excuses, ladies!'

'What kind of Great Exhibition?'

'All the talk is of a sale of women's work that is so interesting, original and picturesque it will open the public's eyes to what the WSPU are capable of. It's to be held at the Princes Skating Rink in Knightsbridge and everything has to be in the colours for impact - purple, white and green. The Actresses Franchise

League are providing entertainment and the women writers and artists have promised work. They want to sign up thousands of visitors to the cause. Oh, and the small matter of £5,000 [£760,000 today] to be raised for the campaign fund.'

'£5,000!' Margaret Eldridge exclaims. 'How will they raise that?'

'A hundred stalls taken by individuals, groups, societies, anyone basically who will undertake to supply items to the value of £100.'

'We can't possibly do that. And we're not even an official group.'

'They've thought of that. As individual members we're urged to take a half, a quarter... even a twentieth of a stall run by a bigger group. Are we agreed?'

A ripple of nods spreads around the room.

'And now you have to listen to this.' Annie peers at an article in 'Votes for Women'. 'There's a new post office regulation which allows the posting and delivery of human letters...'

'April 1st is it?' The women laugh.

'No... listen. A suffragette went to the West Strand Post Office with two women. "I want to send a human letter," she said. She took the form they gave her and addressed her two companions to H. H. Asquith, 10 Downing Street. She paid the threepenny fee and delivered the women to a telegraph messenger with the instruction that they must be signed for on delivery. He marched off towards Whitehall with a suffragette on each arm.'

'Priceless! What happened?'

'They were refused of course. But I'd loved to have seen the look on Asquith's face.'

The suffragettes next attempt to engineer a close encounter with Prime Minister Asquith was to be more successful.

ASQ-TH, LL-G-R-G and GLDST-N (in chorus):
"Booh-hooh! They're coming here again!"
FATHERLY POLICEMAN: "Never mind, my little men,
I'll protect you!"

Chapter Nine
Outrage at Clovelly Court
Spring - Summer 1909

It was part of the suffragette's brief to lobby politicians at every opportunity and there was one above all others they wanted answers from, Prime Minister Herbert Asquith. In London women were finding their political voice, gathering for massed marches on the House of Commons. It was a WSPU tactic that prompted a cynical response from Asquith who threw a cordon of police around Parliament. When the women pressed on they were arrested and sentenced to Holloway Prison. Asquith considered it couldn't be helped if women were determined to make martyrs of themselves and end up in prison. The reality of what awaited them was far from funny, but Asquith's over-reaction was an irresistible opportunity for mockery. Their weekly magazine, *Votes for Women*, was full of information, articles, advice, details of meetings and more than a few cartoons. [The dashes in the caption were to avoid legal action]

The suffragettes had failed to engineer an encounter with Asquith at Westminster, but Elsie Howey discovered that the Asquiths intended to spend their Whit holiday in North Devon. There would be no protective cordon around him there. On the day, crowds gathered to catch a glimpse of Asquith and his wife en route to Clovelly Court, possibly joined by Marie Newby and Annie Ball hurrying over Bideford bridge to reach the station at East-the-Water.

'Will you join us?' Marie glances nervously at her husband sitting beside her in the car. His knuckles are white as he grips the steering wheel, his gaze fixed on the River Torridge.

'I would welcome the opportunity to shake our Prime Minister by the hand but do not wish to be associated with anything Nurse Ball may have in mind.' He nods at Annie pacing the quayside.

'She speaks her mind a little too often. I'm sure it was nothing more than rash words.'

'Rash words! Calling him the Right Dishonourable double-faced Asquith!'

'I know you don't approve of our meetings, but she wouldn't do anything... anything untoward.'

'I strongly advise you to stay with me, Marie. You see how the newspapers speak of these suffragettes. I will not have my wife tarred with the same brush.'

'Tarred with the same...! For years I have done everything in my power to support you, in your career, at home, in the town. Everything. And now you are forbidding me to go? When all I want is to catch sight of the man who seems

resolved to throw every obstacle he can in the way of granting women the same choices in their own lives? Please, Charles. I simply want to see our Prime Minister in person, to make up my own mind. You've always encouraged that in me.'

He bows his head. The lines of age now etched deep into his forehead give him an exaggerated frown. 'I've made my views clear. You must do as you see fit.'

To ask for any more concessions might lose her the one she has already gained. Marie opens the door and hurries after Anne. She is swept up by the crowds surging over the ancient bridge, heading for the station at East-the-Water. For a moment she is glad of the crush protecting her from the full force of the wind sweeping down the river.

THE MAN OF THE WEEK.

THE PRIZE-WINNER.

It's a different matter when she reaches the steps to the platform on the far side. It's a miracle she's not pitched onto the road below with all the pushing and shoving. The whole town seems to have turned out for a glimpse of Mr Asquith. Not that many people know what he actually looks like. The Bideford Gazette featured him in a cartoon, a thoroughly respectful piece about the Right Honourable Herbert Henry Asquith's brilliant career, but it's of little use as an aid to identification.

Annie proves the equal of the crowd and they are soon lodged on the platform. But before long the sun is out and the crush begins to feel unbearable.

'You're looking pale,' Annie stares at Marie. 'Do you feel faint?'

'Yes, a little. I'll move back, get some air. You stay here.'

There's a shout from further up the platform. 'Smoke above the cutting. He's almost here.'

Annie pushes forward. 'I'm going to get closer.'

'What?' The noise of the train drowns out her words. A few shadowy shapes emerge from the steam that fills the space between the Royal Hotel and the station villas. Any one of them could be him. 'Is Mr Asquith there?' Marie says to no-one in particular. Then she catches the whispers.

'He bain't be there. Some of the gentry sure enough but Asquith left the train at Exeter. Afraid of they suffragettes he is so he's coming up by car.'

The Mayor strains to make himself heard above the crowd and the bursts of steam from the engine. 'What's he saying?' Marie asks a woman beside her.

'Probably same thing he said last time.'

'Mr and Mrs Asquith have been to Bideford before?'

'Oh yes. The Hamlyn's at Clovelly Court are some sort of relation. Asquiths came for their honeymoon. That's when the Mayor stood here all preened up like a stuffed turkey waiting to launch into his welcoming address, but they'd come and gone before any of us knew what was happening. I just caught sight of them going over the bridge. Stopped all the traffic they did. Even cleared the road of horse droppings, couldn't offend the delicate nostrils of the gentry. Looks like this time'll be no different.' She nods at the party already making their way down the steps to the waiting cars.

'Did you hear?' Annie appears beside Marie. 'Coward was driven up from Exeter. Good to know we have him on the run though. We have to find Charles, get him to follow them to Clovelly.'

'He won't.'

'Why not? It's not so much further.'

'You were very outspoken in the car. I haven't talked about our activities in such a direct way with him. He's… he's finding it challenging. We have to leave it for today.'

'But…'

'Please, Annie. I don't want this to cause a rift with my husband. He will support us, I know he will, but it will take time and patience.' Marie takes her arm. 'Let's go to Westward Ho! It's years since I've seen the beach there.'

As it happens, Asquith was right to take evasive action, but a quick flight from the train was never going to deter the suffragettes. Travelling close behind were three women on a mission. Elsie Howey, Jessie Kenney and Vera Wentworth were young, fearless and determined to force an interview with Asquith. Jessie was Annie Kenney's sister, someone with a flair for publicity stunts and a passionate commitment to the cause. Elsie and Vera already had mileage with Asquith, both having been imprisoned for demonstrating outside his home, Vera for three months, her third stint in Holloway.

When the papers announced that the Prime Minister would be spending Whitsun in Clovelly it was simply too good an opportunity to miss. Even better, one of his guests at Clovelly Court was Lord Cromer, occasional President of the Men's League for Opposing Women's Suffrage. Two birds in the hand.

But how and when to confront them? A favourite tactic was to heckle government ministers at public meetings. But Asquith had refused an invitation from Barnstaple Liberal Association to be their guest, turning down any public engagements over his Whitsun holiday. The station was the next option but Asquith had ducked out of any confrontation there by being driven up from Exeter. That just left one perfect opportunity.

On Whit Sunday morning Mrs Hamlyn, their host at Clovelly Court, escorted Mr and Mrs Asquith through the grounds to church. It was Mrs Asquith who first spotted something unusual. All the ladies in church were dressed in their Sunday best but none stood out more than the three young women in the pew opposite, dressed respectively in green, white and purple. Did Mrs Asquith realise the significance of the colours? Almost certainly; they were inescapable at suffragette demonstrations in London.

She handed her husband a note. It ruffled Asquith, who kept casting furtive glances in the trio's direction before hurrying out a side door as soon as the service was over. But Jessie, Elsie and Vera caught up with him on the path and asked for a short interview. He was having none of it. 'Not a second,' he said and waved them away. The women were undaunted. Elsie and Vera, despite only being in their early twenties, were seasoned campaigners. A pompous, disgruntled politician wasn't going to intimidate them. 'Miss Woodlock is in prison while you are on your holiday,' they said. 'If you will not give us an interview we will force one.' Miss Woodlock, a Liverpool suffragette, had been sentenced to Holloway a few months earlier.

Asquith was in no mood to listen and hurried back to Clovelly Court. Jessie, Elsie and Vera regrouped at accommodation in the village and set to work creating medallions, rosettes and other suffragette memorabilia. The following morning they were back, playing a cat and mouse game with a police sergeant and a constable until they managed to catch up with Asquith. It was inconceivable that a lady would disturb a gentleman at his leisure on the golf links, but Elsie, Vera and Jessie hadn't got the memo. They shouted their questions. 'Don't be a coward, Mr Asquith, receive our deputation on June 29th,' and 'Why do you not release Patricia Woodlock?' But he refused to reply, ordering the police to remove them. A car was found and the three women were eventually driven back to Bideford.

But the ladies weren't finished yet. They'd endured Holloway for simply wanting to lobby their MPs in Parliament. A Devon bobby wasn't going to scare them off. They deposited their luggage at the station and set off on the eleven-mile hike back to Clovelly, a significant challenge in the pitch black. Arriving back at the Court around two in the morning, they set to work on some horticultural decoration. Before long, bushes and shrubs across the gardens were covered in paper discs proclaiming, 'Votes for Women,' and 'Receive the deputation on June 29'. Copies of *Votes for Women* were strung as bunting along the balustrade and handkerchiefs decorated with paints borrowed from an artist in the village formed banners across the lawn. Even the sundial was draped with a decorated towel.

It must have been tempting to wait for Asquith to discover their handiwork. But it had been a long night and Jessie, Vera and Elsie still had the long walk back to Bideford, a round trip of twenty-two miles, before catching the early morning train to Exeter. This could all have been described as a bit of a jape but an actual medallion left at the scene, and now held in the Clovelly archive, paints a dangerously

radical picture. Scrawled in the purple and green of the WSPU were the words, 'DOWN WITH ASQUITH. DEATH TO TYRANTS.

The local paper wasn't amused. According to the *Bideford Gazette* no-one would give political power to women capable of such tomfoolery. They pitied the mental state of anyone making themselves so obnoxious on the Sabbath. Perhaps it was naive to expect anything else. Even Mary Blathwayt, a steadfast WSPU supporter who offered respite for suffragettes at her home near Bath, called them hooligans. And, apart from Adela's visit a few months earlier, North Devon was virgin territory, full of respectable Liberal Ladies never happier than when chewing over a good scandal. How dare these women approach the Prime Minister? And when he was playing golf!

Curiously, the paper goes on to report, 'The last vestiges of the suffragette's raid had barely been removed on Tuesday, when a lady dressed in black stopped at Clovelly Court and asked to see Mrs Hamlyn. She was asked from where she came, and replied… 'Ilfracombe'. Having in mind that a Miss Pankhurst is reported to be spending a holiday at Ilfracombe, the lady was asked her business. She replied that it had connection with the playing of the organ at Clovelly church, and gave her name as Miss Pond. Although the lady tried to obtain admission at the Court three times, she was unsuccessful.'

There are no more clues as to the identity of the mystery woman. Perhaps Adela, having discovered the charms of Ilfracombe earlier that year? Or Sylvia? Christabel maybe? Or perhaps it was Marie Newby or Annie Ball, the fledgling WSPU supporters making their first foray into positive action.

Few in the south west were ignorant of the suffragettes after that Whit weekend. One of the prime movers in the WSPU, Emmeline

Pethick Lawrence, was speaking at Penzance the following week. The crowd took the chance to heckle her about what they saw as the appalling behaviour of the women at Clovelly. She took the disapproval head on then gave as good as she got. It was time to remind these dyed-in-the wool Cornishmen of one of their own protests that had passed into folklore - and song. 'And shall Trelawney live? Or shall Trelawney die? Here's twenty-thousand Cornish men, will know the reason why!' It went down well. 'If twenty-thousand Cornishmen wanted to know the reason why one of their countrymen was in prison,' Emmeline declared, 'why not three suffragists?'

At the end of July, Elsie and Vera made the headlines again. Earl Carrington, a Liberal MP, was due to address a meeting at the Victoria Hall in Exeter. It was another unmissable opportunity to heckle a government minister. The WSPU's publicity was spectacularly successful, attracting a crowd of over two thousand to hear them speak outside the hall. Vera challenged Earl Carrington as he arrived. 'Why will you not give votes to women?' No answer, of course, as he was escorted inside. But the crowd stayed to hear speeches from the women who more than once almost managed to force their way into the building. Even the *Western Times* was, '…impelled in sheer justice to give them praise for one thing. They posses an enormous amount of pluck and grit, and a great deal more staying power than many men can boast. It was a marvel of female endurance that they withstood the buffeting that they did and yet were able directly after to harangue the crowd from the railings of the station-yard.' The police were constantly forced to retreat, amid great cheering, until Elsie, Vera and Mary Phillips, a WSPU regional organiser, were finally arrested.

In court they thanked the people of Exeter, emphasising that their quarrel was not with the police but with the twenty men who formed the Cabinet who refused to give justice to women. The three women were sentenced to seven days imprisonment. Exeter prison might be a long way from Holloway but the treatment was no less harsh. The women's claim to be political prisoners was denied; it was national policy that all women, regardless of location, were sentenced as common criminals sharing the same conditions as convicted felons.

It wasn't simply the prison conditions that they railed against. When interviewed, Vera and Elsie made it clear at the outset that, '... having been placed in the third division, we felt it our duty to disobey the prison regulations and refuse food until placed in the first division... We refused to go to our cells, but were forcibly removed there... Presently we were told to come and put on prison dress. We refused, and were dressed by the warders and removed to fresh cells... Next day we were visited in turn by doctor, chaplain and governor, who all tried to persuade us to take food, the doctor threatening to feed us if necessary; and when we told him this was illegal he replied he would even certify us insane in order to do so!'

40   EXETER. — *Devon County Prison.* — LL.

Elsie, Vera and Mary became the first suffragette hunger strikers in the West Country. Mary Phillips wrote movingly of her experience in *Votes for Women*:

> Never has a weapon been added to the armoury of women who fight for the Vote more powerful and sure than the hunger strike. It is also a shield against which the weapons of authority blunt and splinter themselves in vain... We told the governor at the beginning that we were going to disregard the rules and we told him why. Remonstrance was tried. Punishment was tried. Both

were useless. Our duty was to "keep on" and we triumphed. When, on the third morning, I could not move from my bed or shout or sing any more to my fellow-prisoners, the doctor told me he would feed me by force. I thought, I cannot be responsible for what happens to my body; but I am responsible for my soul. I must "keep on". I said I am weak and cannot resist you. But I am determined. I will never yield voluntarily. I lay long in expectation of the doctor and his feeding apparatus but he did not come.

Mary Phillips was released after three days over concerns about her health. Elsie and Vera fasted for six days and although were almost too weak to stand, kept their spirits up. After their release, as was often the case, they went to the Blathwayt family home, Eagle House in Batheaston, to recuperate. The family were still supporting suffragettes despite their belief that the Clovelly incident was hooliganism. The women were fed, watered, cared for and restored to health before returning to South Devon, no longer simply Vera and Elsie but 'The Exeter Hunger Strikers'. Exeter WSPU organised a welcome home meeting and Torquay even presented Elsie with a clock. They may have abandoned the ladylike campaigning of the NUWSS but they were still most definitely Ladies!

Chapter Ten
The Bow Street Challenge
Summer 1909

Lobbying for 'Votes for Women' took stamina, resilience and a significant amount of courage. As well as the treatment being handed out in London, the suffragettes were increasingly the target for abuse elsewhere. Annie Kenney decided to heckle Winston Churchill at a Liberal fete in Poole but before she'd said a word she was set upon. 'One man who was wearing the Liberal colours pulled a knife out of his pocket and… started cutting my coat. He cut it in shreds right from the neck downwards. Then they lifted up my coat and started to cut my frock and cut my petticoat. A cry came from those Liberals, who are supposed to have high ideals in public life, to undress me. They took my hat and pulled down my hair...' Fortunately they had a change of heart and dragged her, bruised and battered, out of the grounds. But far from being deterred, Annie was fired with a renewed determination to spread the WSPU message in an intensive campaign across the South West.

She was joined by the Honourable Evelina Haverfield. A typical aristocrat, Evelina tended to be distant and emotionally reserved, until she found her voice with the WSPU. She didn't have an easy ride at times. When presiding in Yeovil she endured catcalls, booing, rattles, raucous singing, laughter, fireworks and missiles - coal, apples, bundles of wet paper and worse. In the chaos, chairs were broken and those on the platform had to beat back the hooligans with sticks. Withstanding this kind of reception was valuable preparation for a challenge she was about to make in the formal setting of Bow Street Court.

The WSPU had discovered an 1689 Bill of Rights that stated, 'It is the right of the subject to petition the King and all commitments and prosecutions for such petitioning are illegal.' As the power of the King had passed to Parliament, their reasoning went, this clause now applied to Parliament's representative, the Prime Minister. Evelina joined Emmeline Pankhurst to challenge Asquith to accept their petition. The call went out for women to witness the deputation, but volunteering for this was no idle gesture. Emmeline wrote in *Votes for Women,* 'Mr Asquith has never received, since he became Prime Minister, a deputation of women on the subject of their enfranchisement... I am hoping that even at this eleventh hour his vision may be restored to him, and he will see the necessity of dealing with this question in a right and proper way... and if not...? We shall not yield one inch unless we are overcome by sheer physical force... And if we are overcome by sheer physical force, and we are arrested, what of that...? They may imprison us... We have not been deterred hitherto by this treatment... we are not likely to be deterred either now or in the future... Come, rally to our standard of freedom, and give yourselves now to the greatest cause in all the world.'

Asquith refused to accept the deputation. The 1689 ball was now firmly in the WSPU's court. Thousands lined the streets surrounding Parliament on 29 June as Emmeline, Evelina and six others marched towards the House of Commons to the sound of the Marseillaise played by the Women's Drum and Fife Band.

Their petition was refused and the eight were arrested. But it wasn't the end of the protest. Wave after wave of suffragettes, furious at the way the women had been treated, hurled stones covered with messages through government windows: 'Grant to the tax-paying women of Britain the Vote'; 'Votes for Women this session'; 'Taxation without Representation is Tyranny'. By the end of the night, 107 women and eight men had been arrested.

The press were divided. *The Manchester Courier* was largely for the women. 'Principles and tact alike are wanting in the Asquith administration, otherwise there would have been none... of the tumult and expense of last night... No-one supposes for a moment that such a large and influential body as the suffragettes would have been denied a hearing by Mr Asquith and his colleagues had it possessed voting power...' Using more colourful language, *The Liverpool Daily Post and Mercury* was uncompromisingly against. 'The shrieking sisterhood has suffered another rebuff. The impudence and folly of the militant Suffragists are passing all bounds. There is no limit to the conceit of these misguided ladies. The unfortunate thing is that the cause of Woman Suffrage as represented by moderate and sensible women and men is being put back for years. It is being entirely destroyed by the methods of fanatic disorder of which yesterday's events in London were only one illustration. Reasonable people who previously have supported the enfranchisement of women where the necessary qualifications exist, are made apathetic on the subject, and even driven into absolute antagonism by the irresponsible outbursts of these howling fanatics who are a public nuisance and must be suppressed.'

'Shrieking sisterhood,' 'howling fanatics,' 'impudence and folly'; how could the WSPU get the nation to take them seriously now? The answer - in that pillar of the British establishment, its courts. The time had come for one of the most significant legal challenges of the WSPU's campaign. The stage was Bow Street Magistrates Court where, in Sylvia Pankhurst's words, '…a sensation was created by the discovery that Lord Robert Cecil, a Conservative MP, had been retained to defend the case of Mrs Haverfield upon which all the others hung.'

Evelina Haverfield (left) and Emmeline Pankhurst at Bow Street.

On the bench was chief magistrate, Sir Albert de Rutzen. De Rutzen had made a name for himself presiding over some high profile cases, including Oscar Wilde and Crippen, and was now an elder statesman of the court. Too elderly according to Sylvia Pankhurst who described him as, 'the old Magistrate with his half-shut eyes, who always reminded me of a tortoise.' But elderly or not, he was still the presiding magistrate and he made his view clear at the outset. 'It is a lamentable thing to see a respectable woman charged with the same sort of offence which is daily charged against small hooligan boys in the street. There can be no justification for women parading through the streets armed with stones and breaking public windows.'

The Bill of Rights defence was debated at length until De Rutzen, looking rather pained and blinking his eyes nervously, passed judgement. 'I agree with Lord Robert Cecil that the right of petition belongs to every subject but when the Prime Minister said he would not receive the deputation, the women acted wrongly in refusing to go away.' He imposed a fine of five pounds for resisting the police, with the alternative of one month in the Second Division.

The women retaliated, claiming they were political offenders, not common criminals, and should be put in the First Division. This would have given them certain privileges, such as the right to wear their own clothes. De Rutzen refused, condemning them to the harshest conditions Holloway had to offer. It was one of a series of judgements against the suffragettes that was later to have explosive significance as a chain of connections began to unravel connecting de Rutzen with the small North Devon town of Lynton.

In contrast to the bitter confrontations taking place in London, in the summer of 1909 both the NUWSS and the WSPU took a different approach with the introduction of Holiday Campaigns. Well-to-do ladies from both organisations travelled from London to resorts across the country, from Blackpool to Torquay, Ilfracombe to Edinburgh, St Ives to Scarborough, intent on recruiting women to the cause - and having some fun in the process. Suffragettes at the Brighton Regatta took to the sea in a motor-boat decorated in their colours - purple, green and white - waving flags and crying 'Votes for Women.' Three women climbed to the summit of Snowdon and held a meeting with fellow climbers. A card was found on one of the highest peaks in the Cheviots that read, 'This is the pinnacle of perfection. May the women of Great Britain rise to the heights of Political Liberty. Three cheers for Mrs Pankhurst and her tribe - by a mere man, Newcastle.' Meanwhile others opted for a more leisurely assignment based at The Hydro in Blackpool.

A great feature of the Holiday Campaigns in Devon and Cornwall was the open-air meetings. *Votes for Women* reported, 'At Plymouth, Torquay and on the Cornish coast these are being carried on successfully.' A distinct advantage of the coastal locations was that, '…in most seaside places meetings are permitted on the sands, there is no expense entailed. Bring out a chair and there you are! The other holiday makers have plenty of leisure, and will congregate in thousands out of curiosity and, as has so often happened before, remain to be impressed and drawn into our ranks.'

The popular holiday destination of Ilfracombe in North Devon was the focus for Mari Pearce, Miss Rind and the Inglis sisters. At all locations the emphasis was on selling *Votes for Women*, a paper packed with suffragette news and comment dedicated, 'To the brave women who to-day are fighting for freedom: to the noble women who all down the ages kept the flag flying and looked forward to this day without seeing it: to all women all over the world, of whatever race, or creed, or calling, whether they be with us or against us in the fight, we dedicate this paper.' Enormous numbers were printed and distributed at a cost of one penny per copy. There was so much interest, the ladies in Ilfracombe easily sold out and urged speakers to come to the town to spread the word.

Across the River Tamar from Plymouth, ladies were invited to a walk through Mount Edgecombe Park followed by tea at Cawsand. Unsurprisingly, Annie Kenney adopted a less genteel approach in her speeches to Totnes and Torquay audiences, reflecting on the fall-out from the 29 June deputation. 'Let all West of England people buckle on their armour, the armour of fearlessness, and take up their sword of justice and truth, and vow their vow like the crusaders of old that they will ever fight against oppression and injustice and stand by the weak and helpless, and resolve firmly that they will never show their back to the enemy. Let us fight like women for our rights, as it is the duty of all to help in this great struggle for the emancipation of our own sex.'

THE ILLUSTRATED
LONDON NEWS,

No. 3634. VOL. CXXXIII   SATURDAY, DECEMBER 12, 1908.   With Supplement SIXPENCE.

Chapter Eleven
The Woman with the Whip
Autumn 1909

Throughout 1909, Annie Kenney worked tirelessly to extend the reach of the WSPU across the West Country. After Dorset, she and Evelina Haverfield moved on to Somerset, holding meetings in Wellington and Street, then Bampton in Devon, the first to be held there. Annie was a powerful speaker but she was constantly heckled on WSPU militancy; particularly when one tactic spawned a hostile headline in the *Pall Mall Gazette*. 'An Outrage Unparalleled in English History'. Suffragettes from the Women's Freedom League attacked a polling station at the Bermondsey by-election, breaking bottles of corrosive acid over ballot boxes to destroy the contents and, it was claimed, blinding the presiding officer in one eye. It was bad enough that suffragettes were now vandalising post boxes and smashing windows but it was beyond the pale for an innocent bystander to suffer.

The truth was rather different. Yes, Alice Chapin had broken a test tube over a ballot box and the liquid, emphatically *not* corrosive acid, did splash the presiding officer, but even he said it was an accident. Far from being blinded, there was just a possibility of a temporary slight haze to his sight. But the *Pall Mall Gazette* reflected the tone of the press. Militancy was in danger of backfiring as the women increasingly lost the battle against press bias - a bias that played to the fears of many.

Condemnation of the suffragette's actions at Bermondsey from the anti-suffragists was to be expected, but an article in their *Review* raised an important issue. 'The very eve of the municipal election was chosen for the perpetration of a silly and dangerous prank, which was certain to exasperate still further the metropolitan constituencies... It bodes ill for the Council elections which are to be held in March, and we regard the fierce sex prejudice, which has grown in volume with such rapidity during the last few months, as a national calamity of the first order.' Their fears were already being realised. In recent Borough and Council elections in London, out of around sixty women candidates only six were successful. The anti-suffragist's had worked tirelessly to support women's involvement at a local level but now candidates were all being tarred with the same militant brush, making it much harder to get elected. They claimed women intent on the exclusive goal of the Parliamentary vote were uninterested in, '...the humbler rounds of usefulness, the sphere in which no one denies the prerogative of women or disputes her capacity.' Were the suffragettes pursuing their goal at the expense of the headway women were making at a local level? It certainly appears that way.

Even those in favour of votes for women were shaken by Bermondsey. When a Mr Hopper spoke to Braunton Women's Liberal Association he was at pains to stress he was ardently pro-suffrage. 'Women had proved themselves capable leaders in other walks of life... it was absurd to keep them out of politics. But, and on this he was unequivocal, no self-respecting Government would give the vote to militants after Bermondsey.' It was a controversy that reverberated across the county. At a WSPU meeting in Exmouth's Temperance Hall on 2 November, Vera Wentworth was uncompromising. The accident of a man being blinded was unexpected and could not be helped - a view that was met with hisses and cries of 'shame' from the audience. Amy Montague was then put on the spot. When asked if she approved of the women's actions at Bermondsey she replied, a little more diplomatically, that she did not blame them. The real responsibility rested with the government who drove the women to take that action.

But some WSPU core supporters were having second thoughts. After getting so close to Asquith at Clovelly, Elsie Howey and Vera tried again when he visited the Kent village of Lympne. But this time Vera, not content with a verbal assault, actually lashed out at Asquith. For a woman to speak disrespectfully to her elders and betters was bad enough, but to physically assault the Prime Minister was an action that sent shock waves through middle England. Emily Blathwayt, previously one of the suffragettes greatest supporters, wrote, 'We hear of terrible things by the two hooligans, Vera and Elsie... Vera was the violent one.' Vera was unrepentant. 'We are driven nearly mad by the unjust treatment all our dear women have received. I am sorry you are grieved but if Mr Asquith will not reccive our deputation we will pummel him again.'

It was too much for Emily. The following morning she wrote to the secretary of the WSPU. 'Dear Madam, with great reluctance I am writing to ask that my name may be taken off the list as a Member of the WSPU Society. When I signed the membership paper, I thoroughly approved of the methods then used. Since then, there has been personal violence and stone throwing which might injure innocent people... People of my village who have hitherto been full of admiration for the Suffragettes are now feeling very differently.' It was a trigger for some women to not only shift their allegiance from the suffragettes to the law-abiding suffragists, but to abandon the suffragist cause altogether, particularly any who read of the events in Lympne in the *Anti-Suffrage Review*. 'The Prime Minister of England was on Sunday last "struck repeatedly" by Suffragists who had followed him to the country and to church in order to molest him.' It's interesting that they used the word 'suffragists'. Millicent Fawcett would have been horrified. Were they trying to tar them all with the same brush?

The antis had a remedy for all those who felt a fierce indignation at such acts. 'Let all employers, public or private, see to it as far as possible that no member of the societies responsible for these abominable acts is appointed to any of the posts under their control.' An interesting suggestion, but the *Review* had only recently covered a WSPU report that it introduced with the words, 'If boundless enthusiasm and energy and the possession of apparently inexhaustible funds are the hall-marks of success then the Women's Social and Political Union have had a most triumphant year.' £31,686 [around £4.5 million today] had been raised in just twelve months. WSPU staff, whether in the offices or acting as area organisers were now salaried, therefore immune to the actions of any employers, public or private. But if adopted, this suggestions would have left ordinary society members at risk.

Emily Blathwayt didn't go as far as joining the Antis. She continued to offer respite at Eagle House for suffragettes released from prison but she became increasingly anxious about their militant tactics. If stones didn't work would the WSPU resort to bombs? The trickle of women leaving the WSPU and joining, or re-joining, the NUWSS was destined to become a flood as dramatic headlines brought yet more negative publicity.

In early December 1909 Marie Newby, Annie Ball and other supporters from Ilfracombe travelled to Barnstaple parish rooms to hear Helen Ogston. It was a controversial choice of speaker given she had come to be known as, 'The Woman with the Whip'. The previous year Helen had attended a speech by Lloyd George at the Albert Hall. Emmeline Pankhurst had warned that the WSPU would heckle if he didn't pledge government action. Of course, there was no pledge, so as soon as he started speaking women sprang up chanting, 'We want deeds, not words!' In her second tier box Helen leapt to her feet crying '*Votes for Women*' and was immediately set upon by the stewards, one even pressed a lighted cigar against her wrist. She reacted immediately, flicking a dog whip towards the men. There was never any intent to harm but it was manna from heaven for papers around the world.

> Suffragettes Riot in Albert Hall
> (*The New York Times*)
> Militant Suffragettes New Weapon in Use at the Albert Hall
> (*Illustrated London News*)

These headlines challenged even the most ardent supporters. Could using a weapon ever be justified? Especially one that had been selected, concealed and carried to the event so deliberately. Helen Ogston wrote to *Votes for Women* to explain. 'On one or two previous occasions when I have been present to heckle Cabinet Ministers I have been subjected to very serious violence, and both I and other women have been disgracefully mauled by the stewards. I determined, accordingly, on Saturday to take steps to prevent a recurrence of such treatment, and to make a protest against it. I therefore took a dog-whip with me.'

If the crowds outside Barnstaple parish rooms were expecting an Amazon they would have been disappointed. Helen Ogston was a mild-mannered, gently spoken lady. Convincing her audience that militancy was justified was a challenge after Bermondsey and her own actions at the Albert Hall, but, she asked, what else could they do? They had tried peaceful, polite campaigning for over half a century and still politicians refused to listen to them. Surely they couldn't be blamed if they'd become a bit disorderly!

There was a falling-out in the hall over the WSPU blanket policy of opposing all Liberals at by-elections but Miss Ogston was convincing. It was, she said, the only way they could force the Liberal Government to live up to its own principles - that taxation and representation should go hand-in-hand, and that the will of the majority should prevail. The majority, that is, of MPs in the House of

Commons and Asquith's own Cabinet, majorities he stubbornly and persistently refused to act on. It could be seen as an abuse of democracy by a man intent on flouting the will of Parliament. But in the suffragettes, the immovable object had met the unstoppable force.

Asquith's personal opposition to women's suffrage was well known. He'd publicly stated that he thought it bad for women and bad for the country. He'd shown his true colours the previous year when he offered to abandon his resistance if it could be demonstrated that enough women wanted the vote. It was a clever tactic on his part. What was enough? How did it need to be demonstrated? Apparently even the thousands of women who turned out for 'The Largest Political Demonstration in the History of the World', as *Votes for Women* titled the mass rally in June 1908, hadn't been enough. Asquith still refused to support a Bill on women's suffrage.

It's interesting to speculate on what fed his opposition. One factor has to be concern that the middle and upper class women likely to be enfranchised would vote Conservative, further eroding the Liberal influence in Parliament. But quite apart from the women's demands, Asquith was preoccupied with insoluble issues connected with Irish Home Rule and the growing power of Germany. And all this on a wafer thin majority. Whatever his reasons, Christabel Pankhurst, now chief organiser of the WSPU, was incensed. 'Women are being defrauded, insulted, and dishonoured,' she said. 'It is time to demand a Bill giving women taxpayers the Parliamentary right of representation. Why should women pay taxes if they have no say in how they are spent?'

There may have been widespread sympathy with the message but the means were still very much up for debate. In December, Kate James, who had spoken at the YMCA debate earlier that year, made her stand at the Albert Hall - Barnstaple's Albert Hall that is, the building that stood on the site of the present Queen's Theatre. 'Speaking as a Suffragist,' she said, 'I strongly dissociate myself from the methods being adopted by militant suffragettes.'

The NUWSS set out to capitalise on the growing number of women who felt as Kate James did. In November alone they publicised meetings at the Public Rooms in Budleigh Salterton and at the Barnfield Hall in Exeter. The *Exeter and Plymouth Gazette* was impressed. 'It shows some courage in the National Union of Women's Suffrage Societies to arrange just at the present time a public meeting such as that advertised for 30 November... It must be to their credit that they have publicly dissociated themselves from the conduct of the militants and have explicitly regretted and condemned it.' That public dissociation came from a resolution passed at a recent NUWSS Council meeting. 'The Council of the National Union of Women's Suffrage Societies strongly condemns the use of violence in political propaganda, and being convinced that the true way of advancing the cause of Women's Suffrage is by energetic law-abiding propaganda, re-affirms its adherence to Constitutional principles.'

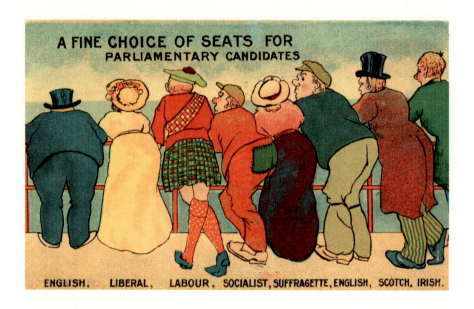

A FINE CHOICE OF SEATS FOR
PARLIAMENTARY CANDIDATES

ENGLISH, LIBERAL, LABOUR, SOCIALIST, SUFFRAGETTE, ENGLISH, SCOTCH, IRISH.

Chapter Twelve
To the Brink and Back
Winter 1909 - Summer 1910

Both the main suffrage organisations were spurred into action when Asquith called another General Election for January 1910. Helen Fraser, previously active in the WSPU but who changed her allegiance to the NUWSS after hearing Emmeline Pankhurst advocating violence, embarked on a tour of the West Country. At a meeting in Budleigh Salterton she outlined their strategy. For forty years the National Union had been tireless in presenting petition after petition signed by thousands of women. But what was the use of petitions signed by the voteless? None. It was time for a new

Miss HELEN FRASER.
Organiser of the Women's Social & Political Union
4, Clement's Inn. Strand, W.C.

approach. They would hand every successful Parliamentary candidate, '…a petition signed by the male electors of each constituency in favour of the extension of the suffrage to women, to be presented at the opening of Parliament. They hoped to get two million signatures at the very least, and that, she affirmed, would exert a greater influence on the House of Commons than any act of violence.' Helen Fraser must have been a convincing speaker; the first to sign the petition, according to the *Common Cause*, was the chairman of a recent anti-suffrage meeting.

In Exeter, despite the bitter cold, suffragists stationed themselves outside polling booths from 8am to 8pm on election day. It was a dedication that paid off; they persuaded 380 men to sign the petition. Our anonymous correspondent, Exonia, commented in the *Western Times* that, 'One of the pleasantest and most gratefully appreciated experiences of Monday… was the unlooked for kindness of residents in the vicinity of nearly all the polling stations attended in offering shelter and hospitality to the Suffragists, even when these were quite unknown to the impromptu hostesses.' Names were also collected through a house-to-house canvas and via their new shop at 13 Queen Street. In her report to *The Common Cause,* organiser Dorothy Edwards commented, '…our highly decorative posters in the big windows attract considerable attention and comment. The educational merits of this form of advertising the movement ought to bear fruit in the way of signatures for the voter's petition.'

Once the signatures were collected, the MP for each constituency was asked to present them to Parliament. In Exeter this meant a deputation to Henry Duke, who received Jessie Montgomery and others most cordially and promised to present their petition, '…at the earliest fitting opportunity.' An interesting turn of phrase, perhaps letting slip his personal stand on the issue. At the next election less than a year later, he actually told the WSPU that he would not be including a pledge for woman suffrage in his election address, a turnabout that was eagerly publicised by the anti-suffragists.

Things were initially even less positive in Plymouth. According to Dr Mabel Ramsay, 'Our work here began badly by one of the members being mobbed in the street on the occasion of Mr Lloyd George's visit. However, we opened our shop and stuck to our colours and have gradually gained ground in Plymouth... It was impossible to get our members to stand at polling stations but we have secured over 600 signatures to the petition... Plymouth is so very backward that what we have gained represents a very real advance, and we are much encouraged by it.' Traditional might have been a better word than 'backward'. Members were more used to meetings such as the cake and pickle sale held in December when, in-between bursts of trading, Miss Laura Jenkins spoke on the social evils of drink. However, she also shared her conviction that because most good women were associated with the suffrage movement it would not fail.

Some Plymouth suffragists suggested their own campaign tactic. In a letter to the *Common Cause*, Mrs Millward wrote, 'My husband has pledged himself to vote either Liberal or Conservative at the general election, according to my direction, and he will tell candidates and their canvassers that it is useless to solicit his vote, as it is absolutely at the disposal of his wife, and they must appeal to her. We expect to persuade several of our friends to do the same and shall write to the local press stating that a number of Suffragists have agreed to adopt this action, so the Plymouth women, at any rate, shall have some sort of representation.' An interesting turnaround from the anti-suffrage belief that women were adequately represented by men.

The WSPU's general election campaign in the south west was typically pro-active and run with their customary military efficiency. Women were briefed on why the WSPU was anti-Asquith, the appalling treatment of suffragettes in prison and why it was so important to fight for the vote. After years of relentless campaigning, suddenly a few weeks of all-out effort could bring them victory. Their message was clear, as printed on their posters.

EVERY VOTE AGAINST THE GOVERNMENT IS A VOTE FOR
HUMAN LIBERTY AND JUSTICE TO WOMEN

EVERY VOTE FOR A LIBERAL CANDIDATE IS A VOTE FOR
FORCE FEEDING AND THE ILL-TREATMENT OF WOMEN
POLITICAL PRISONERS

VOTE FOR THE WOMEN AND KEEP THE LIBERAL OUT

Annie Kenney identified Exeter as a marginal seat, where the Liberal Harold St Maur had scraped in with a majority of just eighty-five votes last time. Mrs Pankhurst's campaign had overturned a majority of more than a thousand in Mid-Devon. How hard could eighty-five be? The women went into overdrive producing posters, pamphlets, leaflets, postcards, badges - none of it pulling any punches. 'The Right Dishonourable Double-Face Asquith' was available in three sizes for hoardings, palings and windows. They were spurred on by reports that Asquith was so afraid of being accosted by suffragettes that his police guard smuggled him into a Bristol meeting through a vegetable patch, then out through the gooseberry bushes. The irony is, there were no suffragettes! They were all busy campaigning on the other side of the city, but the image of their double-dealing Prime Minister cowering amongst the cabbages created better publicity than any encounter could have done.

The WSPU campaign in Exeter was organised from committee rooms at 16 Longbrook St, a double-fronted corner shop overflowing with Sylvia Pankhurst's stunning election posters, leaflets, badges and banners. The women's schedule was exhausting, with four open-air meetings held daily on sites across town: Paris Street, the tram terminus, Sidwell Street, the Iron Bridge, New North Road, Larkbear, Fore Street, Heavitree Road, Queen Street... all the same pitches used by the election candidates. They also held women-only meetings at the smaller Barnfield Hall, frequently full to overflowing.

Votes for Women was keen to report on the response. 'Expressions of encouragement and admiration are everywhere heard. "I should think you have converted every man in Exeter," said one..."You keep on keeping on!" calls out a sympathiser. "That we will," the speaker replies; "we don't know what is meant by giving in!"'

Amy Montague and other local activists led the smaller meetings while Gladice Keevil was drafted in from WSPU headquarters to address the larger ones. She was a flamboyant character, described by The *Daily News* as, '...a particularly striking figure. Robed in flowing white muslin, her lithe figure swayed to every changing expression, and the animated face that smiled and scolded by turns beneath the black straw hat and waving white ostrich feather, was the centre of one of the densest crowds.' She was known for her rousing speeches and panache with hecklers but even she was defeated by the crowd at St Sidwells Street. The meeting was unfortunately timed for 4.30 on a Saturday, just as a large crowd of men and boys poured out of St James's Park after the football. A mob of youths kept up an incessant shouting and singing that made it impossible to hear her.

Campaigning in Paignton could be just as fraught, as recounted in the *Brixham Western Guardian*. 'A Paignton Suffragette who has been rather busy of late speaking at outdoor meetings, visited St Michael's on Monday evening, and succeeded in drawing a large crowd. Except for frequent, but good-tempered, interruptions the speaker was accorded, for the most part, a quiet hearing, but on the Suffragette making an exclusive appeal to vote against the Liberal candidate, the audience quickly showed how much they resented her statement. Almost instantly the quietude of the gathering gave place to very animated scenes. The Suffragette was assailed with showers of various missiles, fortunately without any personal injury, and was obliged to make her retreat towards the G.W.R. station, under the protection of the police, followed by a crowd of youth.'

In the second week of January 1910, Gladice Keevil took time out to support Marie Newby and Annie Ball in Ilfracombe. They were joined by Helen Ogston, without her whip this time, who stayed for an 'At Home' in Barnstaple parish rooms the following afternoon. She was on good form, so fluent on militant tactics that even the local paper described her as a delightful speaker. Gladice then moved on to Torquay where she used a decorated cart to travel the entire constituency, distributing leaflets and exhorting the electors to, 'Vote against the Government that imprisons and tortures women who are demanding the vote. Vote for the Women and keep the Liberal out.' She was alternately cheered and hissed as she paraded the streets, but kept campaigning right to the end of polling day.

Annie Kenney drew unprecedented crowds in Bridgwater - as many as ten thousand according to *Votes for Women*. When the Conservative won the seat with a majority of over 1,500 even the sceptics conceded it was down to the suffragettes. Exeter WSPU were also jubilant after ousting the Liberal. It was tight; the Conservative, Henry Duke, only had a majority of twenty-six, but the women had done it. In seven constituencies across the West Country they had proved they could unseat Liberal candidates. Surely Asquith had to listen now, particularly given his precarious position. He'd only scraped back into power after reaching an agreement with the Irish Nationalists.

But it was another story in Torquay. Workers from the local WSPU had been on a knife-edge during the count. Then came the agonising result. They had whittled the Liberal majority down from 460 to 11 but Sir Francis Layland-Barratt had held on. With a different result here and in a few more constituencies across the country they might even have toppled Asquith's government. Even so, they had certainly shaken things up, giving added impetus to a Private Member's Suffrage Bill about to be presented before the House of Commons.

The women had heard it all before, so many Bills, none making it through Parliament. But this time there were two significant differences. This was a cross-party initiative, so no political point scoring to be had, and the chair of the Committee drafting the Bill was Lord Lytton, brother of Lady Constance Lytton, a committed suffragette who had herself been imprisoned in Holloway. Imagine Christabel Pankhurst's delight. If anything vindicated her policy of recruiting ladies with influence this was it.

It was a pivotal moment. Everyone held their breath as the WSPU and the Women's Freedom League [WFL] discussed a temporary suspension of militancy while the Conciliation Bill, as it came to be known, passed through Parliament. It was an interesting alliance. The WSPU originally had a democratic constitution stipulating annual conferences where members could vote for changes and select the committee. But prior to the 1907 conference a group, concerned about the increasingly autocratic way in which Emmeline and Christabel Pankhurst were behaving, had planned to put more democratic measures to a vote. Emmeline then unilaterally annulled the old constitution, announced a new, hand-picked, committee and cancelled the upcoming conference of members. In *My Own Life* Emmeline is breathtakingly frank about her actions. 'If at any time a member, or a group of members, loses faith in our policy, if any one begins to suggest that some other policy ought to be substituted... she ceases at once to be member. Autocratic? Quite so.' For the Pankhursts the WSPU was an army where unquestioning obedience to the leader, to Emmeline, was demanded. Writing in 1924, Annie Kenney reflected that, 'Nuns in a convent were not watched over more and supervised more strictly than were the organisers and members of the Militant Movement. It was an unwritten rule that there must be no concerts, no theatre, no smoking: work, and sleep to prepare us for more work was the unwritten order of the day.'

Emmeline's stand had caused a split in the ranks that led to the formation of the WFL, a militant but more moderate and non-violent organisation. Significantly, while they agreed with the WSPU on securing the vote for women on the same terms as men, their aims were wider. They wanted equality of rights and opportunities between the sexes and the social and industrial well-being of working women. The Pankhursts, though still interested in the conditions of working class women, were focused on recruiting middle and upper class women who would have more influence in achieving the vote.

Despite their differences, and to the relief of many, these two organisations came together in 1910 to announce there would be a truce while such a positive initiative as the Conciliation Bill was in the offing. It didn't propose the vote on the same terms as men, as the WSPU, the WFL and the NUWSS were demanding, but it would have enfranchised one million women. It was better than nothing. Keen to seize the initiative, MPs on the Conciliation committee issued a letter for publication nationwide, including in the *Ilfracombe Chronicle*. 'Soon after the House of Commons meets, a Bill will be introduced under the ten minute rule, as a private member's measure... The effect will be to enfranchise about a million new electors... a cautious advance which respects the preference of Unionists for a moderate and experimental solution... The committee has no doubt that the Bill could be passed by a large majority. Its fate depends on the readiness of the Government to grant the two or three days necessary for its consideration.'

'Its fate depends on the readiness of the Government to grant the two or three days necessary for its consideration.' Years of struggle came down to this one decision - that rested with Asquith. The WSPU were determined to keep the pressure on. They organised more meetings, more rallies, more sales of *Votes for Women* than ever before. The highlight was to be the most spectacular demonstration yet of public support for the cause - a Great March. But an event no-one anticipated intervened. With heavy black-lined columns, on 6 May 1910 the *Ilfracombe Chronicle* announced, 'His Majesty the King breathed his last at 11.45 tonight.'

After the sombre news of the death of Edward VII the women were lifted by more positive news from Parliament. The first stage of the Conciliation Bill had been passed by the House of Commons. The tide was turning. The Great Procession of Women, organised by the WSPU and the WFL, was rescheduled for 18 June. They would show Asquith, once and for all, that women must have the vote. *Votes for Women* announced, 'The vast army of women which will march through the streets on that day will do more than express an academic belief in the vote; it will definitely be calling upon Mr Asquith to secure the passage of the Woman Suffrage Bill through Parliament... this session.' Devon women would again be marching shoulder-to-shoulder with their sisters, though perhaps not so many this time. Some NUWSS members chose not to participate, unsure whether the WSPU truce would hold.

A personal account in the *Western Times* by 'an Exeter Lady', perhaps our Exonian from 1908, speaks of, '...a tiny contingent from South Devon. Some half dozen Suffragists from Paignton and Torquay, a dozen from Plymouth, six from Exeter...' The women joined a special train at Exeter to get to the embankment by 5.30. As with the 1908 procession, the organisation was impeccable with everyone marshalled into groups, the West of England women allocated to section B3, those, that is, who were able to get there. Our Exeter diarist found the streets so crowded she couldn't reach the rendezvous at Westminster Bridge so diverted to the Ladies Club in Piccadilly. There she found all the women were wearing WSPU or NUWSS colours. When the procession drew near she joined the crowded pavement opposite, watching as sellers of *Votes for Women, The Common Cause* and the WFL paper *The Vote,* worked the crowd. This last was almost exclusively sold by male sympathisers leaving the women free to march.

And then the cry of, 'They're coming!' Evelina Haverfield and Vera Holme, someone else who was to become familiar in Devon, rode up and down the lines like marshals seeing to the arrangement of their forces. A women's drum and pipe band - one of 30 - followed, heralding 617 women all dressed in white, a dramatic representation of the number of prison sentences handed out by Asquith's government. Our correspondent recognised several past visitors to Exeter. 'Miss Christabel Pankhurst, Miss Brackenbury, Miss Annie Kenney, Miss Wentworth and Miss Elsie Howey... A striking cortege, pioneers of the movement, women who have been asking for the vote quietly in a ladylike fashion for thirty, forty and fifty years come next. Groups from all over the country streamed behind them: women graduates, university men, suffragettes displaying the yellow, white and green of the Women's League, nurses, business women, teachers, artists, writers, civil servants, clerks, typists and more. And after the London WSPU branches, the West of England contingent. Bristol, a very strong party, with a handsome banner...' And then came Exeter, and our correspondent joined the procession. She had received some less than positive comments in 1908 so was relieved this time that, '...we are not once bidden to "go home and darn our stockings."'

As before, the procession ended at Hyde Park where they were again greeted by a large crowd, not only of women but also a significant number of men. And this time they were there to support, not heckle.

It was gone 8pm by the time everyone gathered in the crowded Albert Hall to hear Mrs Pankhurst propose the resolution, 'That this meeting calls upon the Government to grant facilities for the Woman Suffrage Bill now before Parliament, so that it may pass into law this Session.' It was an impressive demonstration. The question was, how would Asquith react?

A week later they had their answer. 'The Government cannot afford any further facilities [time] for the Bill this session.'

There was uproar in the Commons. 180 MPs signed a petition demanding Asquith find time for the Bill. Even the press didn't hold back:

Men were deceivers ever. *Nottingham Guardian.*

Mr Asquith has been the drag on the whole of the Suffragist movement. He is convinced of the undesirability of conceding the Parliamentary Franchise to women. That being so, he has found it easy to plead all sorts of difficulties as excuses for not handling the subject. *Aberdeen Free Press.*

Once more the Prime Minister's tactics are exposed as mere subterfuge. *Morning Advertiser.*

Suffragist pioneers… must be getting a little tired of "jam tomorrow, but never jam to-day"; the promised land is always in sight, but it always eludes the weary marchers. *The Globe.*

I may say frankly that their [the militants'] ranks will be reinforced daily by non-militants and by members of the Women's Liberal Federation, of whom many have begun to despair of peaceful methods. *Western Daily Mercury.*

It was a turning point for Mary Frood from Topsham. She was a highly visible member of the Topsham community, operating a school for domestic training from her substantial home. She had been part of the suffragist movement for several years but after Asquith's betrayal felt compelled to write to the *Exeter and Plymouth Gazette.* 'There is not the slightest doubt that thousands of hitherto non-militant Suffragist women will join the militants in their bitter anger and disappointment if they are cheated again, and that militancy will be a far more serious problem than before the truce. I have been for many years a patient, long-suffering non-militant Suffragist, but now I have, without leaving the NUWSS, also joined the WSPU.'

Asquith's announcement was a shock for members of all four NUWSS Devon societies - Exeter, Sidmouth, Teignmouth and the Three Towns. Suffragists in Plymouth launched an intensive campaign distributing bills and pamphlets and holding meetings, often together with the Women's Liberal Association. Frances Sterling, from the National Association, urged her audiences to press their MPs to vote for the second reading of the Conciliation Bill and ensure it passed all the remaining stages.

Magically, Asquith suddenly found two free days in the middle of July for Parliament to debate the Bill. The women were back in the game. It was tight, but there was just enough time for a two day debate on the second reading, a week in Committee, back to the House for the report stage and the third reading then up to the House of Lords before Parliament rose for the summer - provided there was no more obstruction from the Government. Even the most hardened optimist had to face that possibility. At the second reading, the Bill passed with a majority of 109, a larger majority than the Government achieved for the Budget, one of its own principal measures. The Bill was full of compromises but a significant number of male MPs were now agreeing that a small percentage of women should be able to vote. Surely now Asquith would have to honour his pledge and see the remaining stages of the Bill safely through Parliament. The women eagerly awaited news of when.

Just before the summer recess Asquith was at it again, announcing there would be no further time for the later stages of the Bill. He seemed determined to stop women getting the vote, his views as entrenched as in his first major speech on women's suffrage almost two decades earlier. 'The vast majority of women do not want the vote. Women are not fit for the franchise. Women operate by personal influence.' And perhaps most significantly, '…it would upset the natural order of things. Women's place is in the home rather than in the "dust and turmoil" of political life.'

Asquith's cover was well and truly blown. Moderates from the Women's Liberal Association resigned in droves. The Men's Suffrage League recommended an anti-government policy. Even the press conceded a return to militancy would be justified. This Suffrage Bill, that had come closer to passing into law than any before it, was on a knife-edge.

With the WSPU poised on the brink of a return to violence, Keir Hardie, former leader of the Labour party, suggested a way forward. He would press for a third reading as soon as Parliament reopened in the autumn. The logic was overwhelming. Asquith had played his hand cleverly, making his announcement on the cusp of the summer recess. Nothing could be done until Parliament reconvened in three months. The suffragettes agreed to wait, but that didn't mean they would be idle. The WFL issued a rallying call. 'We must go on fighting until, in the face of prejudice and intolerance, we have won our liberties. On the day Parliament closed, the new campaign opened, and from now on, everyone who desires the enfranchisement of women must work unceasingly to rouse the country… the campaign must grow in force and effectiveness until by November we have raised a protest which cannot easily be overlooked or disregarded.'

Chapter Thirteen
Hope Against Hope
Summer - Autumn 1910

In Ilfracombe, Marie Newby and Annie Ball gathered a growing band of supporters around them, enthusiastically playing their part with another holiday campaign. They set their inhibitions aside and took to the streets to demand 'Votes for Women', a step that took enormous courage. Respectable women protesting in the streets! Unthinkable! They may have been shunned by friends and neighbours for whom this degrading activity was a step too far. In London the degradation went even further as women on poster parades were forced to walk in the gutter to avoid being arrested for obstruction.

The campaign in North Devon was boosted by the arrival of Helen Craggs, an organiser from the WSPU's London headquarters. Significantly, two years later Helen was discovered at the country house of a well-known government anti-suffragist in possession of two cans of inflammable oil, two boxes of matches, four tapers, nine 'pick-locks', twelve fire-lighters, a hammer, an electric torch and a piece of American cloth smeared with some sticky substance. She was charged with attempted arson, becoming the first suffragette imprisoned for plotting to damage property. Perhaps she shared her thoughts on militancy with Marie Newby during those summer weeks, thoughts that were to have explosive significance before too long.

Two other WSPU ladies, Margaret Mackworth and Miss Pridders, also stopped off for some campaigning in North Devon as part of a summer tour of the West Country. They settled into the Imperial Hotel in Barnstaple before making their mark, literally, on the town's streets. They introduced the locals to a practice familiar in the capital but a novelty in this rural market town - chalking the pavements. The *North Devon Journal* was intrigued. 'Last week, meetings in support of the Women's Suffrage movement were held on Thursday, Friday and Saturday evenings in the Strand, Barnstaple. The organisers announced the meeting by writing notices in chalk on pavements in leading thoroughfares, "Votes for Women" prefacing the announcements. The young lady who did the chalking in High St about midday on Thursday naturally attracted a good deal of attention. She met with some protests and in several cases the notices were promptly obliterated. There was a fair attendance at the opening meeting and the speakers were afforded a good hearing. Much amusement was caused by the exhibition at the meeting of a notice some wags had prepared. It read, "Blokes for Women". A diverting parody of the familiar war cry of the Suffragettes.'

It was a mild protest for Margaret Mackworth though. The previous year she and Annie Kenney had attempted to speak at Aberdare. In her biography, *Turning the Tide, The Life of Lady Rhondda,* Angela John describes how Margaret was greeted by, '...such a cacophony of sounds - hoots, shouts, a shrill blast from a trumpet, cat-calls, a policeman's whistle and a rattle - that her words were drowned out... The women attempted to restore the peace but herrings, ripe tomatoes and cabbages were hurled onto the platform.' But this

wasn't the end of it. A combination of dead mice on the platform and live ones in the hall, along with snuff, cayenne pepper and sulphated hydrogen gas finally got the better of them!

This renewed WSPU and NUWSS campaigning, spurred on by anger at the stalling of the Conciliation Bill is, however, only one side of the story. *The Anti-Suffrage Review* conveyed a very different response. 'The long expected debate and division on the so-called Conciliation Bill... have come and gone, and every Anti-Suffragist in the kingdom may regard the result with great satisfaction... The present cabinet and the Ministerial majority are so deeply divided on the subject of woman suffrage that to proceed any further than the second reading of *any* Suffrage Bill would break up the Government, and split the party.'

Then came the repetition of a belief that had become central to their opposition. In a speech in Parliament in 1906, William Cremer, a leading opponent of women's suffrage, had declared, '...if we opened the door and enfranchised ever so small a number of females, they could not possibly close it, and this it ultimately meant adult suffrage. The government of the country would then be handed over to a majority who would not be men but women. Women are creatures of impulse and emotion and did not decide questions on the ground of reason as men did.' Controversial now, but at the time it was a commonly held and completely acceptable view, supported by Mary Ward. She repeated her opinion that, 'When it comes to questions of foreign or colonial policy, or of grave constitutional change, then we maintain that the necessary and normal experience of women... does not and can never provide them with such materials for sound judgement as are open to men.'

According to the *Anti-Suffrage Review*, when the Conciliation Bill lapsed, 'The emphatic cheer that went up... gave curious expression to the general relief and satisfaction. In our usual English way we had "muddled through'. The House had... postponed woman suffrage to the Greek Kalends [a colloquialism for postponing something for ever] and everybody was more or less pleased... We have now to use the time given us by the failure of the Bill... so that the coming year may see a striking and definitive change over the whole field of battle.' The suffragists would dispute that everybody was pleased, but ever since Mary Ward had launched her 'Appeal Against Woman Suffrage' in 1889, the anti-suffragists had claimed to represent the silent majority who were against giving women the vote.

In Exeter, WSPU members were focused on challenging anti-suffragists active in the city. At a meeting in Bedford Circus, Mary Frood, Edith Splatt [our 'Exonian'] and other WSPU members took up a prominent position near the wagon from which Mr Calderon, of the Men's League for Opposing Women's Suffrage, spoke. He made his position clear from his opening statement. 'Women had made themselves unbearable by their tactics, and it was time a strong organised opposition met them.' The WSPU ladies plied him with questions and, amidst all the banter, Mary Frood was even invited on to the platform to give a short speech. It has to be remembered that this was a crowd largely in sympathy with the Antis and yet she had the courage to step up and speak in a potentially hostile gathering.

Mary was also a prolific contributor in the press on all matters connected to woman's suffrage, often leading to a frank and open exchange of views. One 'Woman Reader' of the *Exeter and Plymouth Gazette*, expressed her frustration. 'Excitable, hysterical specimens of woman-kind, impatient of control, showing childish anger and dislike against any who may choose to differ from them, or who fail to comply with their demand, cause many of us (men *and* women) to feel doubtful whether (if these typify the sex) the weaker half of creation should have votes or a share in the government at all.' Mary Frood's response was brief. 'I know that many members of the Anti-Suffrage League can be quite delightful people, apart from their movement, and it would, indeed, be very wrong of anyone to indulge in personal abuse of any one of them. But a movement is quite another matter. It has "neither a soul to be saved, nor a body to be kicked."' There is no doubt that this growing movement was given added impetus by the formation of the new National League for Opposing Woman Suffrage - an amalgamation of the existing Women's and Men's Anti-Suffrage organisations.

It hadn't been long since Exeter NUWSS had challenged the Anti Suffrage League to a public debate. At the beginning of March 1910 Jessie Montgomery had done her best to persuade them to send a speaker to debate the subject of Women's Suffrage with Helen Fraser who was "thirsting for the challenge". But they declined. Having ducked this challenge, they were out in force at a prestigious event held by invitation of Sir Thomas and Lady Acland at Killerton House. Mr Calderon was again the speaker. 'The thing at the bottom of the female suffrage movement,' he said, 'was what was called feminism. The point of feminism was that a woman has to do everything that she was not created by Heaven to do. They were in imminent danger, unless they took strong steps at this very moment, of the Suffrage Bill going to the third reading… The chief business of a government was the preservation of the nation and the administration of Justice. It was ridiculous to suggest that those things could be carried on by women.'

One of those 'strong steps' involved writing to all MPs with the question, 'Will you see to it that the will of the nation is ascertained to be in favour of woman suffrage before any measure to that end is passed by Parliament.' In other words, the anti-suffragists appeared to be asking for a referendum on the Conciliation Bill. Aneurin Williams, the MP for Plymouth, responded, 'I am not opposed in principle but at present the only way known to our Constitution is to take the votes of the elected representatives in Parliament and as long as this is the way it must be applied all round.' Aneurin Williams was one of the few south west MPs in favour of women's suffrage.

In early September, Annie Kenney redoubled her efforts in Devon, beginning with Axminster. Interest there had been generated almost a year earlier through the efforts of two women in particular, Edith Clarence of Coaxdon Hall and Mildred Tuker of Ashe House, Musbury. Edith later became the Hon. Secretary of the Axminster WSPU branch. She was subsequently given a special mention in *Votes for Women* for selling eleven dozen copies of the magazine during a six week holiday campaign in Devon and Cornwall in 1911. Mildred Tuker was a prolific writer and active both locally and nationally, having taken part in processions in London. On this occasion she presided over the open-air meeting in the Square where Annie spoke to an attentive audience for over an hour. Annie's next stop, in Seaton, was remarked upon by a correspondent to the *Exeter and Plymouth Gazette*. 'I see the Suffragettes have invaded Seaton at last... one knows how very persevering the Suffragettes are, and there will be no want of effort on their part to make converts at Seaton. After the departure of the Suffragettes no doubt the "antis" will pay the pretty health resort a visit.'

After holding further meetings in Lyme Regis and on the Esplanade at Sidmouth, Annie crossed the entire county to the northernmost point of Ilfracombe. Anticipation in the town was high, with hundreds buying their tickets for the Runnacleave Hall, available for a shilling [£7.50p today] or sixpence reserved, three pence unreserved. *Votes for Women* reported, 'Many new members were made and a local union is being formed at Ilfracombe in the course of a week or two.' A whirlwind had hit Ilfracombe and before they knew it Marie, Annie and other supporters were committed to turning their informal get-togethers into a WSPU branch. In mid October, Annie was back to speak at their inaugural meeting, once again reported in *Votes for Women:*

Ilfracombe and Barnstaple – FIRST REPORT. Mrs Newby kindly lent her drawing room on Thursday last to give Miss Kenney the opportunity of meeting Ilfracombe and Barnstaple members. A good number turned up and the new branch promises to be most active. It was decided to hold a meeting on Saturday, November 12th when Lady Isabel Margesson will speak. Miss Ball wishes all members and sympathisers to call for literature... Any person wanting information should write to Mrs Newby.

Marie, now the Hon. Secretary and Treasurer, and Annie, the Literary Secretary, were joined by Margaret Eldridge, Nurse Simes and seven others on the committee. Flyers were distributed, envelopes addressed, and preparations made for the group's first big event. It was a tight schedule for Lady Isabel Margesson, one of the speakers with membership of both the NUWSS and the WSPU. She was booked at the Victoria Hall in Exeter the previous evening, but everything was in place by the time the stewards ushered the audience into their seats at the Gaiety Hall. The *North Devon Journal* covered her speech. '[Lady Isabel Margesson] presented the case with eloquence and moderation, and urged that as two-thirds of the legislation passed was domestic, women should at least have some voice in it. They had grievances as men had, and should have votes to try and get the grievances remedied. Much was done for the working man but little for the working woman, whose lot was hardly better than it was 50 years ago.' She ended with an appeal to her audience. 'Every Suffragist Society agrees with this [Conciliation Bill] and I hope you will do your utmost for the movement.'

She spoke again in the evening where Lady Margesson was more than equal to the inevitable heckling over militancy. She argued that while anything done by the women was magnified by press and politicians, the rough and harsh treatment of their opponents was often suppressed. Applause greeted her plea for those present not to misjudge the women, but to focus on their work on behalf of those who could not help themselves. It was an effective rallying cry that prompted a rush of new members to the group. Demand was so great, they sold out of copies of *Votes for Women*. Spirits were high. They might be distant from London but the fight for the vote was alive and well across the west country, whether their allegiance was to the WSPU or to the NUWSS.

Lady Margesson's talk at Exeter, the day before her appearance in Ilfracombe, was one of a series of weekly meetings Annie Kenny had organised at the Victoria Hall. Attracting the most interest was a visit by Emmeline Pankhurst, planned for the end of October. It was enough to inspire a local reporter to seek an interview. 'Hearing that the famous leader of the Militant movement for the political enfranchisement of women was expected at Exeter by the 1.52 train, a representative of the *Western Times* went to St David's station to secure an interview with, perhaps, the most-talked-of-woman of the day.' The reporter joined Amy Montague on the platform. 'Greetings and introductions exchanged, Mrs Pankhurst, who was wearing a grey cloth coat and skirt, and a motor bonnet, with a fine black lace veil thrown back from her expressive face, was promptly acquainted with the very full programme laid on for her in Exeter. "This is my first visit to the City," she said, laughing. "You have mapped out so much work for me that I shan't be able to even look at your famous Cathedral.'"

At the Barnfield Hall, Mrs Pankhurst spoke to Amy Montague's resolution calling for the passage of the Women's Suffrage Bill before the end of the year. Independent fact checkers might quibble with her claims, reported in *The Western Morning News*, that, '... they had a majority of people in the country, a majority of the electors, and a majority of the Liberal party, in favour of their reform,' but you can feel her exasperation at Asquith's prevarication. 'All women could do was pay up and shut up, whether they liked it or not. She hoped that efforts would be made to induce the Corporation of Exeter to follow other Corporations by endorsing the resolution.'

It was WSPU policy to recruit women of influence and position in society. During her visit to Exeter Mrs Pankhurst chose a meeting organised by Mildred Tuker at the Royal Clarence Hotel to make, '...a short but impassioned appeal to her hearers, as, for the most part, women of leisure and position, to help the Suffragists in their struggle to better the conditions under which the vast majority of women suffered. "The time has come," she said, "when the fortunate women have arrived at a sense of, shall I say noblesse oblige, and all over the country they are standing shoulder to shoulder with the workers in this struggle.'

One of those present was Juanita Phillips, a significant supporter. She initially became involved with the WSPU when living in London, taking part in deputations to the House of Commons. Now living in Honiton, she had already sparked interest in the town by organising and presiding at a public meeting. Possibly inspired by Mrs Pankhurst's visit, she now arranged another well-attended gathering at the Dolphin Assembly Rooms. Amy Montague moved the usual resolution, calling on the Government to ensure the Conciliation Bill became law before the end of the year, which was carried with just two against.

The Devon Women's Liberal Association was also throwing its weight behind the Conciliation Bill. At their annual meeting in Tiverton the speaker, Mrs Bertrand Russell, moved a resolution, '...cordially approving of the Women's Suffrage Conciliation Bill as being a real instalment of justice towards women, and urging all Associations to help the suffrage movement by taking every opportunity to discuss the matter.'

Meanwhile, the NUWSS pressed on with their own meetings in Exeter, equally determined to keep the subject of the Conciliation Bill alive. In November they even had Lord Lytton, Chair of the Parliamentary Committee that produced the Bill, as the key speaker at a public meeting at the Barnfield Hall - after a leisurely luncheon at the Rougemont Hotel of course. In his speech Lord Lytton posed two questions. When should the vote be given to women and what form should it take? The answers - Now, and in the form that was most acceptable at the present moment to the largest number of people.

Another speaker, Miss Alice Abadam, was also on a tour of the south west. She was a well-known suffragist, who spoke with wit, intelligence and passion on women's struggle for a political voice. Her response to the anti-suffragist view that women could do more at the local philanthropic and municipal level was clear. 'Whereas by charitable tinkering they may remedy individual lives, by laying their hands on the political  machine they would influence the lives of millions of their poorer and unprotected sisters for good.'

It was a message brought home to many by an example of injustice covered in the *Common Cause*. 'At Plymouth this week a servant girl was sentenced to one month's imprisonment with hard labour on a charge of "abandoning her illegitimate child". What really happened was that she left [the child] with a woman to whom she promised to pay 5s a week. She secured work through a labour exchange but... having burnt her arm so badly that she could not work, she fell into arrears with her payments and the woman sent the child to the workhouse. For these 'crimes' this girl, of whom the Chief Constable was able to say she had been an orphan for years, and who had done her best to meet her overwhelming responsibilities, was condemned to prison and hard labour, although the Salvation Army offered to care for her and her child.'

In Exeter, Alice Abadam quoted John Burns, as reported in the *Western Times*. 'As long as you have an overwhelmingly rich manhood, and an overwhelmingly poor womanhood in this country social horrors are inevitable... it was time, and high time, that the women arose, and helped the good men to re-adjust matters... Miss Abadam closed a deeply moving address with an earnest appeal to her hearers not to be content with sympathising, but to do something to further the Suffrage cause. The political enfranchisement of women was the only thing that could mend the terrible evils she had been describing. The ladies before her were, many of them, in a position to bring pressure to bear on the Government, and she asked them to do it, in order to get the Conciliation Bill passed.'

Her words were echoed by the new NUWSS organiser, Marguerite Norma-Smith, who began a series of monthly meetings in Plymouth shortly afterwards. She pressed home her belief that it was not revolution but evolution that made women demand the vote before moving the usual resolution, 'That this meeting calls upon the government to grant the facilities necessary for the passage of the Conciliation Bill during the next session.' They were giving Asquith more rope than the WSPU in mentioning the next session rather than that year, but the message was the same. The Conciliation Bill had to be passed.

Miss Norma-Smith moved on to Teignmouth where a challenge awaited her at the local Women's Liberal Federation. They had been hostile ever since the suffragettes campaigned against the Liberal - who happened to be a good suffragist - at the last election. Although the WSPU in Devon were relatively moderate compared to other parts of the country, the NUWSS were constantly having to fend off criticisms of militancy unfairly laid at their door. On a three day visit, Marguerite Norma-Smith spoke both publicly and privately with individuals and, according to the *Common Cause*, '...completely converted those present from their former attitude of hostility to the Conciliation Bill.'

At what was acclaimed 'the best-attended meeting yet held in Teignmouth', Alice Abadam joined Miss Norma Smith and delivered a stirring lecture on Votes, Work, Wages and Well-being. The *Teignmouth Post and Gazette* made much of her credentials as, '…one of the most eloquent speakers working for the National Union which is well known to be non-militant and law-abiding, preferring to do more by influencing people's judgement than by breaking their windows.' To that introduction Miss Abadam added that they were strictly non-party, neither red nor blue, neither Liberal nor Unionist.

This brief tour was a taster for another a couple of months later when Alice Abadam became a familiar face in Devon, giving addresses more or less every day for over a week in Budleigh Salterton, Topsham, Exeter, Plymouth and Devonport.

Throughout the autumn of 1910, Devon women, whether suffragette or suffragist, put their hearts and souls into the campaign. Women such as Marie Newby and Annie Ball in Ilfracombe, Amy Montague in Crediton, Mary Frood from Topsham, Mildred Tuker and Edith Clarence from Axminster, Mabel Ramsay and Maud Slater in Plymouth, Jessie Montgomery in Exeter and many, many others, were filled with hope. The Conciliation Bill had passed its second reading with such a large majority, surely this time they were almost there.

Suffragette. "Come down this way or you'll fall"

Chapter Fourteen
Betrayal and Reaction
Autumn 1910 - Spring 1911

The women didn't have long to wait. The Prime Minister's response
to Keir Hardie's demand for a third reading was imminent. The
omens were not good. Asquith knew the women expected him to
make time for the passage of the Bill, so why didn't he recall
Parliament sooner for the autumn session? Why did he allow the
House to rise early night after night? Why did he not extend the
session? All very reasonable questions that left the women dreading
yet another betrayal.

    And there had been several.

    June 1906: Asquith announced his intention, before the close of
Parliament, to bring in an Electoral Reform Bill to which a woman

suffrage amendment could be added. Parliament ended without this pledge being honoured.

December 1909: Asquith promised that his pledge would hold good for the Parliament of 1910 and that plenty of time would be given to deal with the whole question. Parliament ended without this pledge being honoured yet again.

June 1910: Having announced there was no time to progress a Suffrage Bill, Asquith buckled under pressure and conceded a second reading, but then dug his heels in, refusing any further time for the later stages of the Bill.

Time after time, Asquith employed delaying tactics designed to take the wind out of the suffrage campaign's sails by promising something. But always next month, next session, next year. It may seem this was solely because of his personal opposition, but he was facing another major hurdle. When any Bill came before Parliament it was debated and voted on in the Commons, then sent to Committee, back for the report stage and the third reading then finally up to the House of Lords. Until reform of the Lords in 1911 every Bill had to pass not only the House of

Commons but an upper chamber dominated by Conservative peers who had complete power to amend, reject or delay any Liberal reform they disapproved of. The 1909 Budget, introducing new taxes to pay for pensions and other benefits, was blocked for over a year by the Lords. It begs the question whether Asquith would have been able to get an extension of the franchise to women through a reactionary House of Lords even if he had wanted to. Giving him the benefit of the doubt, could this have been one more reason behind his delaying tactics?

Suffragists and suffragettes clung to their demand, insisting that Parliament enter the Bill on the Statute Book that year. But a call to arms was not far behind. An article in the WFL's mouthpiece, *The Vote,* made it plain. 'In spite of the obstacles still to be overcome, we believe that the Conciliation Bill can be carried into law during the autumn. But while we are prepared for victory and struggling for it, common prudence dictates that we must hold ourselves ready to meet any and every emergency. We must be prepared for such happenings as will commit us inevitably to a second recourse to militancy – the weapon of the rebel... We cannot repeat, we must progress. We shall find ourselves committed to action upon more drastic lines, to action having more serious effects, to sterner and stronger measures. This will be inevitable.'

Asquith's announcement was expected on Friday, 18 November. Suffragettes gathered en masse at Caxton Hall to wait. If this was to be yet another betrayal they would march on Parliament, spurred on by a missive from Christabel Pankhurst a few days earlier. 'The deputation of women which proceeds to Westminster on Friday must be taken as a sign that women are now determined not any longer to beg for justice but to take it... a new chapter opens in the history of the active movement for the enfranchisement of women. We know perfectly well they will never do anything for us unless we drive them into doing it. This truce has taught us a great deal. It has taught us the absolute necessity for militancy. It is no good sitting at home and talking: it is no good simply wishing for success; we must give some outward manifestation of the feeling that we have in our hearts. We hope that every woman will consider whether it is not right and suitable for her to send in her name, whether it is not her clear and absolute duty.'

Hundreds responded to her call, filling Caxton Hall at noon to wait. Then came the news. There would be no time for the final stages of the Conciliation Bill. No more self-delusion. Asquith had done what Mrs Pankhurst and Christabel suspected he would all along. After every suffragist and suffragette in the country had placed their trust in him, he had betrayed them. Again. The truce was over.

Over 300 women left the hall in detachments of twelve, the first led by Mrs Pankhurst and Evelina Haverfield. Very soon the defenceless women were being buffeted by police brought in from outlying districts. The usual officers had become too sympathetic to the cause, so half-trained recruits from the East End had been drafted in. Sympathisers attempted to help, forcing a passage for Mrs Pankhurst towards Parliament Square. Cheers rang out when she was spotted on the steps to the Stranger's Entrance and each time she was joined by others waving standards declaring 'Where there's a Bill there's a Way,' and 'Women's Will beats Asquith's Won't.'

Within minutes the standards were torn down as police moved in on horseback. Sylvia Pankhurst forced herself to witness the brutality. 'I saw Miss Ada Wright rush the entrance. Several police seized her, lifted her from the ground and flung her back into the crowd. A moment afterwards she appeared again and I saw her running as fast as she could towards the House of Commons. A Policemen struck her with all his force and she fell to the ground. For a moment there was a group of struggling men round the place where she lay, then she rose up only to be flung down again immediately. Then a tall, grey-headed man with a silk hat was seen fighting to protect her, but three or four police seized hold of him and bundled him away.'

This mention of Ada Wright was particularly traumatic for Sidmouth readers. She had moved to the town with her family in 1885, when she was just twenty-three, and had been a familiar face working at a social centre there. For a while she had been part of a small nucleus of women who supported women's suffrage and was active in collecting signatures for a petition to Parliament. But she had become disheartened at the lack of support for the movement. After moving to Bournemouth she joined the NUWSS, but by 1905 she had changed her allegiance to the WSPU and was a committed suffragette. Now aged 48, she had been imprisoned and endured hunger strikes twice before the events in Parliament Square. The image of Ada lying on the ground was circulated in newspapers countrywide.

It was a battlefield. Women battered and bloody were trampled under the hooves of horses, jeered at and taunted by the police and manhandled in the most obscene way. Those who chained themselves to railings were a target for men grabbing at their breasts or pulling their clothes up. Sylvia Pankhurst recalled, 'The cry went round: "Be careful; they are dragging women down the side streets!" We knew this always meant greater ill-usage.' Bystanders challenged the police. If the women were breaking the law why didn't they simply arrest them without the brutality? And if their actions were legal, why weren't they allowed through? Mrs Pankhurst was eventually escorted into the Houses of Parliament, to be told by Asquith's secretary that he wouldn't see her. Over 300 women had faced the brutality of the police only for Asquith to turn them away yet again. For six hours the women kept up the siege of the House of Commons in Parliament Square.

The post-mortem encompassed all emotions. Sylvia was moved to say, 'Never, in all the attempts which we have made to carry our deputations to the Prime Minister, have I seen so much bravery on the part of the women and so much violent brutality on the part of the policemen in uniforms, and some men in plainclothes.' Even an independent Parliamentary investigation concluded, 'We cannot resist the conclusion that the police as a whole were under the impression that their duty was not merely to frustrate the attempts of the women to reach the House of Commons, but also to terrorise them in the process. They used in numerous instances excessive violence, which was at once deliberate and aggressive, and was intended to inflict injury. They frequently handled the women with gross indecency.'

Two women died of their injuries that day. Another, Mary Clarke, was arrested for breaking windows and sent to Holloway Prison, where she endured a hunger-strike and force-feeding. She was released, but on Christmas Day was found unconscious, dying soon afterwards from a burst blood vessel on the brain, most likely a result of her experiences in prison. It was a bitter personal blow for Emmeline Pankhurst. She had lost her sister.

The sombre group gathered in Marie Newby's drawing room would have recognised several names on the long list of those arrested. Among them were Vera Wentworth, Elsie Howey and Helen Craggs, someone who no more than a couple of months earlier had been selling *Votes for Women* alongside them on the streets of Ilfracombe.

Suffragettes waiting to be sentenced outside Bow Street Court

More than a hundred women were brought before Bow Street Magistrates the following morning. But, instead of the prison sentence they were prepared for, the order came for them to be released. It was unprecedented. Questions flew around the courtroom. Why? Who made the decision? The answer soon came. Winston Churchill, then Home Secretary, had decided that convictions were not in the public interest. Events labelled 'Black Friday' by the press had become a public relations disaster for the Government. With another election in the offing the releases were pure expediency, a move to cut off the suffragettes' oxygen of publicity.

But the women were not done yet. Asquith promised another statement to Parliament on the following Tuesday. At noon the women again gathered at Caxton Hall, every seat full, every balcony, gangway and corridor crowded... waiting. Mrs Pankhurst finally took to the stage, Asquith's statement in her hand. She read. 'The Government will, if they are still in power, give facilities in the next Parliament for effectively proceeding with a Bill which is so framed as to admit of free amendment.' There was a strained silence as the women struggled to digest Asquith's words. There was no immediate commitment to the Suffrage Bill, not even a commitment for the next session but for the next Parliament. And women's suffrage was not to be an integral part of a Government Bill but left to the mercy of an amendment. Another worthless pledge to add to the list. Christabel leapt to her feet. It was a mockery, an insult to common sense. 'Negotiations are over,' she proclaimed. 'War is declared.'

The women immediately set off towards Downing Street. The police rushed to form a cordon, stretching two-deep across the road, but Mrs Pankhurst didn't slacken her pace. Evelina Haverfield urged the group forward shouting, 'Shove along, girls!' until the cordon broke. Some managed to get to the Prime Minister's door chanting, 'Mr Asquith, give us the Bill, the whole Bill and nothing but the Bill!' Police reinforcements piled in, thrusting the women back. And not just thrusting. Arms and wrists were wrenched and twisted, women were struck about the head and kicked when they were down. Some were trampled and crushed when others fell on top. Protests continued through the night with cabinet minister's homes and Downing Street targeted for window smashing.

Over 150 women were arrested and brought before Sir Albert de Rutzen at Bow Street Court the following morning. But again, the instruction came from Churchill. All charges of simple obstruction were to be withdrawn. De Rutzen protested, but 106 women were discharged, leaving only those charged with assault and wilful damage to be brought before him. One of these was Evelina Haverfield. Albert de Rutzen addressed the dock. 'Your case, Mrs Haverfield, appears to be a little worse than the rest. When the Constable intervenes and takes you into custody, you strike him in the face, and for a moment or two he is scarcely able to see you, and when you are charged you say that the next time you will come with a revolver, that is what you said. You are charged with assault. I fine you £5 or, in default, one month.'

Evelina was defiant. 'May I say that my whole attitude is a protest against the way the police were instructed to treat our women on Friday. It was the most monstrous thing I have ever known, and when I say I will take a revolver I mean that I will carry on this agitation when I come out of prison with more vigour than ever. We shall carry our point, sir, with all respect to you I am bound to make my protest.'

These protests were a step too far for the Conciliation Committee. Their response was published in *The Vote*. 'This Committee deeply regrets the actions of certain women of the WSPU who yesterday committed acts of violence; it entirely disapproves of such conduct and points out that it can only make more difficult the work in Parliament of Members who are endeavouring to secure facilities for dealing effectively with the question next Session.' The chair, Lord Lytton, added, 'I deplore the hasty action of the WSPU in resuming militant tactics before Suffragists in the House had exhausted the resources of negotiation… It has caused great disappointment and mortification to find that in spite of our efforts to promote the cause of Woman Suffrage during the last Parliament, and the proofs which we have given of our sincerity, we have failed to secure the confidence of many of the militant women.' He concludes, 'Conciliation and militancy cannot go side by side, and until a truce is again declared there can be no more Conciliation Committee. Your friends in Parliament can do nothing while you are fighting outside.'

Militancy was not only turning women in the wider community against the movement but it now risked defeating the cause within Parliament itself.

Then something no-one was expecting caused everything to be put on hold. Asquith announced another election, the second within a year and, as it turned out, the last before 1918. The suffragettes homed in on Mid Devon, again joined by the NUWSS, now extending its reach through the energetic work of Marguerite Norma-Smith.

She had built on Margaret Robertson's work in Exeter, Sidmouth and Teignmouth and supported new branches in Ottery St Mary and Topsham, where Mary Frood was elected as Honorary Secretary. Marguerite was now intent on campaigning with different methods, a different aim and more than a little apprehension. After all, two years previously, Mary Mills and Miss Potter had been completely drowned out by the singing, jeering, shrieking and bell-ringing of the crowd.

Marguerite described in the *Common Cause* how she arrived in Newton Abbot on the day before the Christmas market, '…which, I was told, was the busiest day in the year. All the country people for miles round flock into the town. It seemed a splendid opportunity for sending our message to all the farms and hamlets in this scattered country district. By means of a wagonette, which was put in the Market Square at 12 o'clock with a placard fastened on to it, I advertised a meeting at 3.30. Miss Allen of Teignmouth very kindly came at short notice and supported me. When we arrived in the Market Square a large and expectant crowd was waiting. We went rather in fear and trembling, as the only open-air Suffrage meeting that has been held in Newton Abbot was when Mrs Pankhurst was thrown down by the crowd, her wagonette run into the river and the window of her lodgings broken, and she herself had to be rescued by the police.

'Miss Allen opened the meeting. The crowd at first was not inclined to be very friendly but when they realised, after much telling, that we were not militant or against the government, they were prepared to listen. The interruptions were so frequent, however, that a speech became impossible and the meeting took the form of answers to innumerable questions. The crowd grew in numbers till there were between 500 and 600 people. The questions showed a genuine interest and a real desire to understand. The audience grew more and more friendly until finally they asked for another meeting at night – which I promised to give, but unfortunately, the torrents of rain which came cleared the streets. We parted in a friendly spirit and I look forward to having more meetings in Newton Abbot a little later.'

Miss Norma-Smith's 'much telling' that they were not militant or anti-government had saved the day. The NUWSS acknowledged that militancy had brought more life to the campaign than their forty-five years of peaceful agitation, but saw it as a trap. 'We regard some of the members of the Cabinet as little better than *agents provocateurs* and we are sorry to see women fall into the trap. We conceive one Minister, at least, as rubbing his hands in glee at the success of his plot.' For them, orderly propaganda and public discussion were the way forward, not militancy; and backing for candidates pledged to support women's suffrage more effective than a blanket opposition of all Liberals. The key lay in interviewing candidates and endeavouring to win pledges from them. It was challenging, given the size of the constituencies and demands from so many deputations, but Marguerite was successful in the Ashburton division where she found both candidates prepared to vote for a Woman Suffrage Bill.

Plymouth's Three Towns Society decided to support the Liberal, Aneurin Williams, the only candidate to back the Conciliation Bill. Sadly they hadn't got anywhere with persuading Mr Mallett to change his anti-suffragist stance. He firmly believed that the duty of governing and defending the State belonged to men and the duty of rearing, training and guiding citizens belonged to women. The remaining two candidates, Shirley Benn and Waldorf Astor, were less negative but declined to pledge their support. Mabel Ramsay and others threw themselves into campaigning, holding six meetings nightly in six different districts of Plymouth. Devonport Town Council also passed a resolution requesting that whichever Government was returned, they grant facilities to bring in a Bill for the enfranchisement of women on the same qualifications as men - the first Council in the West to pass such a resolution.

The WSPU stepped up their electioneering in Torquay. A decorated trap and motor car were driven round the whole constituency stopping at polling stations, giving out election leaflets and selling *Votes For Women*. The highlight of their extensive campaign of indoor and outdoor meetings, covering Torquay, Brixham, Dartmouth and Paignton, was an appearance by Miss Decima Moore. She was an actress and active suffragist from London who captivated the attention of a packed audience at the Theatre Royal.

MISS ALISON NEILANS
THE WOMENS FREEDOM LEAGUE

For the first time, the Women's Freedom League [WFL] also campaigned in Devon. Alison Neilans arrived to lead the work, someone whose name may well have been familiar. Just over a year previously, she was one of those who had provoked a backlash after attempting to sabotage ballot papers at Bermondsey. Alison had insisted the liquid poured into the boxes simply contained photographic chemicals, which would produce a black stain at worst, but she was sentenced to three months, her third and longest term of imprisonment. She went on hunger strike and was force fed, something she described as the most unspeakable outrage, but she was undeterred. She became a member of the executive committee at the WFL and was now active in Devon together with fellow member, Margaret Nevinson.

They decided to target constituencies where the Liberals voted against the second reading of the Bill, which meant Sir Francis Layland-Barratt in Torquay and Mr Mallett in Plymouth. Committee rooms were opened at 3 Torwood Street, Torquay which, according to *The Vote*, '...proved a considerable attraction. The boys and girls of the neighbourhood who at first came to jeer and scoff, remained... to fold literature and distribute it for us.' They held daily meetings at Upton, Ellacombe, Union Street and the Strand, and managed to extract a commitment from the Conservative candidate, Colonel Burns, to support a Suffrage Bill if elected.

Their reception by the Liberal, Sir Francis Layland-Barratt, was very different. He refused to answer written questions because they were not presented by electors. 'I am here to represent the men,' he declared, before Alison and Margaret were hustled out of the hall. They must have had a moment of satisfaction when the election result was announced. Sir Francis was defeated by over 100 votes, possibly a result of the efforts of the WFL and the WSPU's blanket opposition of all Liberal candidates. In Ashburton, Tavistock, Torquay and the four seats in Plymouth and Devonport the Liberals were all ousted.

Exeter was on a knife-edge, in more ways than one. In a turnaround from the last election Henry Duke, the Conservative, actually told Amy Montague, Olga Fletcher and the rest of the WSPU delegation that he wouldn't include a pledge for woman suffrage in his election address. But the Pankhursts were adamant - all Liberal candidates were to be opposed. So, incredibly, they still campaigned for him. On the day the Liberal, Harold St Maur, was declared the winner by four votes. But Henry Duke appealed the result and in April 1911 the seat was finally his, by a margin of one vote. Across the country, the WSPU kept the Liberals out in up to forty seats, playing their part in ensuring another hung Parliament. In one sense it was an astounding achievement. This was a time when ladies were expected to confine themselves to the parlour and polite conversation, not make an exhibition of themselves accosting law-abiding gentlemen on the streets. But having crossed that divide, they demonstrated their ability to organise, campaign and challenge with ruthless efficiency.

Politically, it was a case of 'here we go again,' when the new Parliament of 1911 saw yet another Private Member's Suffrage Bill. As always only one thing could stop it - time, or the lack of it. Given Asquith's track record this felt inevitable. However, many women seemed to have developed collective amnesia and again became relentlessly optimistic. Christabel sent out a rallying cry for women to work for this Bill as they'd never worked before. This time they would succeed. The public were with them, a majority of MPs were with them, what could possibly go wrong?

One person who could always be relied on to respond to Christabel's rallying call was Annie Kenney. She was about to bring the big guns to Devon. The instruction came to book venues for one of the most significant speakers in the organisation, Frederick Pethick Lawrence. His credentials were impeccable; barrister, economist, mathematician and, together with his wife Emmeline, a core supporter of the WSPU. He'd written on women's suffrage, co-edited *Votes for Women*, posted bail for women and bankrolled the organisation.

Suddenly it was all hands to the pump confirming the Upper Victoria Hall in Exeter, the Theatre Royal in Torquay, the Gaiety Hall in Ilfracombe and the Imperial in Barnstaple. At each meeting Annie set out her stall, as covered in the *North Devon Journal*. She emphasised that if the present government refused them the franchise, the next would, 'continue to receive their attentions.' They were not asking that all women should have the vote, '…but it is only right and just that all those who pay rates and taxes should have it. Lunatics, criminals, aliens, children, paupers… and women are disenfranchised. A state of affairs that is foolish, unreasonable, illogical and bad for the country. Our demands are moderate. Last year a Conciliation Bill was proposed… this would have meant there would be one million women voters to seven and a half million men - not a great revolution.' Annie continued to regale her audiences with the benefits countries experienced where women had the franchise then took on those who claimed that women were not as intelligent and well-educated as men exclaiming, '…74,000 men voted at the recent election who could not write their names!'

It was a stirring lead-in to the star turn of the evening, Frederick Pethick Lawrence. 'It is very wrong,' he said, 'that only one-half of mankind should be concerned in guiding the destinies of the State.' He dwelt on the inadequacies of a male-dominated state in dealing with the deplorable social conditions of the poor, the sick and the young. 'Women have not been allowed to exercise their judgement in these matters and their point of view has not been listened to… What women want is the driving power that only the vote will give.'

He urged everyone to become readers of *Votes for Women*. Something the women embraced with gusto. 'One Torquay member hit on, propounded and carried out a capital plan for advertising the paper. Miss Baker approached the advertisement manager of the G.W.R. [Great Western Railway] and as a result the front page of *Votes for Women*, in a neat case, has for the past month or so, adorned the railway stations at Torre, Torquay and Paignton.' So much momentum was generated around Frederick Pethick Lawrence's visit to Torquay that the decision was made to hold monthly 'At Homes' in members houses to keep them in touch with each other as well as to sustain and deepen interest in the cause.

W.S.P.U. EDITORIAL DEPT.,

Nationally the WSPU had another fund-raiser to promote - Self Denial Week. Women were urged to give something up and send the money saved to the fund. One suggestion was to go for a few days without a servant. Only in the WSPU! It may have bolstered the coffers but it wasn't such great news for servants struggling to make ends meet without their usual wages. The week was organised with impeccable efficiency from the WSPU headquarters in London. With over a hundred paid workers it's no wonder there was such pressure to fundraise. But money wasn't needed just for staff. They had speakers travelling to all parts of the country, handing out thousands of leaflets. Funds were needed to pay for trains, hire halls, print material and to publicise their campaigns. And a once-in-a-decade opportunity to get their message across was on the horizon. Devon women were about to join a mass sleep-over.

HIDE-AND-SEEK.

HARASSED ENUMERATOR:
"Dear me! I feel sure there are some of those wretched suffragettes living in this house, but hanged if I can find 'em."

Chapter Fifteen
The Great Sleep-Over
Spring 1911

1911 was census year and the Women's Freedom League was urging a boycott with the slogan, 'Since women do not count neither will they be counted'. Census evasion was also adopted by the WSPU. It was a perfect passive resistance tactic given they had agreed a truce on militancy while the Conciliation Bill was before Parliament. Women had a choice; to comply, to evade by absenting themselves from home, or to resist by defacing their returns. There was plenty of encouragement to evade. Dances and whist drives, all night meetings in public halls or houses and other distractions were organised across the country. In London, a midnight promenade was arranged for Trafalgar Square followed by entertainment at the Scala Theatre and skating at the rink in Kingsway to live music. As always, the WSPU thought of everything. The Gardenia restaurant, next to Drury Lane Theatre, was booked to provide refreshments through the night.

It was an action that caught the imagination of several west country women, including the Frood family from Topsham. Mary Frood had mileage with publicising her views. On polling day for the last election she painted 'Taxation Without Representation is Tyranny' along the edge of the pavement outside her home, unavoidable for voters using the street on their way to the polling station. She also painted it along the brick wall of the field they had to pass coming and going to the train. On census night, Mary settled down for an evening of conversation and perhaps a few games of Pank-a-Squith,

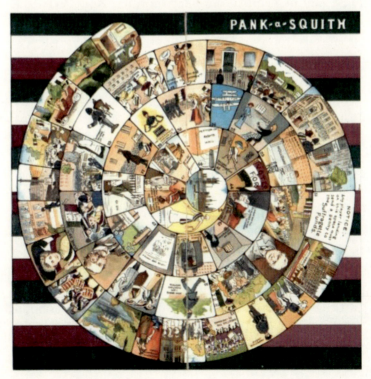

with the women who had taken up the invitation to evade the census with her at Little Broadway House. One of her daughters, a servant and several other women kept her company. The exact number isn't known as she refused to complete her census. She wrote across the form, 'If I am intelligent enough to fill up this paper, I am intelligent enough to put a cross on a voting paper. No Vote No Census.' The census enumerator, Mr. Baker, was instructed to fill out the form with the best information he could muster, which he duly did. He quoted Mrs Frood as saying that she had a 'house full' of boycotters on census night, and promptly decided to add an arbitrary number of six.

Mary Frood wasn't alone in deciding that if she did not count she would not be counted. Amy Scott from Exeter and Juanita Phillips from Honiton also refused to complete their forms while Mary Fausten from Torquay chose a different tactic. She and her daughter wrote under the occupation column, 'Women's Suffrage' and in the infirmity column, 'Unenfranchised.' Nellie Baker also opened her home in St Mary Church, Torquay, for women who wished to avoid being counted. The Registrar recorded, '5 women seen to leave the house before 8 am on Monday morning April 3rd 1911.' Nellie wrote on the census, 'No Vote. No census. Hereby I register my protest against the voteless condition of women [signed] Nellie Baker.'

In Plymouth, The *Common Cause* reported, 'Our members are very grateful to Mrs and Dr Ramsay for welcoming a large party of census invaders, who took shelter under their roof. Every room was occupied, and the comical appearance of the drawing-room, strewn with recumbent forms wrapped in blankets, kept some of the invaders awake from laughter.' The following morning the women had all left by 7am, leaving Mabel Ramsay to await the enumerator. She refused to provide any information but Mr Mears completed and signed a partial return with authority from the Registrar General. Those who spent the night with Mabel Ramsay probably included Maud Slater, Marion Phillips and Hilda Tyerman, none of whom can be found on the 1911 census.

In Ilfracombe Annie Ball made her choice. She announced she was opening up her Trained Nurses' Institute in Ashleigh Road, Barnstaple for anyone who wanted to join her in resisting.

On the evening of Sunday, 2 April, Marie, Margaret and others from Ilfracombe and Barnstaple make their way to Ashleigh Road, pausing in the shadows to check they are unobserved before hastening up the path to slip into the muted glow of the hallway. They carry baskets of food, contributions to the supper party their hostess has arranged. Less usual are the rugs and pillows wedged under their arms. Inside they are greeted by earlier arrivals, sharing an air of suppressed excitement, of conspiracy and daring. After all, they are about to become law-breakers!

Inside Nurse Ball's drawing room, the ladies make themselves comfortable on couches, tucked up with books in their laps, or making a four at the card table. All gratefully accept the cups of tea and biscuits handed round by Nurse Simes and enjoy easy conversation, interspersed with nervous laughter as they recall tense moments with husbands and fathers persuaded, or coerced, into conspiring with them. On a small table at the entrance is a census form with NO VOTE NO CENSUS emblazoned across the orderly columns. Beside it, a dish with a neat sign inviting contributions to the £5 fine [£750 today]. Nurse Ball will shoulder the legal implications; the least others can do is share the financial penalty.

A bridge tournament gets underway, the evening almost eerily normal apart from a creeping tiredness and Annie's constant adjustment of the drapes to prevent any light seeping into the street. Seeing lights through the night isn't so unusual for a nursing home, but they don't want to advertise themselves, not yet anyway. A midnight supper is laid out in the dining room and a toast to the WSPU enthusiastically made by all. As they clear the food and dishes there's a camaraderie in the air; friends and acquaintances sharing a common, illicit, purpose. This is the first time the fledgling group has taken any direct action. They may not be suffering the blows of oppression outside the Houses of Parliament, or the degradation of Holloway, but they have taken a giant stride outside of convention. Their lives will never be the same again.

As night draws on they prepare for sleep. There are one or two beds for the more elderly ladies but most help to lift the couches back against the wall to create space on the floor. Blankets and rugs are laid down as makeshift mattresses or pulled up over fully clothed bodies. No-one expects to sleep. Many talk to pass a restless night and, for some, reservations creep in as spirits wane.

'*Did you read the dialogue in The Times?*' *someone asks,* '*between those pro and anti our protest? They describe it as nothing more than a nursery fit of bad temper and a crime against science!*'

'*What nonsense.*'

'*They say Lloyd George had a radical programme of health and social reform planned for the Liberals. How can he do that without the information he needs to plan for better conditions for everyone?*'

'*Have you read the questions? Wanting to know all about us as wives and mothers. More surveillance than social data collection if you want my opinion.*' *Marie has no doubts. But others are not so sure.*

'*But can breaking the law ever be justified? Perhaps the NUWSS are right, perhaps it is better to make our point in ways that don't antagonise politicians and the public.*'

'*Don't you know?*' *Marie says.* '*The NUWSS are joining in tonight. Dr Ramsay has opened her home in Plymouth. At this very moment ladies will be elegantly strewn across her drawing room floor just like us.*' *There's a moment's silence before laughter catches hold of the women one by one.* '*What reforms have ever been gained without mass protests, all of them breaking the law in one way or another? Why should it be any different for women? If becoming a law-breaker is the only way to achieve publicity and force change then it is our moral duty to act. Just wait for the morning papers. Our protest will be all across them.*'

With the dawn the women set about restoring the nursing home to its former orderliness. But even those who leave take care not to arrive home before noon, the witching hour for being counted. The same day George Mills, the registrar, calls to collect Nurse Ball's return. She hands him the sheet with the columns on the left empty and her statement clearly written on the right .

'*What is this, Nurse Ball?*'

'*It is my return,*' *she replies.*

'*How many persons were resident here last night?*'

'*I refuse to answer any questions.*'

'*I must insist, Nurse Ball.*'

'*And I must decline.*'

'*Come now, Nurse Ball, I am duty bound to report this to the Registrar General. We don't want that do we?*'

'*That is exactly what I want.*'

CENSUS OF ENGLAND AND WALES, 1911.

Annie Ball wrote on her return (above), 'Sir, As one of a large body of taxpayers, householders and employers I have conscientious objections to filling in this paper. We have no guarantee that the statistics supplied by us will not be used to increase our disabilities instead of removing them. We consider also that if we are capable of filling in a complicated census paper, we are capable of making a cross on a ballot paper at a general election. When the Government allows qualified women a voice in the making of laws they are forced to obey, and the spending of the money they are forced to contribute to the State, a privilege granted to men only, we shall not refuse our help.'

It was left to the registrar to complete the form using what he described as 'private sources', presumably the neighbours. He listed three single women at the address in addition to Annie Ball - Miss Grant, Miss Marlow and a general servant, a fraction of the actual number present that night. This tactic of incomplete or spoiled returns was adopted by women nationwide, scrawling 'Votes for Women' or 'No Vote No Census' instead of entering information. Devon resisters left a marker for any family historians unable to find their female ancestors on the 1911 census. Were they evading? Could they have been suffragettes? As a tactic it was inspired. The number of women who refused to complete the census was reported to the cabinet. Businesswomen such as Annie Ball or professionals such as

Dr Mabel Ramsay couldn't risk arrest but at the stroke of a pen their protest reached the very heart of government.

Annie Ball also had another, very public, protest in mind. Women contributed over twenty million pounds [£3 billion today] annually towards the country's economy, but without the vote they had little say in how that twenty million was spent. It was unjust. It

was indefensible. And in 1909 a group of suffragists had decided enough was enough. 'No Taxation Without Representation' was adopted as the clarion call of the Women's Tax Resistance League (WTRL). The organisation was the inspiration of Dora Montefiore who took resistance a stage further. 'When talking this over… with Theresa Billington and Annie Kenney, I told them that now we had the organisation of the WSPU to back me up I would, if it were thought advisable, not only refuse to pay income tax, but would shut and bar my doors and keep out the bailiff, so as to give the demonstration more publicity and thus help to educate public opinion about the fight for the political emancipation of women which was going on… At one time my housekeeper and I counted no less than twenty-two pressmen outside the house…'

'No vote, no tax' was also embraced by Evelina Haverfield, someone who was becoming increasingly familiar in Devon. She was a WTRL committee member and the person who most likely encouraged Annie Ball to join their ranks. This Annie did with a personal letter to Lloyd George explaining that she wasn't willing to pay anything until he granted women the vote. It probably followed the lines of a letter from another tax resister. 'Taxation without representation is tyranny, and although we have to submit to the tyranny, we are not prepared to subscribe to maintain it. To force women out of their earnings to pay salaries to Cabinet Ministers and MPs to legislate for men, who through the ballot box, command attention and consideration is to me such a gross injustice that I offer no apology for my action.'

Official letters dropped on the doormat of the Nursing Home in response to Annie's letter, culminating in a final demand from the Inland Revenue. This was her cue to reply explaining her refusal to pay - and the point of no return. It was not an easy decision. Nurse Ball was a respected businesswoman in Barnstaple and Ilfracombe. She relied on the goodwill of local people to patronise her Nursing Homes. Together with being a census resister, this action marked her out as a law breaker, potentially undermining her standing in the two towns. Yet she still posted her final statement... and waited.

Just two weeks after the excitement of census night, Annie Ball opened the door to some very different callers. Bailiffs had a legal right to enter a resister's property to take items to cover the tax owed, plus enough to cover their costs. Fortunately many were sensitive about this intrusion. Items were generally agreed upon, so Annie would have directed them to the canteen of cutlery and a few selected silver pieces identified as being of sufficient value. Slowly, the tally would be made and her goods removed.

Annie Ball alongside the confiscated items

Having made her stand, Annie's next move was to attract as much publicity for the cause as possible by advertising the bailiff's auction sale of her goods, reaching people who wouldn't have dreamt of attending a women's suffrage meeting. She achieved at least one report in the *North Devon Journal*:

VOTES FOR WOMEN
NOVEL PROTEST AT BARNSTAPLE

Miss Ball of the Nursing Homes at Ashleigh Road, Barnstaple and Larkstone, Ilfracombe, who is the Hon. Literary Secretary of the Ilfracombe branch of the Women's Social and Political Union, recently refused a demand for Imperial taxes as a protest against the exclusion of women from the privilege of the vote, and she wrote to the Chancellor of the Exchequer announcing that she would not be willing pay the taxes until women's suffrage had been granted. But taxes *have* to be paid, despite conscientious objections, and so in this case the usual steps to enforce payment were made. A sufficient number of goods to cover the amount due were seized at the Ashleigh Road Nursing Home and an auction for their sale was conducted on Tuesday morning by Mr 'l'. W. Sanders at the offices of Messrs. Sanders and Son, High Street. The proceedings lasted only a few minutes, the articles (silver and cutlery) being quickly purchased by lady friends who accompanied Miss Ball to the sale. The net result of the protest is that Miss Ball has to pay the amount claimed, plus £1 5s expenses. [£185 today] But Miss Ball is confident that the cause she has so much at heart will be advanced by the procedure.

Marie and others showed solidarity, attending the auction and bidding on items in turn until all Annie Ball's possessions had been restored to her. It was to become a familiar pattern.

Nellie Baker of Torquay, also a census evader, was another member of the WTRL. In 1913 her goods were seized and sold at White, Chatton and Co's Auction Rooms after she refused to pay inhabited house duty. She attracted publicity for her protest with a meeting held outside the public library, just one of a series organised by the WSPU with Mrs Kineton Parkes, the secretary of the WTRL. As well as Torquay, she also spoke in Plymouth, where Frances Latimer chaired the meeting, and Exeter, chaired by Amy Montague.

Mildred Tuker and Hope Malleson of Ashe House Musbury also refused to pay inhabited house duty. A pair of Indian silver bangles were seized but bought back by Mr Phillips, the husband of fellow WSPU member Juanita Phillips from Honiton. A meeting in Trinity Square Axminster brought them the publicity they sought. Mildred tried to publicise her actions through the newspapers but one editor refused to publish her letter on the grounds that it was an incitement to crime.

As well as by direct action, the Ilfracombe group kept up the pressure with letters to the editor of the *North Devon Journal* using the pen name, *Suum Cuique,* a latin motto roughly translated as, 'let everyone get what is due to them'. Their letter opened, 'Woman suffrage is claiming... justice in accordance with two prevailing principles... "No taxation without representation" and "woman is not inferior to man in body, mind, nor spirit."' They followed up with a table of suffrage societies, covering three full columns, representing the full strength of the movement. It's an impressive summary. *Suum Cuique* concludes, '...one common object has brought these Societies into existence, that common object being to obtain for women the Parliamentary Franchise on the same terms as it is, or may be, granted to men, and to establish equity of rights between the sexes.'

It remained a much needed campaign. Woman suffrage had been debated in the Commons no less than twenty times. Twelve Bills were brought before the House. Six passed a second reading. None had become law.

Chapter Sixteen
Different Voices
Spring 1911

Bolstered by the success of their census and tax resistance protests, Ilfracombe and Barnstaple WSPU escalated their activity. Marie, Annie and Nurse Simes, a new member who was becoming increasingly active, began leafleting door-to-door. It was a brave move in this small community where many were adamant that a woman's place was in the home as a wife and mother. Especially when Marie's husband had only recently retired from the important role as surgeon at the Cottage Hospital. It was unthinkable that any woman could disrespect her husband's authority by handing out subversive literature in this way. Marie may well have had doors shut in her face, been given the cold-shoulder at church and become the butt of hostile gossip. It's a testament to her convictions that she refused to be silenced, proudly displaying the WSPU colours and walking the length of Ilfracombe High Street persuading shopkeepers to sell copies of *Votes for Women*.

There was also the small matter of yet another by-election in North Devon, the last thing anyone had an appetite for. But there was no slacking for Marie and Annie. At 8pm on Friday, 21 April they joined the crowds filtering into the Alexandra Hall at Ilfracombe for some reconnaissance on Sir Godfrey Baring, the new Liberal candidate. He addressed the audience on Irish Home Rule and the Parliament Bill but not a word on women's suffrage, a red rag to a bull for Marie. It was time to draft in some significant backup. A few days later a car drew up outside the Newby's semi-detached villa in Broad Park Avenue. The Honourable Evelina Haverfield had arrived. Driving the car was a name familiar from the pages of *Votes for Women* - Vera Holme, a mounted Marshall with Evelina at last year's procession and Mrs Pankhurst's chauffeur.

For many years Evelina had been close friends with Ethel Acland Hood who lived at Brendon, a small village between Lynton and Porlock, and who was undoubtedly the connection that brought Evelina to this remote Devon spot. Evelina acquired a cottage nestling beside the path to Rockford on the north of the East Lyn river, immediately renaming it Peace Cottage. The location was perfect. When not campaigning, Evelina loved to ride; to be so close

to the open country of Exmoor and able to join the Somerset and North Devon Staghounds was all she could ask for.

Her stays at Peace Cottage were mostly for high days and holidays, although that was to change when her relationship with Vera became more intimate. In the privacy of Peace Cottage they set up home together. It was a discreet relationship, although perhaps it wasn't wise to carve their initials on the bed and then ask the landlord of the nearby Staghunters Inn to look after it when they left a few years later.

Having Evelina staying locally was a boost for the Ilfracombe group, particularly when it came to confronting the candidates. On Tuesday, 2 May Evelina joined Marie to drive over to Bideford for an appointment with Mr Parker, the Conservative candidate, at his committee rooms in Appledore. Mr Parker was prepared, '...to go as far as Mr Balfour (the previous candidate) had gone hitherto on the subject of women's suffrage, and was also prepared to mention this subject when speaking in public.' Something of a concession but not exactly a ringing endorsement. They moved on to Sir Godfrey Baring who, Evelina said, '...had a very good understanding of the subject, and was ready to vote straight for any Suffrage Bill which went before the House, and press for facilities as far as he could, without voting against his own Government.' A relatively hopeful response, although of course, he was a Liberal, so they wouldn't be supporting him! Marie and Evelina's interviews had been timely though. Sir Godfrey was duly elected and when the second reading of the latest Suffrage Bill came before Parliament, he voted for the motion, just one of a significant majority in favour.

The women of Ilfracombe were still denied a say in the election of their MP, but the second week of May saw many of them casting their vote in the district council elections. Of 1,639 voters, 355 were women. Equality was still some way off though; the women were allocated a separate voting station in the Alexandra Hall.

In the eight years since the Pankhursts had parted company from the NUWSS, the organisation had continued to lobby in its own reasoned way. Emmeline and Christabel still derided their tactics as ineffective, but the NUWSS was experiencing a surge in membership as more and more women walked away from the WSPU, horrified by the increasing militancy that was getting widespread coverage in the well-read regional papers. Marquerite Norma-Smith took advantage of the by-election to make her first inroads into North Devon. In just two-and-a-half days she addressed eight gatherings, driven between meetings in a car decorated in the red, white and green of the NUWSS and displaying a large placard on the back. She obviously made an impact, recording that people living in the country villages realised for the first time that Women's Suffrage was a living movement. She recounted her experiences in the *Common Cause*:

On Wednesday evening we had a large open-air meeting in the Square in Barnstaple, the first that had been held in the town. Although the Party feeling was very intense and the town very excited, we were treated with the utmost good feeling from first to last, and listened to with genuine interest. At 12.30 on Thursday we held a meeting at Lynton. The audience there was mostly composed of men who showed their approval and appreciation throughout my speech and one announced at the end: "Miss, you have talked more sense to-day than all the men who have been down here electioneering." We drove away happy that a statement of our case had made such a good impression.

By 2.30 we were at Coombe Martin, a long straggling village. Our car soon brought the village women out of their houses and they listened for the first time to an explanation of the meaning of our movement. At 4.30 we held a large and enthusiastic meeting in the main street in Ilfracombe. A drunken man was a little troublesome but the people were so keen to hear that they effectively silenced him. Questions were asked and answered and literature given away, and the people cheered us as we left. At night we had another meeting in Barnstaple.

On Friday we visited the western half of the constituency and had a splendid meeting in Bideford where we again drove away amidst cheering and the waving of hats. In Appledore we had a mixed audience of townspeople and fishermen. When I asked for questions a man remarked, "There is nothing to say: it is all so plain and straight-forward". The vicar of the town, who stood in the crowd to listen, came and spoke to me at the end and said he was "entirely in agreement with our whole movement." In the evening again we had a still larger meeting in Barnstaple and a lively discussion followed.

Capitalising on this interest and the responses she'd received to a plea made through the *North Devon Journal*, Miss Norma Smith decided it was time to start recruiting.

I am delighted to be able to report the formation of four new societies in North Devon. The district was quite new ground when I came here some weeks ago. In Barnstaple, Miss James [the same Kate James who spoke at the YMCA debate two years earlier and decried militancy at a later meeting] gave a small but successful meeting in her garden. Other members have been enrolled by visiting. The society at present is small (about 30 members) but we hope after a public meeting which we propose to have in the early autumn, the numbers will be considerably increased.

At Instow, Mrs Preston-Whyte gave an afternoon meeting in her delightful drawing room. The meeting proved a great success and quite a number of people gave in their names as willing to join a local society. Since then Miss Preston-Whyte and I have collected more members and now Instow can boast a Suffrage Society of its own duly affiliated to the National Union.

The quaint little fishing town of Appledore has yielded a surprising number of Suffragists. We have had two meetings in the church schools at both of which the vicar, the Rev G. Scholey has presided. Thanks to the energy and help Miss Martin has given, the Appledore Society now numbers some 51 members. Miss Martin has worked splendidly and I am delighted to leave the secretarial work of the society in her hands.

On Tuesday of last week by kind permission of Miss Abbott, a meeting was held at West Bank School, Bideford, which has resulted in the formation of a Suffrage Society there... I am hoping to have another meeting in Bideford soon as many people are asking to be told more about our movement. Four keen and enthusiastic societies in one constituency ought to make both political parties regard Women's Suffrage as a vital question.'

A noticeable absence in this list of new NUWSS societies is Ilfracombe. While the rest of the region was more comfortable with the moderate approach, Ilfracombe remained an island of militancy, with no suffragist group ever forming in the town despite Miss Norma Smith's apparently successful meeting there.

Elsewhere in the county, Mary Willcocks addressed Sidmouth's first annual meeting in February. The large gathering which turned out to hear her and Annie Leigh Browne was impressive given the significant anti-suffrage support in the town. But the antis seemed to have gone quiet of late. Exeter NUWSS was also forging ahead. A house-to-house canvass of women municipal voters culminated in an invitation to the Queens Hall to hear Mary Willcocks, now the South West Federation's Hon. Secretary, Marguerite Norma-Smith and Jessie Montgomery. They were obviously successful in motivating their audience; twenty women signed up then and there. Exeter was also one of the bookings for Alice Abadam, back for another tour of the region. She held eleven meetings at five branches in all, including Plymouth where, according to the *Common Cause*, 'the audience was deeply stirred by Miss Abadam's fine fighting speech.'

In April the NUWSS South-Western Federation held their first meeting in Plymouth, part of a major push to increase suffragist influence there. The list of attendees gives an interesting snapshot of the branches and individuals that were particularly active at the time. Miss Baly, Mrs Penry, Mrs Fletcher and Mrs Ross were all present from Exeter; Lady Lockyer (Mary Leigh Browne) from Sidmouth, Mrs Knight Bruce, Miss Wild and Mrs Hole from Newton Abbot and Mabel Ramsay, Clara Daymond and Maud Slater from Plymouth.

At the Birmingham conference in 1896 Mrs Taylor had recommended strategies for covering 'those blank tracts of land' such as Devon. That plan was now coming to fruition. Mary Willcocks took to the floor to urge that the larger and stronger

Societies should organise the small towns in their neighbourhood, recommending that there should be at least one branch in each constituency. The need, as always, was for more speakers. If each branch ran speaker's classes then, when the organiser was ready to arrange a public meeting in a new place, she would have local speakers to draw on to form a new branch.

Alongside this pro-suffrage activity, the anti-suffragists in Plymouth were still making their views felt. In April and May there was a flurry of correspondence in the *Western Morning News* following a letter from Lieut-Col Purchas, Hon. Secretary of the Plymouth and Three Towns Branch of the League for Opposing Women's Suffrage. He referred to the Conciliation Bill as the thin end of the wedge claiming that, '...the vast majority both of the electorate and of women are opposed to "votes for women".' It was an irresistible challenge for Annie Ramsay, Dr Mabel Ramsay's mother. 'When women are enfranchised - as they will be - they will not be dragged to the polling booths to record their votes... They can abstain if they wish - just as men do now. The anti-suffrage attitude to my thinking is somewhat like the dog in the manger, "I don't want it, and you shan't have it".'

Maud Slater, another Plymouth NUWSS member, took on the anti's claim that they represented the silent majority. 'If the large majority of women are anti-suffragists why do they not intimidate the councillors into passing a resolution against the Bill?' She asked for evidence of a single instance. 'Meanwhile... the number of Town Councils [supporting] the Bill is steadily mounting. I gave it as 81 a few days ago and now have a further list of 13 towns.' In another letter she pointed out that 26 societies, nearly all managed and financed by women, were working to persuade men to give them the vote. Whereas only one society, half managed and chiefly financed by men, was working against women obtaining the vote. How did that prove that the majority of women did not want the vote? Pro-suffrage women also held two or three hundred meetings a week, 30 in Plymouth alone during the last ten months. But they rarely heard of an anti-suffrage meeting.

Marquerite Norma-Smith had a few disheartening encounters with anti-suffragists when canvassing Town Councils. But she was even more exasperated with the man who claimed to support the suffragists but when asked for his vote answered, 'Oh, no, I could not promise that...' followed by all sorts of excuses. 'All this makes one come away with a feeling of hopeless resentment, and makes one wonder what lever can be used to further our cause. It takes big courage to go on and on with no weapon! [Thinking of militancy perhaps] No wonder sometimes our hearts fail us, and we are inclined to think it is all time thrown away! But then comes the wonderful part of it. When we realise that no word in the cause of truth and justice is ever lost... powerful thoughts envelop and surround us; convincing first of all the people near us, then the community at large... If we could once convince ourselves of the truth of this invisible power, we should never falter or get downhearted.'

These challenges from the anti-suffragists did have one positive outcome. They provided a way for the women to get suffrage news and arguments into papers that definitely wouldn't have published their propaganda otherwise.

Making banners at WSPU headquarters

Chapter Seventeen
Loud and Proud to London
Summer 1911

It had been an eventful twelve months in Devon with three elections, two Suffrage Bills, endless procrastination from the Prime Minister, several blistering talks from Annie Kenney, the official launch of the Ilfracombe and Barnstaple WSPU, the arrival of the NUWSS in the North of the county plus… the biggest sleepover Devon had ever seen. But the icing on the cake was still to come - the Great Procession in London on Saturday, 17 June. Unlike the procession the previous year, all the suffrage organisations would be taking part in this event, including the NUWSS.

At drawing room meetings across the county Annie Kenney carried her audience with her in a passionate bid for everyone to involve themselves in the cause in whatever way they could. Would they write immediately to their Liberal candidate asking him to support the latest Suffrage Bill? Would they vote with their feet and show Devon's solidarity with the movement at the demonstration planned for 17 June in London? And would they join Mrs Pankhurst at a meeting in the Albert Hall afterwards? (Tickets available but going fast).

It was a pivotal moment. In 1910 the first Conciliation Bill had achieved majorities in two debates before Asquith, after several delays, halted all further progress by calling a general election. On 5 May the second Private Member's Conciliation Bill had passed with a majority of 255 to 88 and the government were now considering whether or not to grant further time for it. In a stirring call to action, Annie urged her listeners to overwhelm Asquith with demands that he progress the Bill. *The Ilfracombe Gazette* had a unique take on her address. 'With great power and knowledge of her subject, Miss Annie Kenney spoke on the Women's Suffrage Bill now before Parliament. Really though, if women eventually obtain that much craved boon, the franchise, will not the first few general elections at which they exercise their right to vote be highly reminiscent of Gilbertian opera?' [Usually taken to mean wildly comic and improbable] Perhaps it was this comment that inspired a member of the WSPU to respond.

'Sir, I have just returned from a political meeting at which the women were urged to use their influence over men, what we suffragists call the 'backstair influence'. How weak men must be if they can be so easily persuaded for whom to vote!... No doubt a few women use the charm of their sex to influence men to their way of thinking, or wives importune their husbands till from very weariness these are induced to vote against their judgement. This kind of influence is, in my opinion quite illegitimate and will become, one hopes, more rare when women have some real political power of their own.'

Inspired by Annie, women from Crediton, Exeter, Axminster, Honiton, Ilfracombe, Barnstaple, Plymouth and Torquay committed to join the procession in London. Members from Axminster either took part themselves or arranged for deputies to march for them. Ilfracombe and Barnstaple made an occasion of it by arranging an excursion to London for their members. Plymouth NUWSS representatives proudly advertised their participation with a banner and by wearing 'Plymouth' badges. As Maud Slater commented in the *Common Cause*, it was hoped that, '...being seen by many people before and after the procession... would help to show the strength of the movement in the provinces.'

Volunteering for the procession was no idle gesture, as a contributor to the magazine graphically illustrated. 'A good many of us don't like "processing"... Physical discomforts and burdens we are so used to that we treat them as almost negligible. But it is no joke to be up half the night and travel and walk all day, knowing you have another sleepless night of travelling before you and thence a day's work demanding your remaining energies.' But this faded into insignificance against the sacrifice of the large contingent of Northern working women who, '...had been fined - every one of them - to the extent of a day's wages.'

In addition to the practical arrangements, all groups, NUWSS as well as WSPU, were sent copies of the song, 'March of the Women'. Especially composed by Ethel Smyth, this was to be sung throughout the demonstration and learning it by heart was obligatory.

Dedicated to THE WOMEN'S SOCIAL AND POLITICAL UNION.

THE MARCH OF THE WOMEN
(Popular Edition in F. To be sung in Unison)
By ETHEL SMYTH, Mus.Doc.
Price: One Shilling & Sixpence net

Life, strife - these two are one,
Naught can ye win but by faith and
daring.
On, on - that ye have done
But for the work of to-day
preparing.
Firm in reliance, laugh a defiance
Laugh in hope, for sure is the end
March, march, many as one
Shoulder to shoulder, and friend
to friend.

The last of four verses to be memorised.

The timing for the procession was perfect. George V's coronation was scheduled for 22 June, just six days later. People were gathering in London from all over the Empire; it was a once in a lifetime opportunity to show the whole world the strength and determination of the movement in the UK. Women in Australia and New Zealand already had the vote. If they could be represented, why not women from the birthplace of the Empire? Given the ongoing truce over militancy, every suffrage society in the country was planning to be there; the WSPU, the NUWSS, the WFL, churches, actresses, writers, graduates, Young Suffrage League and more. It was to be a mass celebration of the sisterhood of women. Nothing was going to keep Devon women from saying loud and proud that they were part of this mass movement.

The leadership of the WSPU were in no doubt about the importance of the event. 'The Great Procession of Women... will be the most memorable which has ever taken place in history. It will stretch for seven miles in length and will be made up of forty-thousand women who have chosen this method to demonstrate their determination to win the franchise for their sex.'

Participation demanded dedication. Workers were tasked with organising the women into sections, each under the command of a marshal. Teams of volunteers advertised the event, distributing thousands of handbills and chalking pavements, including the whole of the route of the procession. The familiar figure of Helen Craggs was in charge of the *Votes for Women* Corps, boosted by volunteers from Plymouth, Torquay and Paignton. They were phenomenally successful, selling over 10,000 copies throughout the day.

Common Cause sellers were also out in force, with many women having already worked the corridor trains on the way to the capital. They were helped enormously by Annie Leigh Browne lending her carriage to deliver fresh supplies of the magazine to the women. One seller was struck that, '...there was nothing of the spirit which tells you to, "Go home and behave yourself" among the women. Not *one* said it to me, and I offered the paper to thousands. This slavish bitterness seems to have died out." Although this correspondent then adds that she was still greeted by a man on the club steps with, 'Oo's making the 'usband's tea?' The anti-suffragists were also present through paying, '...some dozens of forlorn unemployed to ramble about with sandwich-boards proclaiming that "women do *not* want the vote." A pitiful procession, pitifully disregarded.' Even *The Spectator*, usually a supporter of the Antis, had to agree. 'The file of anti-suffrage sandwich men appealed neither to the eye nor to reason and the crowd thought so too.'

For the women in the procession itself, there was copious guidance:

> Don't... wear gowns that have to be held up; be later than 4.30 in joining the Procession; leave your ranks once you have taken your place; look behind once the Procession has started; wave handkerchiefs; break line; break step; crowd up if the ranks in front of you are halted; run to catch up the line in front.

> Do... wear white if possible, with a gay display of the colours; wear your badge; wear a small hat and no long hat pins; be punctual; take up your place five abreast in the Procession and remain there; bring some provision lest you suffer from want of food; leave a clear space in front and behind every banner; keep step with the marcher on the left; march eyes front like a soldier in the ranks; march with the left foot first; make quite sure you know the Marching Song by heart.

> Do... realise that the work of the organisation on so enormous a scale would be impossible except for the fact that the WSPU relies on the intelligent, self-restrained and hearty cooperation of each and all its members.

There were even detailed instructions for turning a corner.

> For a line of five people to turn a corner with neatness and precision is a very difficult achievement which calls for the

exercise of great care and attention. Upon its successful accomplishment depends the good effect of the Procession. The person on the inside of the corner should mark time, without advancing at all, the second should advance very slightly, also marking time, the third must take longer steps, the fourth longer steps still and the fifth has to step out and swing round in fine style without for one second breaking the straightness and solidity of the line.

Fully briefed, on Saturday, 17 June Devon representatives, including women from Sidmouth and Plymouth with their banners, hurried from Paddington Station to take their places, the WSPU contingent in section A3, the NUWSS in E6. Then came the signal to move, all part of a mighty stream. Fellow marcher, Miss Skrine, shared her experiences in the *Bath Chronicle:*

There was something unusual about the crowd itself. What was it? Why yes, of course, the colours! They were everywhere. Purple, white and green, gold and white, gold, green and white. WSPU, Freedom League, Church League, Men's Society, many more still, but everywhere, outnumbering the rest, the red, white and green of the National Union of Women's Suffrage Societies... So on we went... Now the stress of the march made itself felt... slowly and with constant halts, the great procession unwound its six miles of orderly length.

It was a new and trying experience, this slow intermittent journey through a lane, sometimes all too narrow, of the watching faces of a great and silent crowd. Their silence struck the attention at once. No cheering yet, no demonstration of enthusiasm - but scarcely an unkind or sneering word. To those among us who had had experience of petition work at the polling booths of 1910 this was indeed a significant fact.

Presently we became conscious of a curious undercurrent of sound among them, a low throbbing, regular beat, like the sound of a tom-tom, the steady clapping of hands from friends who had the courage of their convictions.

Encouragement was indeed welcome, for the physical strain on processionists was severe. The necessity of moving with the muscles braced to halt at any moment, the halts themselves, the long standing and slow marching through the hot airless passage cleared by the police were all exhausting. One could not wonder that some faces grew white and strained... As we turned into St James's Street, our case was altered. Here the sunset light from a glorious evening sky lit up the waving banners. A cool breeze brought freshness... Best of all, our friends had mustered. We knew it in a moment. Silence and attention had meant respect, but from this point on we found enthusiasm. Cheers, clapping, friendly words were heard from every side.

But more was to come. As the golden banners dipped suddenly before a decorated balcony, every right hand was raised to salute a certain grey-haired, sweet-faced lady. For Mrs Wolstenholme Elmy, rising, bent over the parapet, waving white old hands in greeting to these her younger sisters in the cause. [One of the first women to petition Parliament for the vote almost half a century earlier.]

That was a moment to remember. Then came another. When each rank reached the point where Piccadilly sloped downhill, those marching could for the first time see something of the procession they helped to make. That mile-long spectacle of moving banners winding away quite out of sight... must have brought to many a strange moment of realisation. To know oneself less an individual than a living part of a great movement, is an experience which comes to most men at least once in a lifetime. To most women it is denied. But here it came to forty-thousand... And so marching, tired but triumphant, we reached the open space behind the Albert Hall.

To the multitude of Suffragists, who could not be with us, to the innumerable friends who watched us pass, to the processionists themselves has come immense encouragement... Finally, has the greatest result - the Franchise - been won? At least one influential paper has called the Procession, "The Women's Victory." May that victory, which seems indeed so near as to be almost ours, come without bitterness and further struggle.

Mrs Pankhurst took up the theme when she addressed the sea of white-uniformed women finally gathered inside the Albert Hall. 'What does this demonstration of ours mean? It means victory! And here we are tonight, not only in the sure and certain hope of victory, but with a sure and certain knowledge that victory is very near. We who began as a small insignificant band of women only a few years ago, are now a mighty army, an irresistible force, a force that is bound to win... because it is an army composed of individuals all animated with a burning desire for freedom.'

It had been a long and exhausting day, but one that those in the Devon WSPU and NUWSS contingents would never forget: a day when a few determined women came to know themselves less as individuals, '...than a living part of a great movement'. According to *Votes for Women,* 'On Saturday last all previous records were broken and surpassed. It can be said without fear of contradiction that no such procession ever walked through the streets of London or any city of the world before. Whether it be judged by the standard of the numerical strength, of beauty of design, of enthusiasm, of consummate organisation, the Women's March of Saturday, June 17 will stand out for ever as a great event in the history of this world.'

Interestingly, the press agreed with Miss Skrine's observation that the red, white and green of the NUWSS outnumbered the rest. The *Times* commented, 'The surprise of the demonstration, however, was the unexpected strength of the Constitutionalists which it showed. The Women's Social and Political Union and the Women's Freedom

League combined were outnumbered and over-shadowed by the National Union of Women's Suffrage Societies.' A reflection of the increasing numbers of women moving to the NUWSS. But whatever their affiliation, the message was loud and clear.

Women wanted the vote.

Women deserved the vote.

Women must have the vote.

It was a message that seemed to be finally bearing fruit, as Christabel Pankhurst confirmed in *Votes for Women*. 'The Prime Minister has now assured us that the Women's Enfranchisement Bill is to be allowed to pass within the first two Sessions [of the new Parliament] Consequently the measure will have the security, afforded by the Parliament Bill, of becoming law before the next General Election.' The mention of the Parliament Bill is significant. This recent legislation made it much less likely that the Lords would be able to sabotage progress on the Bill. Christabel continued, '...far more valuable still is the Prime Minister's assertion that the Government, though divided as to the merits of the Bill, are unanimous in their determination to give effect not only in the letter, but in the spirit, to their promise in regard to facilities [time].' The suffragettes now effectively had an assurance that the Bill would become law before two Sessions of the current Parliament were over.

The chief danger, as Christabel identified, was for their opponents to make a last desperate attempt to snatch victory from them by moving wrecking amendments. Their task was clear. 'There must not be in the House of Commons one Member who can say that the men and women of his constituency are indifferent or opposed to the Women's Enfranchisement Bill... Already this Union is planning a great and extended campaign for the purpose of making certain the promised victory. From now until the Bill is carried the country must ring with the cry of Votes for Women.'

Young New Zealand: "Oh Grandpapa! What a funny old machine. Why don't you get one like mine?"

Printed and Published by the Artists' Suffrage League, 259, King's Road, Chelsea.

Chapter Eighteen
A United Front
Summer - Autumn 1911

Press across Devon proclaimed the success of the Great Procession. Under the headline, *March of the 40,000,* the *Ilfracombe Gazette* declared, 'Pageantry, artistic and of high merit, marked the great women's Suffrage demonstration held in London in brilliant sunshine on Saturday.' Picture Halls, including Ilfracombe, put on showings of the procession, presumably filmed by the WSPU, an inspired piece of propaganda. Thousands were able to witness the scale of the involvement, of not only women but men too, in the suffrage movement.

The Great Procession marked a rite of passage for Marie, Annie and their fellow WSPU members. Ilfracombe now had a fully fledged, fully committed suffragette movement. And there was work to do. 'Miss Ball and Mrs Du Sautoy Newby will give an At Home at the Nursing Home for members and sympathisers tomorrow... The Women's Great Procession has done much to convert people to the cause.' The meeting was a great success attracting new members and boosting sales of *Votes for Women*.

But their elation was short-lived. Christabel's fears were realised when news came that Lloyd George had proposed an amendment to include married as well as single women and widows. The Conciliation Committee had laboured long and hard drafting a Bill that stood a chance of being passed by Parliament. They knew that if they included married women up to seven million would be enfranchised, something bound to create a backlash amongst MPs. Settling for one million, as in the Bill as it stood, was the women's best and, for now at least, only hope of the legislation being passed. They feared Lloyd George's amendment would create a Parliamentary rebellion, sabotaging the Bill.

Marie and Annie were quick to respond with letters to both the *Ilfracombe Chronicle* and the *Ilfracombe Gazette*. 'The very large procession of women through London recently, and the friendly and respectful attitude of the large crowds who viewed it, show that the determination and unanimity of women are turning the scale of public opinion in their favour. But the wide and sweeping amendments, by altering the reasonable and conciliatory character of the present Bill, will certainly reduce its majority, and thereby leave a loophole for escape from promises.' The suggested amendment was sabotage in all but name. They appealed to readers to lobby their MP to insist the Bill was passed as it stood. 'The alternative will mean another long round of discussion and delay and for women the certain conviction that they are being played with by the Government.'

Victory, which had seemed so certain after the Great Procession, was again on a knife-edge. They had to open the eyes of the women of Devon to what the government was doing. Two weeks later the *Ilfracombe Gazette* published another letter, this time from Christabel Pankhurst herself. 'Mr Lloyd George, or any other, who asserts that a Bill enfranchising seven million women can be carried... is obviously throwing dust in the eyes of the women who are waiting so anxiously and working so hard for political enfranchisement... The pursuit of wrecking tactics by those who seek to deter indefinitely the enfranchisement of women will only have the effect of increasing the enthusiasm and energy of those who are endeavouring to get the Conciliation Bill carried into law.' And for once she was not only speaking for the WSPU.

At the end of July both groups unusually found themselves working side-by-side, perhaps encouraged by their successful cooperation during the Great Procession. Under the heading 'Union is Strength', the *Common Cause*, announced, 'The news that the Women's Social and Political Union is going to work at all by-elections to support the candidate who will support the Conciliation Committee is the best news we [the NUWSS] have heard for a long time. It is a really statesmanlike resolve on the part of their leaders, and suffragists will feel themselves happy that now from end to end of the country their ranks are closed, their objects and methods are the same.'

It was a union that Devon embraced, but perhaps a triumph of optimism over experience nationally. At a WSPU meeting just four months earlier Christabel had made a characteristic rallying cry in favour of militant action. The NUWSS commented at the time, 'Unfortunately, far from emphasising the points of unity between all Suffragists, as Mrs Pankhurst had done, she [Christabel] denounced in vigorous terms those who chose to work by constitutional means, declaring that, in her opinion, they must, as women of intelligence, believe in militant action, and only abstained from taking part in it through cowardice.' Hardly a ringing endorsement of a united approach, but in rural Devon both approaches were still relatively moderate so cooperation was achievable.

The two organisations shelved any differences as news came of another by-election, this time in neighbouring West Somerset. Devon suffragists and suffragettes moved into the constituency. Marguerite Norma-Smith coordinated her campaign from Taunton while Annie Kenney established her headquarters in Wellington, immediately organising meetings everywhere from Minehead to Dulverton, Porlock to Milverton. The choice to campaign against the Liberal was an easy one this time. Dudley Ward was committed to wrecking the Suffrage Bill, while the Conservative, Colonel Boles promised to do everything he could to get the Bill through. As always, the WSPU campaigned with military efficiency, drafting in speakers from across the country - and beyond. Their star speaker this time was Vida Goldstein, President of the Women's Political Association of Victoria, Australia.

It was a constant thorn in the side that, while women in Australia had been able to vote since 1902, the UK government remained intransigent. Not only were Australians able to vote, but Vida Goldstein became the first woman in the British Empire to stand for election, albeit unsuccessfully, to a national parliament - inconceivable in Britain. Here was someone who could talk at first hand about the difference having the vote made. No more hypothesis, no more speculation, no more ill-founded prejudice. She countered wild assumptions, fears or notions with the facts and painted a vivid picture of how things were when women had the full support of their Prime Minister. Andrew Fisher, the Prime Minister of Australia, couldn't have been more different from Asquith, believing that no country could progress without the assistance of women, obtained through the vote. It was a belief reinforced by his wife. Both arrived in London in June 1911 - Prime Minister Fisher to attend the King's Coronation: Margaret Fisher to lead the Australian and New Zealand women in the Suffrage Procession.

All the familiar faces from the WSPU were out in force campaigning in West Somerset. Mrs Pankhurst was tireless, addressing crowds in Minehead, Taunton and Wellington, driven of course by her chauffeur, Vera Holme. The *Western Morning News* was quick to

comment. 'The crowd... showed some desire to catch a glimpse of the famous leader of the Suffragettes, and crowded round the motor car... The Suffragists lose few opportunities to have a thrust at mere man. Even the chauffeur was a lady, and she certainly handled the car with considerable ease.'

Evelina Haverfield was also on the campaign trail, alongside Anne Martin, a former history professor at the University of Nevada. The good folks of rural Somerset must have struggled to understand these guest speakers, lurching between the antipodean twang of Vida Goldstein and the American drawl of Miss Martin. It was an equally a baptism of fire for her. 'I have never before been to a country by-election, and since I arrived in the motor car with Mrs Haverfield and Vera Holme last Monday, have been living in a sort of whirlwind of political activity with Annie Kenney as its centre and driving force.' Their gruelling schedule of open-air meetings often meant speaking at a crossroads in the middle of nowhere with an audience of a few farm workers and some cattle. But they would still deliver a full-blown speech. And Annie proved herself over and over again. At Dulverton a man was heard to remark, 'Jove she can talk! If only we had a few like her in Parliament instead of the muddlers we send there now!'

Marie Newby had arrived to support Annie. It was challenging at times, particularly when they addressed a crowd on the Esplanade at Watchet, yards away from a rival rally supporting the Liberal candidate. The paper reported, 'After a few words of introduction from Miss Kenney's companion, Mrs Newby, Miss Kenny commenced her address... [she] had proceeded without much criticism, the crowd listening to her being comparatively thin, but with the termination of the Liberal meeting... the audience began to gather in strength and opposition. Miss Kenney preserved her sang-froid, in spite of persistent interruptions, and challenged her hecklers to put questions to her.' But the last thing the Liberal supporters were interested in was a reasoned debate. They continued jeering and chanting until a riot threatened. Fortunately PC Penny, Watchet's village bobby, bravely escorted Marie and Annie to safety.

The women claimed victory when the Conservative held the seat with a majority of 604. Their success was acclaimed in *Votes for Women,* alongside an advertisement featuring none other than Evelina

Haverfield. She is depicted giving a ringing
endorsement for the 'Omne Tempus'
Raincoat, the ideal coat, or so the advert
goes, '...for Town, Country on
Campaigning'.

While Marie was away, Annie Ball
concentrated on the holiday campaign in
Ilfracombe, arranging a daily WSPU stall in
the market. Ilfracombe was inundated with
visitors each summer and Annie Ball set her
sights on converting as many as possible.
She put an advert in the paper inviting
visitors to buy 'Votes for Women' tea as
well as the newsletter. It was a way to draw
women in, get them talking and encourage
them to join a meeting. Meanwhile,
someone who was becoming a core
member of the group, Miss Simes, was out
and about on the streets selling *Votes for
Women*, with great success.

WSPU holiday campaigns in the rest of Devon were also in full
swing. Annie Kenny put out a plea for any ladies holidaying in
Torquay, Brixham, Dartmouth, Teignmouth, Dawlish, Seaton or
Sidmouth to get in touch. Edith Clarence from Coaxdon Hall, the
Hon. Secretary of the Axminster group, was also increasingly active.
She had joined Elsie Howey for a six week speaking tour in Cornwall
and was now busy putting up posters in the coffee rooms of all the
principal hotels in Lyme Regis, Seaton and Axminster, advertising
Votes for Women. She also spent two weeks helping the campaign on
Dartmoor, selling at least two dozen copies in Princetown. The
following year she went even further afield, on a speaking tour of the
west coast of Scotland.

Someone else covering as much ground as possible was the Rev
Hatty Baker, co-founder of the Free Church League for Women's
Suffrage. She held the controversial view that women should trust in
their own vision of God, not rely on a version handed down by men.

Spiritual independence reached much further than the church. It was an essential step towards equality in all aspects of women's lives, including their fight for the vote. She was also someone who bridged the two groups. She had joined the WSPU Hyde Park demonstrations and was also a speaker with the NUWSS, making quite an impact according to the *Western Daily Mercury*. 'Miss Baker is a lady who arrests attention. Dressed in a Geneva gown, surmounted by a conspicuous white collar, she possesses a commanding presence.'

On a speaking tour of Cornwall and Devon she was accompanied by Maud Slater from Plymouth, fresh from her debate with anti-suffragist Lieut-Col Purchas in the columns of the *Western Morning News*. Maud gave a colourful account of their tour.

'You feel such a fool when you mount the sugar box in the empty village street and address two small boys and a girl as "Ladies and Gentlemen" but the dear little folks, with the courtesy of childhood, enter into the spirit of the pretence and array themselves before you with the manner of first arrivals among a thousand. A white apron flickers at a distant cottage door, you aim your voice at the apron and painfully explain the non-militant policy... That apron has disappeared, but the owner presently issues in bonnet and Sunday gloves. Slowly the audience grows. The Hobbledehoys pretend to swagger past but slip behind the women and stay to listen. A workman fills his pipe and smokes it just within hearing. Someone leans from a window, doorways are filled, the children are backed by larger figures, and you are free to step, quaking, from the tub and call upon the speaker. Now the real thing begins. The women nudge each other with frank appreciation, the men's pipes go out, the crowd has forgotten itself. It is no longer concerned whether Mrs Overtheway will imagine it has suffragette sympathies, it is picturing the women forging chains at Cradley Heath...'

After more than a dozen meetings in Cornwall Hatty Baker moved on to Tavistock, where a lack of volunteers made for a disappointing attendance, and Plymouth. At the close of the tour, Hatty Baker offered a heart-felt reflection. 'My personal thanks are largely due to my colleague, Miss Maud Slater, [with whom she was to forge a close relationship] who, a stranger to me at the beginning of the tour, rapidly proved herself indispensable... Not the least striking feature of suffrage work is the splendid way in which our sex is coming to its own, realising the depth of the comradeship possible between women, and that the whole-souled friendship of woman is perhaps one of the most beautiful - because wholly altruistic - things in the world.'

The end of Hatty Baker's tour was marked by a Suffrage Saturday afternoon picnic and public meeting, significantly promoted by the NUWSS jointly with the WSPU. These combined events were a new initiative and something they planned to continue the following summer. While nationally the suffragists were keen to distance themselves from the militant tactics of the suffragettes, in South and East Devon, the atmosphere was more one of cooperation than confrontation. Exeter NUWSS were planning a winter programme where they hoped to work jointly with the WSPU. Meanwhile Plymouth intended to unite to provide lecturers and speakers for all the societies who would accept them. In an outbreak of bonhomie, WSPU members such as Marion Phillips and Gwyneth Keys became active in both organisations. It was an initiative that carried through to the following spring when the two groups, along with the newly formed Plymouth branch of the Free Church League for Women Suffrage, met in conference to discuss future cooperation. They decided on a united weekly campaign during March and April 1912 with a meeting to be held in a different Plymouth ward each week.

Maud Slater was particularly keen on uniting with church attenders, a view she shared in the *Common Cause*. 'Political organisations touch only a small proportion of the population... yet when we look at the churches and chapels we find that they draw support from an enormous proportion of the population of women. It is not only that women form the congregations of listeners - they form the committees of workers... Why not follow the line of least resistance and through the religious leagues extend the area of our work?'

Another entry in the *Common Cause* from the South West Federation is curious. 'This month should have been a specially busy one in the Federation, and it is much to be regretted that many meetings have been given up for no better reason than the action of another society.' This is likely to be a reference to the anti-suffragists who continued to make themselves felt, particularly in the east of the county. After a relatively quiet time, Sidmouth had affiliated with the newly formed East Devon Branch of the National Society for Opposing Women's Suffrage. Through weekly adverts in the Sidmouth Herald, the group announced a series of meetings to be held in March 1912. They were so keen readers shouldn't miss the advert that they added hands pointing to it from above and below.

The autumn of 1911 was a time for farewells, some brief, some more final. The Ilfracombe group had lost Evelina after the summer break, she was now back in London, busy chairing the Paddington branch of the WSPU. More of a blow was the news that Annie Kenney was returning to her roots, organising a special campaign for the pit-brow women in Wigan. It's true that one or two Devon branches had found their feet, Ilfracombe and Torquay particularly, but others remained in need of Annie's passion. She would be sorely missed. Annie left as she'd arrived, with a plea that the women get sewing for an upcoming Fair. 'I am most anxious that the West of England stall should look the very best, have the largest stock, take the most money. I recommend weekly sewing meetings and visits to shops to ask if they'll help by giving linens, silk or cotton to make bags with. Each member should visit her dressmaker and milliner and ask for remnants.'

Another lighter moment in the calendar was the annual Bideford carnival. On 6 September Mrs Nash, a member of the WSPU and enthusiastic seller of *Votes for Women,* won second prize for the best decorated bicycle; a brave appearance given anti-suffrage feeling there.

It was tame stuff compared with the momentum they'd built up through the spring and summer, but patience was to be the suffragettes biggest challenge through the autumn of 1911. Asquith eventually caved in, or so it seemed, to outrage over the wrecking tactics announced by Lloyd George with an assurance that the latest Suffrage Bill would be progressed. 'I have no hesitation in saying that the promises made by, and of behalf of, the Government in regard to giving facilities for the Conciliation Bill will be strictly adhered to both in letter and in spirit.' But not yet. Not even this year, but next.

Amazingly, Christabel took the Prime Minister at his word, responding with the offer of a continued truce over militancy. 'The women's movement for political emancipation has gone through testing times. Physical violence, ridicule, abuse, persecution, imprisonment, torture. Now the movement is undergoing the hardest test of all – the test of peace and postponement, the test of a long truce from militant action in return for a definite pledge of facilities next year for the Conciliation Bill.' Evelina, however, was sceptical. *The Bath Chronicle and Weekly Gazette* reported her speech to Bath WSPU. 'After remarking that women were capable of making any sacrifices for love of their country, Mrs Haverfield condemned the doctrine of patience and supported that of impatience and concluded by expressing a hope that next year would see the success of all their efforts.' Timely words given that Government prevarication was about to sink the best chance women had ever had to claim the vote.

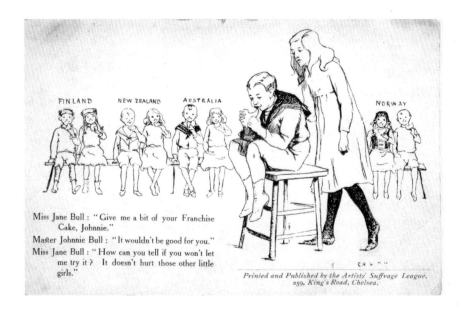

Miss Jane Bull : "Give me a bit of your Franchise Cake, Johnnie."

Master Johnnie Bull : "It wouldn't be good for you."

Miss Jane Bull : "How can you tell if you won't let me try it? It doesn't hurt those other little girls."

Printed and Published by the Artists' Suffrage League, 259, King's Road, Chelsea.

Chapter Nineteen
Worthless Words
Late Autumn 1911

On 10 November *Votes for Women* broke the news. 'On Tuesday last, the Prime Minister made the announcement that it is the intention of the Government to introduce a Franchise Bill next session... [This Bill] will be confined to adult males; women will be excluded.'

Women will be excluded! Asquith had made a public commitment to proceed with the Suffrage Bill. He had promised. Despite so many past betrayals, he had been believed. No more. Now both suffragists and suffragettes could see that his word was worthless. The article continued. 'From this announcement it will be seen that the Government have decided to range themselves definitely in opposition to Woman Suffrage. In spite of the fact that there is an agitation for giving votes to women which is national in its scope and unprecedented in its magnitude... the Government are proposing to give more votes to men and none to women. In consequence of this attitude, the Women's Social and Political Union have decided to resume immediately their militant anti-Government policy.'

Some of the press were uncharacteristically sympathetic:

We are no friends of female suffrage, but anything more contemptible than the attitude assumed by the Government, it is difficult to imagine. *The Globe.*

Any male, however regardless of his civic duties, is to be endowed, without effort on his part, with the right to govern his fellow citizens; no female - if Mr Asquith has his way - is to have any share in the government of her country, however great her capacity, however large her contributions to the public revenue. *The Daily Graphic.*

For our part, if there were to be any question of Adult Suffrage we should oppose to the last any partial measure which excluded thousands of educated and responsible women from the Suffrage while opening the gates of political power to mobs of utterly ignorant men. *The Daily Express.*

The advocates of Women's Suffrage will, of course, be furious. Mr Asquith's bombshell will blow the Conciliation Bill to smithereens. *The Evening News.*

The Government have certainly dealt a deadly blow at the Women's Suffrage movement in Parliament. *The Yorkshire Post.*

The WSPU immediately announced a deputation to demand that the proposed Manhood Suffrage Bill, giving the vote to all men over twenty-one who satisfied a simple residency qualification, be abandoned. There had been no groundswell of demand from men for an extension of the vote. This Bill was simply an attempt by Asquith to duck commitments made to the women. They intended to confront the Prime Minister and the person they now considered just as much the architect of their downfall - Lloyd George. 'It is an open secret that the whole idea of the introduction by the Government in 1912 of a Manhood Suffrage Bill emanated from the brain of Mr Lloyd George, who has for a long time been scheming to wreck the Conciliation Bill. Baffled in other attempts at mischief, the Chancellor of the Exchequer has devised this latest scheme of destruction, which he trusts will effectively achieve his end.'

Asquith's duplicity was predictable. His next move was not. A letter arrived at WSPU headquarters addressed to Mrs Pethick

Lawrence. 'Dear Madam - I am desired by the Prime Minister... to inform you that arrangements have already been made for the Prime Minister to receive a deputation from various suffrage societies at 11.30 on Friday, November 17th at 10 Downing Street, including your own society if you desire it.' After years of refusing to admit deputations, resulting in the brutal treatment and imprisonment of hundreds of women, the WSPU was finally being invited inside Downing Street. They immediately began formulating their demands. The latest Conciliation Bill was dead. It was time to regroup. They had always campaigned for the vote on the same terms as men and they would accept no other solution. They would call on the Government to abandon the Manhood Suffrage Bill and introduce instead a measure giving equal franchise rights to men and women. It was a knee-jerk reaction that was to have significant consequences.

On a damp November morning, representatives from the WSPU, the NUWSS, the WFL and other suffrage societies made their way to Downing Street for the meeting with Asquith and Lloyd George. Asquith was quick to take control. He reassured the ladies that a private member's amendment could be made to the Manhood Suffrage Bill to extend the franchise to women. Despite his personal belief that this would not benefit the state, his government would respect the view of Parliament on this.

The NUWSS issued a strongly worded protest, describing the omission of women from the Bill as a gross insult and injustice. They declared a woman's suffrage amendment would certainly be moved. The WSPU, on the other hand, were adamant that no private member's amendment would gain a majority. It was a trick, another tactic to sabotage their efforts. They left the meeting determined to resume militancy with immediate effect. Their campaign would go forward with more vigour than ever, spurred on by Christabel's rallying cry. 'Some people, and of them the WSPU is made, do not shrink from their mission... They do not fight with their own strength, they do not speak with their own voice, they are the instruments of a Power greater than themselves. Ours is a great crusade. We ask you all to join us. March under our banner. Share the victory that is before us.'

*Marie closes the door to the sitting room and settles herself in her favourite chair.
She folds back the pages of 'Votes for Women' to reveal a piece by Christabel. 'A
Call to Arms,' the headline announces. 'On Tuesday next at 7.30pm Caxton
Hall will be crowded with women who will assemble for the purpose of resolving
upon such action, whether militant or otherwise, as the Prime Minister's statement
of to-day may render necessary. It will be an historic gathering, perhaps the most
important since the movement began. Names are coming in steadily for the
deputation to the Prime Minster (should this be necessary) - volunteers should
write at once to Miss Christabel Pankhurst... You want the deputation to go; you
want the protest to be made; but how can you expect other women to do anything
if you do nothing yourselves? Who are you that you are privileged to stand aside
and clap your hands at the sacrifices that others are making? Why is it more
difficult for you to join this deputation than it is for others? It is most important
that all those who are prepared to take action if action be required should write
without delay to Clements Inn.'*

> *Marie sighs. Halls in London were overflowing with women cheering and
applauding Mrs Pankhurst and Christabel's call to arms while she sits here in her
comfortable armchair. Even Mr Pethick Lawrence, whom she so admired when he
came to Ilfracombe, stated such treachery could only be met with action. She reads
on. 'I know all the things people say to prevent your going. They will say you
cannot go because you are too much missed in your home; you are too much wanted
outside Holloway Gaol. Well, you would not be worth very much if you were not
wanted, whatever your circle of activities and energies happen to be! It is because
of that that you ought to be on this deputation. It is not idle women, but thinking
women who should be there... every woman who feels like that should be with us
on that deputation on Tuesday.'*

> *Marie's hands tremble. How can she restrict her activities to the streets of
Ilfracombe and leave other women to carry this burden? It is time to fully embrace
Deeds not Words. But if Asquith refuses to give the answer they want, as Marie
knows in her heart will be the case, then she will face violence, arrest... and
prison. Holloway. Simply a word to her now, but her decision has been made. She
picks up the telephone.*

> *'Annie? It's Marie. Donations for the Christmas Fair, can you take them in
for a few days?'*

'*I can, but…*' *she hesitated.* '*You're going aren't you.*'
'*Yes*'. *It was said now, no going back.*

A notice appeared in the 17 November edition of *Votes for Women*. 'Bags when finished must be sent to Miss Ball as the secretary will be in London for the deputation.'

Marie steps onto the platform at Paddington station and picks her way through the bustling atrium towards the waiting taxis. At first the crowded London streets are the usual mix of visitors, families and businessmen but as she pays her fare outside Caxton Hall, she is swept up by a swathe of women. At the door she is handed a typewritten sheet giving a list of instructions about what to do when she is arrested - not if, when. She is to refuse to go to her cell, refuse to undress, refuse to be medically examined, refuse to scrub out. It's a brutal wake-up call, this piece of paper telling her she will be put in solitary confinement in punishment cells. Her reality in a few short hours? Yet all around women are chatting and laughing, carried along on a wave of nervous excitement. They are on the verge of making history. The future of women across the country, the world even, depends on what they do next.

The stewards check her name and direct her to seats reserved for volunteers for the deputation. Somewhere in the crowd is Evelina, an old hand at these demonstrations. She is sure to get arrested, given her moment in court and sent to Holloway. These experienced protestors are easy to spot, they are the ones padded with cotton wool and cardboard to protect their ribs from the blows. But this is Marie's first time. There will be no shame in taking things step-by-step.

The hall bursts into life as Mrs Pankhurst, Christabel and others take the stage. Handkerchiefs are waved and cries of 'Bravo' ring out. It's the first time Marie has seen Emmeline and Christabel in the flesh. Suddenly she understands. Perhaps it's the noise, the charged atmosphere or the crush, but even at this distance their charisma is obvious. Mrs Pankhurst raises her hand to speak. 'The Government's pronouncement is a trap which we decline to enter. I move the following resolution. This meeting condemns the Government's announcement of a Manhood Suffrage Bill as a grave and unpardonable insult to women; (Cheers) firmly refuses to allow the political enfranchisement of women to depend upon a mere amendment to the Manhood Suffrage Bill; (Cheers) demands that the Government abandons the Manhood Suffrage Bill and introduces and carries in the next Session of Parliament a measure giving precisely equal franchise rights to men and women. (Cheers) And further, the meeting declares its resolve to enforce this reasonable demand upon the attention of the Government and of the electors by vigorous and determined militant action.' (Cheers and applause)

Mrs Pethick Lawrence steps forward. She has been alongside Emmeline Pankhurst since the early days of the WSPU. She and her husband, Frederick, publish 'Votes for Women' and contribute thousands to the campaign fund. She also knows what it is like to experience the degradation of Holloway. 'The objective of the deputation,' she opens, 'is to protest on the floor of the House of Commons, in the presence of all the members, against the deep insult of manhood suffrage that has been offered to the womanhood of the country. Nothing will make us turn our backs except, of course, physical force.

'But we who are on the deputation tonight are already outside our body. We know that our hands, our feet, and all that we have are being used by the Great Spirit to carry out the great purpose of His will. It is that which destroys any possibility of anxiety or fear or consciousness of pain. We know that here we offer and present ourselves, our souls and bodies, to be a living sacrifice for all those great sins of the world whose taproot is in sex discrimination. We go tonight not only to fight for the freedom of the women of our own country, but to carry a message of deliverance to the whole world.'

Marie knows the sustaining force of her religion, but to hear the words used like this… she is simultaneously fired with zeal and shot through with apprehension. But there's no time for indecision. The speeches are over and she is swept out of the hall, a small particle in an unstoppable mass. No more than a few yards on they are confronted by a cordon of police. A struggle begins until, suddenly, the cordon breaks and the leaders are let through. It closes again, but then another small group is let through. It's soon clear. The police are briefed to break the demonstration up into small parties, thwarting their intention to become a procession. Marie follows when her turn comes. As she reaches the corner of Parliament Square she sees women caught up in the fiercest of struggles. Even the small groups are scattered by the surging crowd and the mounted policemen. In the melee she recognises Vera Holme seizing a horse's bridle and trying to turn it around, fearless of the mounted policeman's attempts to beat her away.

Women hurl themselves at the police cordon surrounding the House of Commons but again and again they are forced back into the crowd or manhandled away under arrest. Marie finds herself separated and set upon in the crush. Her hair is grabbed, and she is dragged along the road, her head pulled back until her eyes water. She makes herself a dead weight until, suddenly, she is released. She drops to the ground, curling up to prevent being trampled.

Unknown hands half-support, half-carry her, barely conscious, free of the crowd. The relief is overwhelming. She'd felt threatened by the rowdy Liberal supporters in Watchet but that was nothing compared to this. She watches from the sidelines. Her protest is over - for now.

The mood in Ilfracombe was sombre. How had it reached this point? *Votes for Women* provided an answer:

In the last century by a succession of great meetings and monster petitions, including in all over three million signatures, women demonstrated their intense desire for the franchise. A majority of MPs pledged to support 'Votes for Women' but by a succession of despicable tricks, politicians continued to defraud women of their rights. The cause retrogressed and women lost heart.

Then in 1906 a handful of women determined on new tactics. A militant campaign was inaugurated and carried on for several years. The Cause made progress. At first they inflicted no injury on person or property but suffered themselves to be assaulted by the police, arrested and imprisoned.

In 1910 it was suggested that if militant tactics were suspended the Government would give facilities for a Conciliation Bill. The WSPU decided to give it a trial. The Bill seemed likely to pass but Lloyd George opposed it and facilities were refused.

In 1911 a similar thing happened but with a definite promise of facilities for 1912. In the light of this promise The WSPU continued to hold its hand.

On November 7th Mr Asquith announced the intention of the Government to introduce a new Franchise Bill where women were excluded... The WSPU called on the Government to introduce instead a measure giving equal franchise rights to men and women. At Downing St on November 17th, Asquith & Lloyd George refused to consent to the Government introducing a Woman Suffrage Bill.

Only one reply was possible - the events of 21 November.

Mrs Fawcett and others in the NUWSS saw it very differently. The editorial in the *Common Cause* condemned the '...wrecking policy of the WSPU [which] can only be regarded as madness,' and insisted other solutions were still available. These included, '...a great combined suffragist movement of men and women together. Women suffragists have always been agreed upon the object of their agitation - "to obtain the vote on the same terms as men." They were united upon a measure which many of them did not wholly like, the Conciliation Bill, because it was the only measure at that time which had a good chance of becoming law... but the movement lacked leadership among men... We believe that a hearty and frank cooperation between all societies having for their object the enfranchisement of women, and all Members of Parliament having the same object, is possible and immensely desirable.'

It was a cooperation that groups in Devon, in Exeter and Plymouth in particular, were working hard to achieve. But after several months of attempts at unity between the radicals and the moderates at a national level, the divide was growing ever wider.

Mrs. Partington again: "WAIT, WAIT, WHY CAN'T YOU WAIT?"

Chapter Twenty
An Island of Militancy
Winter 1911 - Spring 1912

While Ilfracombe WSPU were preoccupied with national events, the NUWSS were determined to increase their activity in South Devon. But this wasn't easy, as Mary Willcocks and Marian Penry, Hon. Secretaries of the SW Federation, summed up in the *Common Cause*. 'For many reasons this is a difficult Federation to work; the area covered is very large, the towns are for the most part small, and the branch societies very poor, while the absence of large industrial towns makes it hard for us to bring home to well-to-do women those black things that lie behind the votelessness of women—the sweated labour, the moral degradation, the narrow outlook. All this makes it practically impossible to make headway, or even to hold the position now gained, without an organiser. But an organiser is not all. We have societies on our list that cannot pay the expenses of a meeting, societies that have never had a public meeting at all through lack of funds, societies too poor to send delegates to Federation meetings.' They go on to thank both national and local donors, including Ethel Mathieson, Adelaide Baly, Olga Fletcher and Jessie Montgomery, for their financial support.

Although struggling with their own debts, Plymouth NUWSS had hit on a strategy that seemed to be working. In November they were busy organising smaller meetings reported, with obvious satisfaction, by Mabel Ramsay in the *Common Cause*. 'We have congratulated ourselves that they [the meetings] have been convened for the most part at the expense and by the efforts of others.' Those 'others' included Ebrington Street Young People's Guild, Saltash Baptist Literary Society, Morley Street and Mutley Men's Adult Schools and the YWCA. Mabel Ramsay, Maud Slater, and Marion Phillips were the most active speakers, together with Mrs Merivale Mayer, on a tour of Devon tour speaking on 'How the Vote was won in Australia'. All these events were a lead up to a mass meeting in the Corn Exchange on 23 November addressed by Mrs. Philip Snowden, the wife of a prominent labour politician and a leading campaigner for women's suffrage. According to the *Common Cause*, it was the most successful meeting the Plymouth branch had ever held. Sadly, the report doesn't say whether Ethel Snowden treated the assembled crowd to her party piece - mimicking the renowned anti-suffragist, Lord Cromer.

Budleigh Salterton also formally launched as a branch. They had held their first public meeting back in 1909 when a crowded hall listened with interest to Jessie Montgomery and Helen Fraser. But it was only now that Ethel Mathieson, who not only arranged but also financed the 1909 gathering, was elected as Hon. Secretary. Forty new members signed up, a number later boosted at a packed evening meeting presided over by Mary Willcocks. Mrs Merivale Mayer reprised her talk on Australia before moving on to Ottery St Mary, this time accompanied by Jessie Montgomery.

At the end of November, The *Common Cause* reported on Exeter's 'Suffrage Day' where, '...an American Fair was held at the Barnfield Hall, which was decorated in the colours and soon became crowded with all the notabilities of the neighbourhood. Guessing competitions, side shows, an exhibition of sweated industries, [where women worked long hours in poor conditions with low pay] music and entertainments of a great variety kept everyone amused and busy.' This was followed in the evening by a public meeting when the Barnfield Hall rang with a rousing rendition of 'The March of the Women' during the half hour while the audience assembled. 'It was a fitting prelude', according to the *Express and Echo*, 'to Mrs Snowden's speech that, idealistic and enabling, and yet practical to a degree, found an echo in almost every heart.' It was a message she repeated the following day for an audience in Plymouth, although they had to wait until 14 December for their own American Fair. It was obviously successful though, Mabel Ramsay was able to report that the profit from the day almost cleared their remaining deficit.

December also saw a Special Meeting of the NUWSS South Western Federation at Exeter to welcome Miss Davenport, the new organiser. Fund raising during the autumn had made her appointment possible, and not a moment too soon. The Federation had grown from ten to seventeen branches since May. Jessie Montgomery was elected incoming President while Mary Willcocks stood down as secretary. She was leaving to concentrate on speaking engagements and had a packed programme planned.

Miss Davenport laid the ground for their winter campaign with an advert on the front page of the *North Devon Journal*, emphasising the non-party, non-militant stance of the organisation and inviting all sympathisers to get in touch with her at 2 Park Villas, Barnstaple. At a meeting in the Parish Church Room on 11 December there was only one possible focus for Miss Davenport's address - the positive, non-militant alternative the NUWSS provided to the WSPU. Her message was embraced with enthusiasm. The Barnstaple and

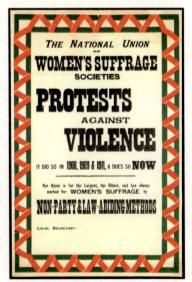

THE NATIONAL UNION
OF
WOMEN'S SUFFRAGE
SOCIETIES
PROTESTS
AGAINST
VIOLENCE
IT DID SO IN 1908, 1909 & 1911, & DOES SO NOW
Our Union is far the largest, the oldest, and has always worked for WOMEN'S SUFFRAGE by
NON-PARTY & LAW-ABIDING METHODS
LOCAL SECRETARY:

District Suffrage Society was boosted by nine new members and a committee was formed, with Mrs Elsie Mangan as Honorary Secretary. Plans were made for a series of eight meetings commencing in February.

Miss Davenport and Mary Willcocks repeatedly criss-crossed the county throughout the winter months. In December, Mary visited Newton Abbot then addressed the inaugural meeting of a new Totnes branch at the Seymour Hotel Assembly Rooms. A committee formed with Mrs Chapman elected President, Mrs Cowper Lee and Mrs Arrowsmith joint Vice-Presidents and Miss Mills Young as secretary.

Then in the New Year, they were both back in North Devon, speaking in Appledore and Instow. The *Common Cause* reported, 'A most enthusiastic meeting was held on January 11th when Miss Willcocks (from Exeter) spoke on "Why Women Want the Vote" and Miss Davenport on the political situation. The hall was brightly decorated with posters and the colours and the meeting roused great enthusiasm, one old inhabitant offering the speaker "her heart's blood". The wives of sailors and fishermen are determined to help to get the vote. The one difficulty in this branch is the extreme poverty of the township. The largest subscription received is five and a half pence.' [£3 today]

Miss Davenport spent a week in Bideford, addressing both the Bideford Women's Liberal Association and a cottage meeting at Northam. The following day, there was a get-together at the regular Bideford venue, the Cut Round Tea Rooms, before she concluded her North Devon tour with a social hosted by Appledore. Miss Davenport had fulfilled her brief as an organiser, appointing, advising and offering support to local women who would now take the branches forward. The Barnstaple group immediately followed up on her recommendation that they get workers interested, holding their second meeting at Pilton Glove works. The *North Devon Journal* reported, 'The meeting was in furtherance of the educational campaign inaugurated a few months ago; and under enthusiastic management, the Barnstaple branch of the Society is making rapid progress.'

On 24 January Mary Willcocks was again in South Devon at a meeting hosted by the Women's Liberal Association in Sidford, a small village just inland from Sidmouth. She delivered her talk on women's suffrage from an industrial, social and political point of view to an audience of over 50. According to the *Common Cause* this was, '...particularly gratifying as the outlying villages of Sidbury and Sidford were new ground, worked up in a short time in the face of great opposition and the most discouraging weather.' The weather was unlucky but the 'great opposition' most likely referred to a resurgence of the Sidmouth anti-suffrage group.

A letter appeared in the *Sidmouth Herald* on the 13 and 20 January announcing that, 'The Sidmouth Branch of the National League for Opposing Women's Suffrage has now been affiliated with the newly formed East Devon Branch of the above Association.' Committee members included Mrs Clements, Mrs Scott, Mrs Richmond White, Mrs Secker, Miss Boyd and Miss Purcell with Mrs Tindall as Vice President, Miss Browning as secretary and Mr Browning as treasurer. Top of the agenda for the re-formed group was a series of public meetings, the first to be held on 7 March and addressed by Mrs Greatbach and J. Arthur Pott Esq. In the light of imminent future actions by the WSPU, the timing of this meeting couldn't have been better for the anti-suffragists.

While most pro-suffrage women in Devon, including many in the WSPU, continued their non-militant approach, Ilfracombe, and to a lesser extent, Torquay, were moving in the opposite direction. But how to convince others this was the way forward? *Votes for Women* had an answer. 'There is nothing at the moment so important from the political point of view as increasing the circulation of the paper. Even those who believe in a vague and general way that women ought to have the vote jump to the conclusion that though we have been right in our militant methods in the past, we are wrong in the very last and latest development. For are not all the daily papers, whether Conservative or Liberal, saying so? And what everybody agrees in saying must of course be sound sense! The only people who do not get bamboozled in this way are the regular readers of VOTES FOR WOMEN.'

In December 1911 Ilfracombe had the perfect opportunity to promote the paper. A meeting had been arranged at the Gaiety Hall

The Promenade, Ilfracombe.

for WSPU members and the general public to hear someone who had been active in Devon longer than anyone else, Amy Montague, Honorary Secretary of the Exeter branch. Appearing alongside her was Jessie Smith from Bristol, arrested at the recent protests in London and someone well able to bring the horror of Holloway to this Devon town.

On a dark Monday evening, Marie escorts Amy Montague and Jessie Smith to the Gaiety Hall. She is buoyed up by the work she and Jessie have done over the past week. Jessie has sold over a hundred copies of 'Votes for Women' in the shops and on the streets, engaging so many women in conversation. It's an invaluable opportunity for Marie to listen and learn, to see how women warm to Jessie's passion and conviction. No more hiding in the shadows. She will be a passionate advocate for the cause, claiming a prominent vantage point in town by the market arch to sell 'Votes for Women'. To make sure she is seen, she will wear the bold apron Sylvia has designed to advertise the magazine. Emmeline Pethick Lawrence is right. The only people not bamboozled by the mainstream press are the regular readers, as Jessie had reminded the Ilfracombe members.

Now a much bigger crowd is pouring into this sea-side theatre, set in a terrace of shops and cafes opposite the magnificent glass house on Ilfracombe's promenade. Its modest entrance through one of the shops belies the scale of the auditorium at first floor level. Capable of holding 650, it is almost at capacity as Amy Montague opens the meeting. Her message is clear. 'Women are denied the rights and privileges of citizens simply because they are women… when women get the vote they will use it to better their conditions, just as men did, and to get their grievances redressed, which is impossible as long as they are not enfranchised. Mr Asquith has said that the only opinion he considers is the vote at the poll. Women wanted the vote in order to express their opinion there. While men who were supposed to be the stronger sex, were armed with a weapon [the vote] with which to defend themselves, women were unarmed. Slavery had been defined as government without the consent of the governed, therefore women who were governed without their own consent were really slaves.'

It is fighting talk. She moves on to the increasingly complicated issue of the Suffrage Bill. 'The government is going to introduce a Manhood Suffrage Bill without including women. Yes, it is open to any amendment but this will not get enough votes. It will be defeated'.

Jessie is next to speak; her mission - to arouse the audience's sympathies. 'Yes, I am a militant suffragist. But history would never have been written but for the successful fights for justice and for people rising against bad laws and making good laws instead. There are women in the industrial markets living under conditions no better than slavery. Women's influence is needed in politics for they understand some social evils better than men. Militant methods have been described as disgraceful and unwomanly, but it is more unwomanly and disgraceful to tolerate the conditions of life under which women suffer. A number of MPs signed a petition protesting against the recent conduct of the suffragettes but they do not protest against the damage done by men when they strike - simply because they have votes and women do not.'

Jessie Smith's mention of 'a number of MPs' is an understatement. Over a hundred MPs condemned the actions of the WSPU, convinced that their conduct made the organisation of an effective campaign in favour of women's suffrage difficult, if not impossible. Even Ramsay MacDonald, leader of the Labour party, was uncompromising. 'One would prefer to be oblivious to, and to forget, the degrading and disgusting scenes at which we have just been looking. Those of us who have any regard for womanhood, those of us who have any ideals regarding woman's intelligence and woman's conduct, must simply bow their head in shame. If I felt the cause had come to this I would go into the lobby every time against it.' On this December evening in Ilfracombe, Jessie Smith is in the firing line from those in agreement with Ramsay MacDonald.

'Do you not think,' a questioner asks, 'that in bringing about meetings of this kind you would do more to further your cause than by breaking windows and damaging the facial appearance of ministers?'

'We have tried to arouse public opinion by meetings,' Jessie replies, 'but that in itself has failed. So we have followed the example of the men when they were agitating for the vote. But we do not go so far, for the men attacked individuals and burned houses.'

'Are the majority of the members of the Women's Social and Political Union in favour of militant methods?'

'They are all in favour.' Jessie seeks out a familiar face in the audience. 'Ilfracombe was represented in the person of Mrs Newby at the last demonstration and I hope the next time Mrs Newby will take honours by graduating at the suffragette university at Holloway.'

Only a few days earlier at Braunton Liberal Club, a Mr Smith had quoted Asquith. 'If female suffrage became law it would be an unknown, unmeasured disaster and a calamity to the nation.' A view shared by his cabinet minister, William Harcourt. 'I believe that for women to become part of the political machine is bad for themselves and bad for the country. I think that it draws them from the spheres in which they shine, from duties which they adorn, from duties which can adequately be performed by none but themselves. Women of course possess emotion and charm. These are great assets, but I do not think they are conducive to sober political judgement. Then there are physical and physiological circumstances in their lives which are more fitted for discussion in the consulting room than on the platform, circumstances which unfit them for public duty or judgement.'

Enough to raise hackles amongst many then and now. But militancy had found a home in Ilfracombe and new members continued to swell their meetings. Miss Warren, Mrs Dovell, Mrs Mumford, Mrs Turiss, Miss Bendle, Miss Wormall, Miss Bull, Miss Heselton and many more gathered to discuss some interesting news. Despite Ramsay MacDonald's reaction to the events in London, the Labour Party had carried a resolution that, 'This Conference, in harmony with previous decisions, is of the opinion that the enfranchisement of all adult men and women should be included in the Reform Bill to be introduced by the Government in the coming Session of Parliament.' A controversial stance given they were repeating Lloyd George's pledge of enfranchising all women, seen as sabotage at the time. But the Conference report continued. 'It further requests the Labour Party in Parliament to make it clear that no Bill can be acceptable to the Labour and Socialist movement which does not include women.'

Over Christmas 1911 the Ilfracombe WSPU group had been boosted by the arrival of Evelina at Brendon. It was the perfect place for her to recuperate from a recent incarceration in Holloway, filling her days with gentle walks by the East Lynn and long rides across the moor. There was also time to catch up with Marie, Annie and all the new faces in Ilfracombe. Coming so close to Jessie's visit, Evelina's account of her experiences in Holloway may well have been too close for comfort, particularly for Marie. What was the point in being part of the protest and simply returning home? Getting arrested, refusing to pay the fines, being imprisoned was the whole point. It was a call to action she could no longer ignore.

Marie paces the carpet, Emmeline Pethick Lawrence's words ringing in her ears.
'We are intellectually convinced that unless we can make trouble for the
Government we must remain in the political subjection which penalises women in

every aspect and avocation of their life and heaps misery upon the wretched and degradation upon the wronged. This intellectual conviction, united with the strong moral compulsion that has welded us together in this Movement, obliges every woman in our ranks to take her place in the demonstration of protests that will be made on Monday, March 4th against the exclusion of women from the Government's programme of electoral reform.

'There is not a woman in the world who is not indispensable to some person in her own circle. Not one but has had to leave husband or brother, sister or mother, who she loved better than herself, not one who has not caused grief in hearts intensely dear to her, not one who has not incurred disapproval, not one who has not linked the loss of friends to the withdrawal of affection. That is the price they have paid for a great ideal and for the deliverance of those too weak, too poor, or too rigidly held in bondage to help themselves.'

For Marie, March 4th 1912 must mark a turning point. Mrs Pankhurst was demanding that she stand up and be counted. 'I cannot say too often that the success of the next protest depends upon its size. We have courage and determination in this movement. What we lack is actual fighting members. Come if it is humanly possible for you to come! We cannot go into the conscience of every woman. We cannot weigh her reasons for and against coming with us. That is the responsibility upon each of us, but I can say, and my colleagues can say with me, that we believe the call now is so great that nothing but the most vital necessity should prevent women from coming to take part in this protest. I believe from the bottom of my heart that if we are determined enough, if we are courageous enough, the enemy will be glad to bring this struggle of ours to a speedy close.'

Marie looks again at the letters from women who had already answered the call.

'Will you please put my name down for the protest on March 4th. I have not joined in any of the other protests but feel it is my duty to do so.'

'Will you put my name down for the demonstration for the sake of the children…'

'Though I am almost an invalid, I have still strength enough to volunteer to throw a stone of protest and I cannot be a coward any longer. I am not at all heroic over physical suffering but if you will have my name I shall feel honoured to be permitted to swell your fighting ranks on March 4th.'

'If only we could muster in our thousands and show this tyrannical so-called Liberal Government (whose methods of treating political prisoners are worthy of

the middle-ages) that the just demands of the women of this country can no longer be ignored.'

No more hesitation. Marie sits at her desk, takes an envelope and addresses it to Miss Christabel Pankhurst, 4 Clements Inn, London, W.C. She will be standing side by side with these women on Monday, 4th March.

Within days Marie received a letter thanking her for rallying to the cause and informing her she would be given specific instructions when she arrived at Clements Inn. The letter also contained a card of admittance to the London Pavilion and a stark slip of paper telling her she would be arrested. She should bring a change of clothes with her but she is to carry nothing. No umbrella, nothing. She may leave a portmanteau at Clements Inn which will be transported to Bow Street for her appearance there. So methodical, so matter of fact, so final. Marie has crossed an invisible line, now committed to actions that were inconceivable only a year before.

Chapter Twenty-One
Graduating at Holloway
Spring 1912

They stand in silence at Ilfracombe station waiting for the Barnstaple train. Marie
draws her overcoat closer, wincing as the biting sea air sweeps across the platform.
Her husband grasps her arm a little tighter than necessary. How easy it would be
to return to their homely villa in Broad Park Avenue. Easy, but not an option,
not this time. Marie checks her portmanteau. Cotton wool, newspaper, small
stones, identification, a change of dress, the bare essentials. 'I've left menus with
Annie,' she says, anxious to break the silence between them. 'You just need to give
her your schedule each week. And Sarah will attend to any household matters.'

'I'll be perfectly well taken care of. I just wish I could say the same of you.'
He squeezes her hand discreetly; his touch is reassuring. There's no turning back,
Marie knows that, but shivers at the prospect of what lies ahead. Three days
before dozens of women had been arrested at a similar protest. It was one thing to
witness the appalling brutality from the sidelines, but this time she will be standing
shoulder to shoulder with her sisters.

With a final wave, Marie boards the
7.30am train and settles herself into a
compartment. There's an annoying wait of
over an hour at Barnstaple for her
connection but she arrives in London by
1.30pm, plenty of time to get to the briefing
at Clements Inn. There she joins a growing
queue of women. Hundreds have answered
the call. It is to be a protest the like of
which London has never seen. They must
never doubt their cause is just.

> **MEN AND WOMEN**
> **I INVITE YOU TO**
> **COME TO**
> **PARLIAMENT SQUARE**
> ON
> **MONDAY, March 4, 1912,**
> at 8 o'clock,
> TO TAKE PART IN A
> **GREAT PROTEST MEETING**
> against the Government's refusal to
> include woman in their Reform Bill.
>
> Speeches will be delivered by well-
> known Suffragettes, who want to enlist
> your sympathy and help in the great
> battle they are fighting for human
> liberty.
> (Signed) **E. PANKHURST.**

They are ushered inside to receive their instructions. 'On arriving at
Holloway you are to refuse to go to your cells until you have seen the governor. If
forcibly taken, you must refuse to be medically examined. You are to protest at
being held as common criminals and refuse to wear prison clothes. If, as is likely,
you are forcibly undressed you must remain calm and polite with the warders. Your
strongest weapon is passive resistance and endurance, whatever the cost. As a
protest against insufficient air, you are to wait for a bell to ring at 1pm and then
break a pane of glass with the heel of your shoe. We shall most likely be in
solitary confinement, in punishment cells, probably in separate prisons. But we will
be together in spirit. Now, please ensure your portmanteaus are clearly labelled
with your name and leave them in the hallway. You will be given a typewritten
sheet as you leave telling you where to go. It is vital you follow your instructions to
be sure that you are all where you need to be when the time comes.'

At 3pm she follows others as they make for the London Pavilion. Noise and
warmth swamp her as she climbs the stairs where she is swallowed up in a mass
of 800 women. Someone clasps her hand and guides her to a seat at the front,
those reserved for the deputation. On the stage, Mrs Pethick Lawrence waits for
silence. 'They thought the women of this country were inured to political
subjection; they have found out their mistake. The worm has turned at last.'

Marie is riveted as Mrs Pethick Lawrence and Christabel speak for almost two hours, inspiring everyone with their revolutionary fervour.

Marie joins a group directed to wait at the Gardenia restaurant in Catherine Street. She shuffles anxiously on her chair, convinced that every man who approaches is a plain clothes policeman intent on apprehending her. This time there will be no gentleman to carry her to safety. This time she will be arrested. At 6.15pm she makes for the door, seeking out her small group of three. After the unannounced mass window-smashing just three days before, the police are on high alert. She is to strike more covertly. Her companion grasps her arm and they walk along the Strand, past Charing Cross station to Trafalgar Square. She catches sight of others heading for Regent Street but Marie is hurried on to Whitehall, towards her target. She quickly identifies the Home Office, and, without pausing, grasps the stone in her pocket and throws. It finds its target, the glass shatters.

GLASS - SMASHING FOR VOTES! SUFFRAGETTES AS WINDOW - BREAKERS.

Her arm is grabbed. The policeman's grip tightens as he propels her forward, through the London streets towards Bow Street Police Court where women are spilling out of the building. They cheer as she joins the throng. Ushers push and pull them until every nook and cranny of the building is filled. The Magistrate, Mr Curtis Bennett, scans the room, nods to the clerk, and prepares himself to weather the inevitable cries of 'Votes for Women' as he processes the prisoners.

Marie waits her turn. She finds herself alongside Olive Wharry, from Holsworthy, a familiar face from the Church League for Women's Suffrage.

'First time?' Olive asks.

'Yes.'

'Who are you?'

'You know who I am, Marie Newby from Ilfracombe.'

'I know, but he don't.' She nods at the magistrate. 'You've family at home. Might want to think of an alias.'

'Alias?'

'Joyce Locke, pleased to meet you,' Olive holds out her hand in mock greeting. Olive, Joyce, winks as an usher grabs her arm and pushes her towards the rail. Women cheer as she raises her hand in salute.

Marie shuffles forward, her alias ready. There will be no record in the papers of the arrest of Mrs Kathleen Marie Anstice du Sautoy Newby. She is less prepared for the sentence. Two months imprisonment with hard labour. She gasps. Two months is bad enough but the hard labour means she will be denied her own clothes, time to exercise and speak with others. She is about to experience Holloway at its worst. Too soon she is lined up against a stone wall, watching as female warders make their way towards her. No amount of fine words or mental preparation is enough to withstand the violation of hands removing her dress, leaving her humiliated, shamed. And this is only the beginning.

Marie is thrust into a cold, dark cell, much like that described in *Prisons and Prisoners,* by the aristocratic suffragette, Constance Lytton:

> In the cell - a shelf near the door which is honoured by the name of table, a wooden chair, and standing up against the wall, a plank bed. Then at the far end of the cell there is a hot water pipe, and on the floor a row of tins, a dustpan and brush, small basin, tin to

hold water, a pail, also - a plate. On a low shelf there is a bundle of bedding consisting of a thin, hard mattress and an even harder pillow, two blankets, a pair of sheets, and a sort of rug. The shelf above contains a slate and pencil, a case with the prison rules, a mug, spoon, salt-cellar, and toothbrush. There, too, one finds a Bible, hymn book, prayer book, "The Narrow Way", "A Healthy Home and How to Keep It", and a brush and comb.

Confined in separate cells, the suffragettes smash windows to call to each other to bolster their resolve. As a stream of women arrives from the courts the prison becomes more and more overcrowded. Perversely this makes it easier to organise and support one another, support that will be needed as they prepare to go on hunger strike. Hunger strike, a phrase familiar to Marie from reading *Votes for Women* in a comfortable armchair by her fireside. But here, within the stark, cold walls of Holloway, the reality is very different. Hunger pangs assault her, intensified by the sweet-smelling food left in her cell to tempt her to eat. When this fails, the harrowing noises from adjacent cells bring her to breaking point. Ada Wright, in Holloway at the same time as Marie, gives a graphic description of force-feeding:

When the hour of torture arrived, the door of my cell was suddenly flung open, and four to six or seven officers entered and seized me. There was a deep breathless struggle while I clung to my iron bedstead, and held on to it with all my strength. I was against five or six, but it was always some minutes before the wardresses, after using much force and pressure, could unlock me from that position. Naturally I got much bruised, but of that I do not complain, as bruises were mutual. I was then dragged to the chair, and tied down and my hands and arms were tightly held by wardresses on each side so that I could not move.

Two doctors came in and began their objectionable work. One stood behind me and one in front, and they proceeded to force open my jaw. When my lips had first been forced open, a steel gag was, with force again… inserted between my teeth and my mouth was then prised open, and kept so by the doctor behind, who worked the gag and who held my head so that I could not move it, while the doctor in front rammed that unspeakable instrument of disgust and torture - so to me, at least - the stomach tube, down my throat, causing me to writhe and retch and cough and choke at every twist with which he sent it down. At first it absolutely used to suffocate me till I grew almost black in the face for want of breath.

While in Holloway the women, including Marie, somehow managed to pass handkerchiefs between them, recording their imprisonment. On the first (above) her signature is bottom left, upside down. On the second, a rougher piece of material, it is in purple just above the centre on the left, above Margaret Macfarlane. This one was also signed by Emily Wilding Davison, bottom right. She was a committed hunger striker and barricaded herself in her cell to resist force-feeding, a protest that was ended by the use of a water cannon.

Women arrested alongside Marie included:

Olive Wharry: sentenced to six months for breaking £100 worth of glass at Robinson and Cleaver, four months more than an Edinburgh man who broke his wife's skull.

Jane Pascoe: from Falmouth. Sentenced to one month for breaking two panes of glass at the Board of Education. Value 10s. She said at her trial, 'I came up from Cornwall to protest against the Government's refusal to include women in the Reform Bill. Women have worked constitutionally for years, and it has not been any use, and now we are going to fight as the men fought for their rights until we get the franchise.'

Elsie Howey: sentenced to six months

Alice Parker: niece of Lord Kitchener and WSPU organiser for Glasgow. She said at her trial, 'If I had thrown a stone as a striker, or even as a man who is intoxicated, I suppose I should have received a very light sentence... men in Swansea, when they were held up for rioting, got a fortnight's imprisonment, and the ringleader of them got only six weeks.' Sentenced to four months.

Ada Wright: sentenced for four months

Zoe Proctor: like many of the women, she came from an affluent background and initially had trouble adapting to prison routine. Much to the amusement of the other prisoners she expected her bed to be made for her. Sentenced to two months.

Marie Newby and Olive Wharry weren't the only west country women facing a prison sentence. Edith Clarence, Hon. Secretary of the WSPU Axminster branch, had booked national speaker Georgina Brackenbury to address meetings in the town on the 28 and 29 February. Georgina was an artist whose studio, according to Diane Atkinson in *Rise Up Women!*, was used to share the militants' campaign plans during February 1912. Given that Edith almost certainly provided hospitality at Coaxdon Hall during Georgina's visit, these plans were probably discussed. Was this when she made up her mind to respond to Emmeline Pethick Lawrence's plea for volunteers and join Georgina at the protest the following Monday? Georgina had speaking engagements in Bath on Friday and Saturday but may well have reciprocated with accommodation in London on the Sunday.

On the Monday any thoughts they had of repeating the mass window smashing of the previous Friday were thwarted by the immense police presence. *Votes for Women* reported Georgina Brackenbury's description of how, '…I was walking towards Westminster perfectly quietly, when the police suddenly appeared, seized me roughly by the shoulders, and said, "You must go the other way"… Then other policemen came and when they couldn't move me… they took hold of my scarf and pulled it, and I fell down senseless, being nearly choked… then the men got frightened and sent for an ambulance.' In court the constable described the encounter rather differently. 'I took hold of her [Georgina Brackenbury] not using any unnecessary violence, but she struggled violently and fell down. I assisted her to her feet and gave what attention I could.'

Both Georgina and Edith joined dozens of other women, arrested on Friday, 1 or Monday, 4 March and brought before Mr Curtis Bennett at Bow Street Police Court. Edith was charged with insulting behaviour and obstruction and ordered to pay sureties or serve a sentence of one month's imprisonment. In some ways she was fortunate. As *Votes for Women* reported, 'Mr Curtis Bennett explained that those arrested after Friday [who had smashed windows] had been given hard labour.' This included Marie Newby.

We don't know if Marie endured force-feeding but she did go on hunger strike. When she finally emerged through the gates of Holloway at the end of her sentence, she was presented with a WSPU medal 'For Valour'. Her name was inscribed on the reverse, and presented in a silk-lined case with a gold blocked inscription on the lid. 'Presented to Marie du Sautoy Newby by the Women's Social & Political Union in recognition of a gallant action, whereby through endurance to the last extremity of hunger and hardship a great principle of political justice was vindicated.'

TORPEDOED!

Chapter Twenty-Two
Disappointment and Division
Spring 1912

The violent protests in London provoked a backlash from all sides, including from one paper traditionally supportive of the suffragettes, the *Manchester Guardian*. After the first protest on 1 March, under the headline 'The Madness of the Militants' it stated:

> Hundreds of windows, including some of the most valuable in London, were yesterday wantonly broken by the small body of misguided women who profess to represent the noble and serious cause of the political enfranchisement of women, but who, in fact, do their utmost to degrade and hinder it... [these actions were] the follies and excesses of a small and fanatical sect, led by a few persons of... great enthusiasm and capable of great self-sacrifice, as is the way with revivalists, whether religious or political, but

without balance and incapable of conceiving or carrying out a sustained and practical policy. To them the movement owed much of its original impetus, but the time has long passed when they can render it any effective assistance, and they have of late become... the chief obstacle to its success.'

The paper considered Christabel's plea, that they were only emulating the miners and proposed to attain their end by force, to be farcical. 'A vast and orderly assertion of the power of organised labour is treated as on a par with the petulant outbreak of a few sincere but unbalanced women. The thing would be laughable if it were not pathetic.'

The protests also created a challenge for the NUWSS - how to further distance themselves from the actions of the suffragettes? Speakers from HQ were dispatched to all parts of the country to reach as many women as possible with their non-militant message. The person on her way to Devon was Clara Rackham, chair of the national executive committee. On 16 March she arrived in Sidmouth, ready to give an address on 'Women's Suffrage and the Present Situation,' to a substantial audience assembled at the Winter Gardens. Was the choice of Sidmouth deliberate? The Antis had certainly stepped up their activity there after the recent violence.

The Right Hon. Sir John Kennaway, President of the East Devon Anti-Suffrage branch, chaired a meeting at Ottery St Mary on 5 March immediately after the events in London. Mrs Greatbatch regaled a crowded room with her belief that a woman's place was in the home. '...If women kept the place that nature intended for them, they would have in the world better mothers and better wives, better husbands, better sons and better legislators'. They could do much more good on local governing bodies and County Councils than they could in Parliament.

The following day, a meeting was held at the Temperance Hall in Exmouth where, according to the *Anti-Suffrage Review*, Mrs Greatbatch was so convincing 80 new members immediately signed up. An editorial in the *Exmouth Journal* agreed. 'It was particularly apt that at a time when the Suffragettes forcibly distracted attention to their cause by an epidemic of window-smashing in London, the National League for Opposing Woman Suffrage should be holding a meeting in Exmouth. The anti-suffrage movement has a great amount of sympathy in Exmouth... the outrageous methods adopted by these irresponsible Suffragettes have killed practically every ounce of public sympathy for the woman's movement.'

The following night saw yet another meeting, this time at the Manor Hall at Sidmouth. It was something of a coup when Sir Ernest Satow, in the chair, read a telegram from Major Morrison-Bell. The MP for the Honiton division had previously voted *for* the Conciliation Bill, and had given a pledge to do so again, but, '...In consequence of the recent Suffragist disturbances, and a study of the leading speeches made at our Albert Hall meeting, [an anti-suffrage rally in February] he now intended to vote against Woman Suffrage.' In his view the interests of the country were too complicated and vast to justify the risks that might be run were such an experiment to be tried as giving all women the franchise - repeating the Antis view that giving any women the vote was a likely precursor to giving it to all.

This blanket coverage of East Devon by the Antis concluded with a meeting in Exeter on 8 March covered by the *Western Times*. Mr Roberts, in the chair, opened with the topic everyone was expecting. Window smashing by the militants was, '...a senseless and wanton destruction of property... [that] had alienated the sympathies of many of the Suffragettes' strongest supporters and had done incalculable damage to the cause they advocated. The incidents only showed how utterly deficient these women were in the common sense which was the first qualification of anyone claiming to vote on national issues.' A compelling argument that many women in homes across Devon would silently have agreed with.

A letter from Sir Thomas Acland introduced the thought that female suffrage would, '...bring women into purely party politics, from which local administration ought always to be protected.' A fair point, but surely this applied to men as well as women? He was also of the opinion that opening the doors of Parliament to women would double the number of uneducated and ignorant voters. His letter was greeted with a cheer of approval; with no opportunity for the dozen or so suffragists in the audience to point out that perhaps the answer lay in better education for women, not denial of the vote.

Mrs Greatbatch couldn't believe that it would be to the national good for the country to be governed by a preponderance of women. Yes, they should cooperate with men in the administration of the country but they should still remain uncompromisingly women. In her view the suffrage movement had been engineered by a small number of extremely able women who had attracted a following of young and impressionable girls. What they lacked in numbers they made up for with astuteness in advertising and creating a lot of clamour. It was a perceptive comment, but in her view the day for clamour was practically done.

New branches of the Anti-Suffrage League formed in Ottery St Mary and Exmouth after these meetings. Added to those in Exeter, East Devon, Plymouth and Torquay this now made a total of six in Devon. Given this swelling of the anti-suffrage ranks, the Sidmouth suffragists may well have felt in need of support, although Clara Rackham's visit marked the eighth NUWSS meeting in the Sidmouth neighbourhood that year, signalling an increasingly vigorous fight back.

Mrs Rackham then moved on to the Barnfield Hall for the annual meeting of Exeter NUWSS. After condemning the recent actions of the WSPU she invited her audience to consider the possibility that if they had all done more, militant tactics would never have arisen. It was a thought she repeated at the Seymour Hotel Assembly Room in Totnes. After her speech a resolution was moved expressing disapproval of the militant outbreaks but urging every MP who supported the principle of the enfranchisement of women to still vote for the latest Conciliation Bill.

Unsurprisingly, women were becoming increasingly confused about the legislation coming before Parliament. The first Conciliation Bill, which passed its second reading in July 1910 with a majority of 109, was delayed by Asquith then lost when he called a general election. The second, introduced in May 1911, passed its second reading with an increased majority of 167 but was delayed by Lloyd George's amendment to include married women, then overshadowed by Asquith's proposal for a Manhood Suffrage Bill. While discussion rumbled on over whether a women's amendment could be added to

Asquith's Bill, March saw a third attempt to pass a Conciliation Bill. It was a vote on this legislation that was just five days away.

The following day saw the end of Mrs Rackham's tour at the annual meeting of the Three Towns and District branch, held at Plymouth Corn Exchange. It was a meeting given a boost by an editorial in the *Western Mercury* which lauded the, '... sensible and dignified way in which the National Union of Women's Suffrage Societies has met the crisis created by the window smashers... Last night at Totnes, Miss Mills Young had the satisfaction of seeing a resolution carried which at once condemned the tactics of the hammer brigade and asserted the justice of the women's cause.' The piece goes on to hope that, '...the antics of a few women, however idiotic, ought not to prejudice the overwhelming case of the whole sex... We trust that the meeting in Plymouth tonight, with Miss Willcocks and Mrs Rackham speaking, will show that there has been no local defection from the cause.' If the number of NUWSS groups now established in Devon was anything to go by, the opposite was the case. Branches were listed in Appledore, Barnstaple, Bideford, Budleigh Salterton, Exeter, Exmouth, Instow, Newton Abbot, Ottery St Mary, Sidmouth, Teignmouth, Three Towns, Topsham and Totnes.

In contrast, these were trying times for the WSPU. Police had raided their London headquarters with warrants for the arrest of Mr and Mrs Pethick Lawrence, Mrs Pankhurst and Christabel. Christabel evaded arrest by exiling herself to France, recalling Annie Kenney to take charge in London. But it was delegation in name only. Christabel retained control, briefing Annie on her regular trips to Paris.

Her determination to hold onto power was fuelled by the belief that others were plotting to challenge her leadership. And there were challenges. Although the WSPU had dismissed the Conciliation Bills as being dead in the water, the latest one still came before Parliament on 29 March. At the vote, the previous substantial majorities evaporated and the Bill failed to pass its second reading. The Women's Freedom League, as reported in *The Vote,* were in no doubt why. 'There is little doubt the Bill would have passed its second reading if it had not been for the recent militancy. Many MPs who voted against the second reading or abstained declared that their action was a protest against militant methods and not a final judgement on the general question.'

The piece continued. 'It is impossible to view this defeat with any other feeling than the deepest pain and regret. The woman's movement in Britain has received an undoubted blow. We cannot and do not share the view that it is a good thing the Bill is killed. The WSPU have said repeatedly that they were not interested in the Bill and did not care whether it was defeated or not. Indeed, it seems likely that the militancy which took place only three weeks before this critical second reading was deliberately designed to wreck the Bill.' The cracks in the militant movement were deepening, and the WFL was in no doubt that the blame lay in the increasing recklessness of the WSPU.

In Plymouth, Mabel Ramsay, also expressed her keen disappointment at the defeat of the latest Conciliation Bill in the *Western Daily Mercury*. 'We shall have to work harder that is all. "Even Sir John Spear" [Tavistock MP], she remarked bitterly, "is a man not to be trusted - and I thought he was. I thought he was the one straight man on the job, but he had a sudden wavering of conscience at the last.' Devonport was also represented by two men who were not prepared to support woman suffrage. '[She] hadn't realised so much and so bitterly how they were being laughed at until she interviewed the MPs for Plymouth... Members who were sent up to represent the people "laughed behind us." They were polite but had not the slightest conception of the views the women wished to lay before them... They [Mabel and others] went to ask the Members for Plymouth... What were they prepared to do? Were they prepared to do anything? "Absolutely nothing, was the message."' According to Mabel Ramsay they had reached a critical stage in their campaign where there was not only an element of pessimism about, but also of hysteria; a reflection on the recent WSPU activities in London.

At a meeting later in the year she went even further. 'We are sick to death,' the *Western Daily Mercury* reported, '...of arguing the cause... They wanted finality, which meant the vote... [she] went on to allude to Mr Asquith as "our big stumbling block." The inspiring force of the opposition to women citizenship, Dr Ramsay described, "...is all prejudice, prejudice right the way through". And we have got to beat down that prejudice.' It was with that renewed passion that Mabel Ramsay concluded that the movement was going favourably in the West. She had never received so many requests to launch new branches and their membership had doubled to over 200 members. More and more women were joining the NUWSS in protest at the escalation in militancy and the intransigence of the government.

One benefit for Mabel Ramsay and the Plymouth group was increased subscriptions, useful in continuing to weather a tricky patch financially. She shared her attempts to be philosophical about the situation in the *Common Cause*. 'When we have deplored the state of our finances we have frequently been advised to have a jumble sale. Apparently it is what every Society in need does once – and vows never to do again. Accordingly we had our jumble sale, and spent a warm sunny day sorting old clothes in an airless room off a back street. The sale was soon over; one crowded hour of glorious life realised £5, [around £750 today] and we are now in a position to pass on the good advice to other branches.'

Other NUWSS groups across Devon also stepped up their activity during 1912. Barnstaple forged ahead with Kate James still very much involved and planning for a suffrage summer school on Dartmoor in August or September. Names for this were invited by the group's new organiser, Miss Christine Wodehouse, someone already well known for her work with young people in her father's parish at Bratton Fleming - and even more famous for her family connections. She was a cousin of author and humorist, P.G. Wodehouse.

The Exmouth group was also going from strength to strength. Interest had waned after their first tentative beginnings in 1904 but the branch had re-formed with Joan Retallack as Honorary Secretary. They organised fundraising Musical Entertainments at the Temperance Hall, with adverts emphasising their strictly non-militant, non-party stance. The group welcomed Helen Fraser back as their speaker. She opened by saying that the NUWSS was the greatest force in the country to secure the Parliamentary vote for women, given there were now 365 branches country-wide and an increasing membership. [The NUWSS 1912 Annual report puts this at 42,438]

Exmouth residents were treated to a balanced view at a follow up meeting with speakers from both the NUWSS and the National League for Opposing Woman Suffrage. They even took a neutral approach with their choice of chair as reported in the *Western Times*. 'Miss Duke explained that she was asked to take the chair because she was in the peculiar position of not being at all interested in the suffrage question.' When it came to a vote on whether the Parliamentary Franchise should be granted to women, Miss Duke declared, amidst good humoured laughter all round, 'You are very evenly divided, ladies and gentlemen.'

At a joint meeting with the Budleigh Salterton society, Exmouth committee member, Mary Oliver, introduced Frances Sterling from the NUWSS executive. Miss Sterling tackled the thorny issue of political loyalties. The Union was not affiliated with any particular party but supported candidates from any that fulfilled their pledges to support suffrage. Her emphasis was very much on the word, 'fulfilled', as reported in the *Exeter and Plymouth Gazette*. 'There were some seats hopelessly anti-suffrage, some held by wobblers, and some held by men who had pledged themselves up to the hilt to their constituents to support the suffrage, but who had broken their pledge. Those men of all men wanted polling out.'

Yet, despite their increase in numbers and undoubted enthusiasm, the NUWSS women were still relying on the tried and tested formula: meetings to raise awareness, polite lobbying, support to get as many men into Parliament as possible who were good Suffragists... and endless motions, all calling on the Government to extend the Parliamentary Franchise to women. And the result of all this activity? The answer is best summed up by Mr Duke, K.C. M.P. When reminded of the numerous meetings in Exeter where resolutions in favour of Women's suffrage had been passed practically unanimously, he said he would only consider a decision at the polls as giving him a mandate on this matter. The perfect dilemma. To influence their local MP to give them the vote, women had to have the vote.

THE SPLIT.

Budding Suffragette. "I say, Prissy" (*with intensity*), "are you a Peth or a Pank?"

Chapter Twenty-Three
Matters of Divided Principle
Summer - Autumn 1912

In contrast to all the NUWSS activity, WSPU groups in Devon seemed to have lost impetus. There were exceptions. Ilfracombe remained active, Edith Clarence continued to post reports from Axminster and Torquay shared news of a successful 'At Home'. But even this ended with a plea for those who took the paper to become more united and to offer to host meetings. There were no more entries for a while so perhaps offers were hard to come by. The Exeter and Plymouth groups had also gone quiet. This hiatus may have been part of a national reaction to militancy, persuading some women to transfer their efforts to the NUWSS, at least partially. In the spirit of recent cooperative working, several women retained membership of both groups, active in one or the other, or both, at different times. This was true for women such as Mary Frood in Topsham, Mary Willcocks in Exeter and Marion Phillips in Plymouth.

Marion's changing allegiances are particularly difficult to pin down. In July she defended WSPU militancy in the *Western Daily Mercury*. 'The non-militant party seem to suggest that the Government's promise [of an amendment to the Manhood Suffrage Bill] offers the prospect of at least some votes for women. The WSPU think this promise a mere trick to defeat our ends. Every day it becomes more evident that the Government are determined no amendment shall be carried... We believe that trust in the Government is quite misplaced, and that strong pressure must be brought to bear, of a sort they can understand, if success is to be attained. With the imprisonment and torture by forcible feeding of our leaders it became quite impossible for the WSPU to quench (even if they wished) the militant spirit which the Government's treachery has aroused. Who would be free, must strike the blow.' Any lingering doubt of her continuing support for the WSPU is dispelled with a subsequent letter replying to criticism of her defence of militancy which she signs Marion Phillips, Militant Suffragette.

Yet in November she and Gwyneth Keyes joined Mabel Ramsay in a NUWSS deputation to the Three Towns Parliamentary Debating Society. Mabel Ramsay's comments suggest how close the two groups had become. '...The Government proposed to give to those [thoughtless] lads what they refused to give to women, for which they had suffered torture, imprisonment, and obloquy. [Strong public condemnation] Can you wonder then,' she enquired again, 'that some women are militant. My wonder is that more women are not so!' Marion Phillips then took to the floor, prompting what the *Western Daily Mercury* described as 'ironical laughter'. She opened by saying she was, '...very proud that she had belonged, from the very first, to the WSPU led by Mrs Pankhurst and her gifted daughter.' A combination of the two messages, both militant and non-militant, must have been confusing for the lay person, possibly damaging both causes.

In July the Torquay and Paignton WSPU branch was revitalised by the arrival of Greta Allen from Brighton as organiser for the holiday campaign. It was the start of a busy programme that turned out to be so successful Torquay was given its own review in *Votes for Women*. 'From Torquay come accounts such as we always like to receive from workers. Not only were hundreds of copies disposed of to casual purchasers, but also from shops where it is now, as a result of the campaign, being regularly ordered for customers, as well as of paper sellers established for street selling. The campaign included a decorated motor boat, many meetings, (only the rain prevented still more) a tea and fete at Oddicombe beach turned at a moment's notice into a Town Hall entertainment paid for by a local member, a march with the band playing Ethel Smyth's "March of the Women" and columns in the local papers... Bravo Torquay!'

Despite the rain, eighteen meetings were held in nineteen days, including open-air ones on Paignton Green, chaired by Mary Mills. Local members were once more actively involved, chalking the pavements and selling copies of *Votes for Women*, over fifty in one week alone. Mary Fausten, a U.S. citizen who had just returned to her home at Livermead in Torquay after an extended stay in America, became the new Hon. Secretary. She considered this a pivotal moment for the group. 'During these critical weeks, members are earnestly requested to do their upmost to increase interest and scope of the work.' She wasn't alone in her support for the movement. Her husband, Oscar Fausten, was a member of the Men's Political Union for Women's Enfranchisement. In October 1912 the Union even gave them a special mention in the *Suffragette*. 'Thanks to Mr Fausten who, with the help of Mrs Fausten, keeps the flag flying in Torquay by holding meetings and doing other propaganda work.'

Mary continued to be the driving force in the Torquay WSPU, but possibly struggled for support at times. In November she posted in the *Suffragette*, 'The general work and interest is increasing, but many more helpers are needed. Will four members volunteer for paper distribution? Another "At Home" is earnestly desired. Will a member kindly offer?' The group benefitted from her dedication until she moved away in July 1913. Mary Phillips posted a notice in *The Suffragette* of her farewell tea at Goodbody's café. '...the latest portrait of Mrs Pankhurst, especially signed, was presented to her as a small token of the great appreciation her fellow members feel of her splendid work for the cause in Torquay.' Mary Philips was obviously concerned that the momentum might be lost with her departure. She continued, 'It is up to members now to show it [their appreciation] in a still more practical way by carrying on the work. This will please her more than anything.'

A year before this parting of the ways, the Ilfracombe WSPU group was particularly active. Annie Ball was again in the news for refusing to pay her taxes. 'A Tax-Resistance Sale of goods seized from Miss Ball, Matron of the Trained Nurses Institute of Ilfracombe and Barnstaple, took place recently at the Auction Rooms, High-Street, Barnstaple. A previous sale had taken place a fortnight earlier at Ilfracombe. Members of different suffrage societies were present, and leaflets were distributed. The tax collectors and other officials concerned in the distraint and sales have invariably acted with the greatest kindness and courtesy, and seem fully to grasp the principle of tax resistance as practised by the women of the Tax Resistance League.'

By 7 June 1912 Marie had been released from Holloway and was busy arranging their next public meeting. Significantly the speaker was Georgina Brackenbury who was sentenced alongside Marie and Edith Clarence for the March campaign. On the afternoon of Thursday, 27 June the Gaiety Hall at Ilfracombe was filled with women eager to hear Georgina speak. And if they missed out on an invitation to that event, they had a second chance. At 8pm she was again in action addressing a crowd at Montebello Lawn, the venue behind the Gaiety where visitors gathered for Ilfracombe's season of summer concerts.

Things were going well for the Ilfracombe branch. Membership was growing, prestigious speakers were regularly arriving, and they had a Liberal candidate for the Barnstaple constituency, Henry Harben, who was brave enough to stand and be counted when it came to Votes for Women. But ironically his support of the cause was about to deprive them of a valuable ally. In June 1912 George Lansbury, the Labour politician, confronted Asquith in the House of Commons, denouncing the government for their treatment of suffragette prisoners. 'You are beneath contempt. You call yourselves gentlemen, yet forcibly feed and murder women in this fashion. You ought to be driven out of public life. It is the most disgraceful thing

that has happened in the history of England. You will go down in
posterity as a man who condemned innocent women. You will be
remembered as a Government that has tortured women.'

It was a stand that resonated with Henry Harben, prompting him
to write to Barnstaple Liberal Association withdrawing his
candidature in protest against the
forcible feeding of suffragist prisoners
and the Government's proposal to give
more votes to men, while leaving women
unenfranchised. He wrote, '...what is
the good of it all? If the authorities want
to vindicate the law, let them first avoid
making it ridiculous. If they only want to
treble the income of the WSPU they
might find some more humane way of
doing it. This policy of pusillanimous
persecution is not my idea of Liberalism.
The bullying of voteless women by a

Government that is actually proposing to widen the franchise of men
is quite without excuse. Unmanly, ungentlemanly, unsportsmanlike,
and uncivilised it can serve no purpose but to disgrace those who are
responsible for it and those who acquiesce in it. The Liberal party in
the House of Commons having endorsed this policy, I feel compelled
to make the only protest open to me by withdrawing my active
support altogether from the party at the present time.'

The leadership of the WSPU was jubilant, applauding his actions
in surrendering the chance of a safe Liberal seat. The Ilfracombe
group was quick to add its support. 'A great impression has been
made here by the splendid action of Mr Harben in resigning his
Parliamentary candidature as a protest. It has brought home to a good
many people the abominable treatment of suffragist prisoners by the
so called Liberal Government.'

Just three months later they had cause to regret their enthusiasm
when Mr H. A. Baker, whose views on women's suffrage couldn't
have been more different, was adopted as the new Liberal candidate.
He stated that he, '...could not pledge himself to vote for women's
suffrage if returned. It was not in the interests of women or the

country. There was no evidence the majority of women wanted such
a change.' The women of the Barnstaple constituency were now
saddled with a confirmed anti-suffragist. Those gathered for the
AGM of the Devon WLA, held in Bideford, begged, '...all Members
of Parliament who desire the well-being of the country to support
such amendments to the Reform Bill as shall place the self-protecting
power of the vote in the hands of women.' But this was tempered by
the now familiar reservation. 'Rational, logical plans for female
enfranchisement have been hampered by misguided women going
about the country in the name of militant suffragists. Despite them,
the great principle will be carried into law. We mean to struggle for
the vote until we have it.'

Their concerted voice made no difference to Mr Baker who
couldn't have been more dismissive. He announced that he didn't
intend to deal with several questions handed to him on Women's
Suffrage, remarking that it was evident the views of the questioners
differed from his own. WLAs historically backed their candidates,
with the ladies throwing themselves into campaigning whenever the
call came. But their new candidate's emphatic rebuff pushed them
into unprecedented action. Most of these women were not
suffragettes, or even suffragists, but they issued a public challenge to
Mr Baker in the *Ilfracombe Gazette*:

Dear Sir,
We the undersigned Liberal women, note with great regret
your views against the enfranchisement of women.
We think you lost sight of the fact - amongst others - that in
the event of your being returned to Parliament as member for
this Division, a considerable part of your salary would be
forcibly obtained from women who feel strongly the injustice of
taxation without representation.
We are, of course, aware our present member has consistently
voted in favour of Women Suffrage, and urged the justice of
their claim. We could, therefore only regard the election of an
anti-suffragist as a distinctly retrograde step which would make it
very difficult, in some cases impossible, for us to work in the
Liberal interest in future.

We beg you will give the subject your further serious consideration and hope you may find it possible to modify your views on the subject.

Mr Baker did not mince his words. He did not approve of the Parliamentary vote being extended to women, and would not in any way bind himself to help them to get it. Ilfracombe WSPU probably regretted applauding Henry Harben's principled resignation now. What a different reception he would have given them. And they were soon to be faced with another parting of the ways.

In October 1912 the WSPU were on the move to bigger, better, more imposing London premises at Lincoln's Inn House, Kingsway. A lack of space at Clements Inn, also the home of the Pethick Lawrence's, was given as the reason for the move. But a statement issued soon afterwards offered a very different view.

Along with Mrs Pankhurst, Mr and Mrs Pethick Lawrence had been sentenced to nine months after the window-smashing campaign. They went on hunger strike, and suffered the violence of force feeding. Mrs Pethick Lawrence resisted so vigorously it took nine wardresses to hold her down. Frederick Pethick Lawrence suffered force-feeding twice a day for ten days before being released in a state of near collapse. They travelled to Canada soon afterwards to recuperate and reflect, increasingly concerned about the direction the WSPU was taking. They now feared the mass window-smashing was the precursor of ever-increasing violence to come.

When they returned in early October it was to a mixed homecoming. Christabel and Emmeline made it clear that they intended to pursue a new militant policy of all-out war against the government, inciting WSPU members to strike however they could, particularly through the destruction of property. On this they were intransigent. *Votes for Women* reported, 'At the first reunion of the leaders after the enforced holiday, Mrs Pankhurst and Miss Christabel Pankhurst outlined a new militant policy, which Mr and Mrs Pethick Lawrence found themselves altogether unable to approve. Mrs Pankhurst and Miss Christabel Pankhurst indicated that they were not prepared to modify their intentions and recommended that Mr and

Mrs Pethick Lawrence should leave the Women's Social and Political Union.'

The Pethick Lawrences retained control of *Votes for Women* and expressed their shock and pain at the turn of events in their first editorial after the split. 'Severe as is the shock which we know this will be to our readers we can assure them that no pain which they suffer in consequence of it can possibly exceed the pain which we feel ourselves... or the distress which we have experienced before deciding to take this course.'

Christabel and Emmeline had combined to oust two core supporters of the movement who had been alongside them every step of the way. A sympathetic view might be to argue that they believed their plans for increased militancy, including the destruction of more property, would place Frederick at further risk of bankruptcy unless he severed his connections with the WSPU. Whatever the truth of it, rather than create a schism in the ranks, Mr and Mrs Pethick Lawrence agreed to go quietly. It was the first of several expulsions that eventually even included Sylvia and Adela.

Negotiating the politics of the split at a local level must have provoked some interesting discussions. Traditionally, *Votes for Women* included a section for groups to provide local news. After October, this section disappeared so the only option for WSPU groups was to post in the Pankhurst's new publication, the *Suffragette*, advertised as 'The Official Organ of the Women's Social and Political Union'. This was an easy choice for the Ilfracombe members, now separate from Barnstaple, who posted once in November and never again. Torquay and Paignton is the only other group who moved at the same time as Ilfracombe, with a revitalised Plymouth posting again the following February and Exeter in March. Both of these bursts of activity coincided with the arrival of Mary Phillips as the new organiser, well known in Devon as one of the Exeter hunger strikers and an outspoken advocate of militancy.

The editorial content of the *Suffragette* became increasingly militant, as did some suffragette actions. The WSPU had a new aim - to make life, not only for the government but all electors, so unbearable that they would give women the vote to put an end to the disruption. Sylvia Pankhurst summarised this escalation from petty injuries and annoyances to large-scale damage:

> Street lamps were broken, 'Votes for Women' was painted on the seats at Hampstead Heath, keyholes were stopped up with lead pellets, house numbers were painted out, chairs flung in the Serpentine, cushions of railway carriages slashed, flower-beds damaged, golf greens all over the country scraped and burnt with acid... A mother and daughter, bearing an ancient name, spent much of their time travelling in trains in order to drop pebbles between the sashes of carriage windows, hoping the glass would smash on being raised. Old ladies applied for gun licences to terrify the authorities. Bogus telephone messages were sent calling up the Army Reserves and Territorials. Telegraph and telephone wires were severed with long-handled clippers; fuse boxes were blown up, communication between London and Glasgow being cut for some hours.

Part of this escalation was a campaign to destroy the contents of post-boxes. May Billinghurst, another signatory alongside Marie Newby in Holloway, was the driving force, setting out in a wheelchair with a rug concealing packages oozing a dark brown sticky fluid. She went from one pillar box to the next dropping a package into each, destroying many people's Christmas greetings. The government claimed over 5,000 letters were damaged this way. Post boxes were to become a target in Devon but for the moment these tactics remained at one remove, something west country women could read about in detail in the papers but of which, on the whole, they had no direct experience. Women such as Olive Wharry, Marie Newby and Edith Clarence had taken part in national protests but in Devon, reason not rebellion remained the weapon of choice, for now at least, even in Ilfracombe.

SHUT YOUR EYES AND OPEN YOUR MOUTH AND TAKE WHAT ASQUITH SENDS YOU!

Chapter Twenty-Four
Enraged and Rebuffed
Winter 1912

Ilfracombe WSPU were becoming skilled at using the press to influence public opinion, often inciting controversial responses. In what feels like deliberate provocation, a correspondent to the *Ilfracombe Chronicle,* who simply signed himself Junius, referred to women campaigning for the vote as 'people with fads and crotchets,' and 'legislative hobbies.' It was a step too far. The following week a letter appeared from an 'Ex-Liberal':

Dear Sir,

We absolutely refuse to have such a fundamental and world-wide question as the enfranchisement of women relegated contemptuously to the ranks of "legislative hobbies, fads and crotchets". If poor Junius has made this classification honestly and in good faith, I can only assure him that he is in the most pitiable state of ignorance as to the extent and strength of the movement for the enfranchisement of women. Women are not clamouring for the recognition of fads and crotchets; they are demanding, as men once did, justice, liberty and equality.

The letter is anonymous but a prime candidate has to be Margaret Eldridge, who had no compunction about signing her name to a second letter:

We hope by refusing to do anything for Anti-Suffrage candidates we may stir the sluggish conscience of the whole party on this subject, and awaken them to our great need... Do men fear women will corrupt politics...? It is not a question of rivalry as many seem to think. Co-operation will prove to be a mutual aid, men will be benefited by the new order of things quite as much as women, and perhaps a century hence they will admit it.

Week three and Junius is back, making a stab at contrition. 'If I used any words which my critics think may belittle their views, I wish to express my regret, as no one doubts their sincerity, even if not agreeing with them.'

Immediately beneath this response is a letter from Richard Havilland of Chambercombe, Ilfracombe:

Dear Sir,

John Stuart Mill held to it, in all seriousness, and as a part of practical politics, that, "Women ought to be treated as beings equal in intelligence to, and having rights equally with, man, and should no longer be classed with children and idiots and lunatics, who need to have everything done for them." That being so in the time of Mill, when the masses were so illiterate, how much more true is it at the present time, when education has made such strides... Woman is intellectual enough to be taxed: she has been found intellectual enough to sit on the British throne more than once... to be schoolmistress, doctor of medicine, civil servant and voter at municipal, school board, county council and other elections. Yet it is asserted that she is incapable of equal intelligence with the town and country elector whose "intellectuality" consists, it is very often alleged, in discovering the candidate who will give him the biggest jug of ale. Or again with the many electors who are even now classed as illiterates, being unable to read the English language on the ballot papers!

Cries of 'hear, hear!' are sure to have rung round Annie Ball's sitting room. Mr Havilland's arguments are not new, but for a man to voice them so publicly was welcome support. But then the question of militancy reared its head. Mr Havilland continued:

> But for the suicidal policy of the Militant party during the last few years in deliberately flouting and estranging the more moderate party, on whose votes they are bound to rely, the question of female franchise would have stood today on a much firmer basis.

His views stir Marie to write to the *Ilfracombe Chronicle*, publicly identifying herself as a militant. It is our first opportunity to hear her speaking in her own words:

> Dear Sir,
>
> One hears much of the Militant Suffragists and what they are doing, may I say a few words on the need for such militancy. First of all I should like to mention why we militants are so keen on getting the vote that we are ready to leave our homes - and most suffragettes have very happy home relations - for prisons. We know that the women, with the power of the vote behind them, working with the men, would be able to improve existing conditions. For surely questions concerning housing, children's welfare etc would be better understood by the former... Then there is the injustice of the laws. For example, take those relating to injury to person - a few weeks imprisonment for the men who assault little girls if they have not already been let off with a fine, and those relating to damage to property - months of imprisonment for breaking a window!
>
> I should like to ask those gentlemen who say, "I have always been in favour of Woman Suffrage, but will do nothing *now* to help because of this militancy", a question. What did they do to

help the women before they were militant? The answer, in most cases, is *nothing...*

Many say war is a necessary evil, and yet in every war damage is done to private property and thousands of "innocent" people are rendered homeless. Remember no windows were broken or other damage done until time after time women were arrested and imprisoned as common felons for going quietly on deputations to the House of Commons, which any man is permitted to do, and not only arrested but knocked about and disgracefully treated, not by the crowd who are favourable, with the exception of a few hooligans, but by the police who had their orders. I am not blaming the police as a Force, they are splendid men, and great friends of the suffragettes, but amongst any large body of people some will be always found who would behave as brutes if occasion permitted, and some times as many as 20,000 police have been called out to "protect" the Houses of Parliament.

We do not wish those concerned to like it if their windows are broken or their game of golf spoilt. Have our non-militant friends ever heard of the London bus-driver, until then perfectly indifferent to the political enfranchisement of women, who, being held up by a suffrage procession shouted in tones of exasperation, "Oh! Give 'em the vote, but don't let them stop the traffic."

Yours faithfully, M.du Sautoy Newby. Hon. Secretary. WSPU

There is no doubt where Marie stood on the issue. But any hope she had of winning over public opinion was undermined as soon as readers turned to the next page and read the headline:

SUFFRAGETTES MEAN TRICK - Ilfracombe Victims. One of the latest dodges worked by the spiteful members of the "Votes for Women" party, was carried out this week all over the country by means of letters posted in several of the large towns in the North of England. The method adopted was to wrap a halfpenny in a leaflet advocating Woman Suffrage, and post the letter without a stamp... On Wednesday, a number of such trick letters were delivered at Ilfracombe, each involving a payment of 6d. [£3.65 today]

The letter contained a leaflet asking anyone annoyed, inconvenienced or financially injured by the tactics of the suffragettes to remind themselves of women's fight for the vote. A familiar message, but with a fundamental change in tone and target:

> The Government that withholds this reform is our arch-enemy. By every means in our power we are making it impossible for them to continue to govern women without their consent. Many think that our actions hit chiefly at people who are innocent in the matter. There are few who have had no opportunity of informing themselves as to the justice of our cause, and the glaring reason for urgency. If the public will not rise and demand for women their emancipation, they cannot complain if they receive some of the knocks when the women are fighting their own battle. All these tactics that you perhaps so much dislike will instantly cease directly you demand Votes for Women and get it. Your would-be fellow citizen, A Suffragette.

The *Ilfracombe Chronicle* was defiant. 'These spiteful tricks will most certainly not make the public, "rise and demand for women their emancipation" but will retard the movement. Voters will not be bullied into any course of conduct by methods of terrorism…' Many Ilfracombe readers will have agreed. What did the suffragettes hope to gain by antagonising ordinary people? Did they think the citizens of Britain would rise as one to demand that the Government end this nuisance and give women the vote? Whatever the reasoning, many now questioned the escalation of tactics that had already caused the WSPU to fracture at its very heart.

For over a year Asquith had sounded like a broken record promising that his preferred Manhood Suffrage Bill could be amended to include woman suffrage. The more optimistic campaigners had taken him at his word. Even Christabel had held back on more extreme militancy while there was still a possibility, however remote, that a women's amendment would succeed. They were about to receive an emphatic wake-up call. Asquith couldn't deny time for his own Bill but that didn't stop him looking for another way to sabotage its progress.

In January 1913 he approached the Speaker of the House of Commons, James William Lowther, with a loaded question. Would adding an amendment result in the abortive employment of parliamentary time? Unsurprisingly, the Speaker concluded that if a women's amendment were passed it would add a very large class to the electorate and establish an entirely new principle. Therefore, he was driven to the conclusion that it would practically constitute a new Bill. With staggering pretence, Asquith thanked the Speaker for saving the House from what would have been a regrettable waste of Parliamentary time. It was the end of the Bill and any chance of an amendment including women.

At a NUWSS meeting in Exeter, Mary Willcocks proposed the motion, 'That the meeting, seeing the great injustice done to women by the present Parliamentary situation calls on Mr Asquith to fulfil his pledge given to the NUWSS in November 1911." No more Private Members Bills doomed to failure, the NUWSS would be content with nothing less than a Government Bill.

The WSPU's reaction was significantly less nuanced. The *Dartmouth and South Hams Chronicle* reported, 'Simultaneously with the withdrawal of the Franchise Bill the suffragettes declared war. Militancy is to be fiercer than ever, and Mrs Pankhurst, at a meeting of the Women's Social and Political Union, said that while they would regard human life as sacred they would stop at little short of it.'

The WFL also announced that the time had arrived for greater militancy, but while the WSPU were introducing tactics making life as difficult as possible for the ordinary citizen, the WFL had a much more specific focus. Militancy was directed towards the Government and Laws which failed to acknowledge the citizenship of women. Their tactics were also more muted, eliminating attacks on people or property, other than ballot papers. And there was one militant tactic they emphatically drew the line at. Arson.

MORE ARSON BY WILD WOMEN.

Bristol University's athletic pavilion, which has been destroyed by fire. It is supposed to be the work of suffragettes. The building was only erected two years ago at a cost of £2,000.

Chapter Twenty-Five
Wild Women
February - March 1913

'It was in February 1913 that militancy as it is generally understood by the public began,' wrote Sylvia Pankhurst, '...militancy in the sense of continued, destructive, guerrilla warfare against the Government through injury to private property. Some property had been destroyed before this time, but the attacks were sporadic, and were meant to be in the nature of a warning as to what might become a settled policy. Now we indeed lighted the torch, and we did it with the absolute conviction that no other course was open to us... we had to do as much of this guerrilla warfare as the people of England would tolerate.' These words heralded a time of unprecedented destruction:

> When the campaign was fully underway... a certain, exceedingly feminine looking young lady (Grace Roe) was strolling about London, meeting militants in all sorts of public and unexpected places, to arrange for perilous expeditions. Women, most of them very young, toiled through the night across unfamiliar country, carrying heavy cases of petrol and paraffin. Sometimes they failed, sometimes succeeded in setting fire to an untenanted building - all the better if it were the residence of a notability - or a church, or other place of historic interest.

On 19 February 1913 two suffragettes made their final preparations to attack their most strategic target yet. A second home was being built for Lloyd George next to the Walton Heath golf course in Surrey. Just two weeks earlier, Lloyd George had refused to see a deputation of suffragettes to discuss the vote, making himself a prime target for reprisals. In the early hours, they broke into the house and left two bombs on timers. One detonated causing extensive damage but another failed to ignite. The WSPU always insisted that their actions would never harm anyone. Lloyd George's house was empty; but workmen had been due to arrive around 6am. The crude detonation techniques could easily have resulted in the bombs exploding when they were on the site, with deadly consequences.

Speaking in Cardiff the following day, Mrs Pankhurst declared, '...we have blown up the Chancellor of the Exchequer's house, a way of trying to wake up his conscience'. She was unrepentant, firmly convinced that the only way to get the vote was to make things intolerable for most people in the country so that they would demand MPs get rid of the nuisance. Significantly she declared, '...for all that has been done in the past I accept responsibility... I have advised, I have incited, I have conspired'. It was all the police needed to act. She was arrested for procuring and inciting women to commit offences and sentenced to three year's penal servitude.

Mrs Pankhurst immediately went on hunger strike, creating a problem for the authorities. Force-feeding the leader of the WSPU was deemed to be out of the question but the last thing they wanted was a martyr. Their solution was to rush The Prisoners' (Temporary Discharge for Ill Health) Bill through Parliament, allowing for the release of hunger-strikers so that they might recover, before being returned to prison. It swiftly became known as the 'Cat and Mouse Act', one of the most notorious pieces of suffrage legislation ever passed.

This escalation of militancy caused waves in Devon. Mabel Ramsay and Adelaide Baly, from Exeter, were presiding at a meeting in Totnes in February when they read a letter from Mr Mildmay MP, reported in the *Western Times*. His opening words were encouraging. 'In his opinion there was much to be said for the inclusion of women as voters upon the lines of the Conciliation Bill and he had before now supported such a proposition, but… his sympathies had been greatly alienated lately by the injudicious actions of the advocates of the cause… It would seem that they were bent upon persuading the public that women were wholly unfitted for the vote. If they had to resort to such methods as these to keep their cause before the public eye, the only conclusion he could come to was that they had no weight of female opinion behind them.'

It was an understandable but unfortunate conclusion. The opinions of thousands of women lobbying for the vote within the NUWSS were being overshadowed by WSPU militancy. It was a concern that was on the agenda in May when Exeter hosted a meeting of the NUWSS Provincial Council, largely organised by Olga Fletcher. Delegates arrived from places as far afield as Norwich, Leeds, London and Manchester. Local delegates included Mabel Ramsay and Maud Slater from Plymouth, Miss Kelsall from Westward Ho!; Miss Leng from Sidmouth; Miss Palmer from Torquay; and Miss Waring and Miss Misick from Tiverton. They joined familiar faces Margaret Robertson, Marguerite Norma-Smith and Evelina

Haverfield, who was clearly now more involved with the NUWSS than the WSPU.

The meeting marked the launch of a new educational campaign, introduced in *The Common Cause*. 'The suffrage cause has all to gain and nothing to lose by the education of the public, not only on Suffrage itself, but on all questions of public interest.' But first the matter of militancy had to be addressed, as the *Exeter and Plymouth Gazette* reported. Sir Robert Newman, in the chair, acknowledged the great setback they had experienced in recent months and knew there was only one cause, the actions of the militant suffragettes. But he was anxious to impress on the meeting that a few lawbreakers, whose actions they wholeheartedly condemned, was no reason to set the whole principle of women's suffrage aside. He had yet to learn, '… that London had gone to the dogs, or that their County Council of Devon was becoming corrupt or incompetent since ladies had had a voice in the selection of its members.'

It was a plea echoed by Lady Courtney of Penwith, Hon. Secretary of the NUWSS. 'The folly and unwisdom of the militants almost broke one's heart, and she could not think of them without condemnation. What was it these women were doing? They were burning houses, trying to destroy the treasures of their own country, and they were doing these things not for their own selfish aims or because they they had anything to gain by it, but out of sympathy and devotion to a cause which really they were ruining.'

The NUWSS were determined that peaceful propaganda would win the day, whether through their new educational campaign or a grand event now being planned, the Great Pilgrimage. They would reach the public throughout the entire country in a way it had never been reached before, bearing the message of the law-abiding Suffragists. There was a phenomenal amount of organisation to do, pilgrims would be marching from all parts of the country before assembling in Hyde Park, but one essential was, of course, choosing a song. Members were invited to send in suggestions, with John Brown's Body given as an example of one with a good rhythm for marching.

Re-energised, Miss Kelsall returned to host an 'At Home' in the Station Hall in Westward Ho! Around two hundred people gathered for a debate between Mr Griffiths (for woman suffrage) and Mr Rivington (against). The *Bideford Gazette* reported, 'The Resolution was defeated, but only by five votes, which must be regarded as a great victory in such an anti-suffrage neighbourhood.' Despite healthy suffrage groups in Instow, Appledore and Bideford itself, much of the Torridge district remained not only anti-militancy but anti-suffrage. This was demonstrated when Miss Walford, a NUWSS national organiser, spoke in Bideford, as reported in *The Gazette:*

A disgraceful scene took place at a Suffrage Meeting in the Town Hall on April 3rd when Mr Cameron Grant and Miss Walford were refused a hearing. After an hour's booing, shouting and singing... the speakers and the Chairman... retired from the platform. Thereupon three quarters of the audience rushed from the Hall to be ready to receive their visitors in the street. Many of the orderly members of the audience however remained in their seats and someone conceived the idea of asking Mr Cameron Grant to return and give his address. He did so and the motion "that this meeting believes that the extension of the franchise to Women is a measure of Justice and will be for the good of the country" after being seconded by Miss Walford, was carried by a large majority. Meantime the crowd outside did their utmost to drown the voices of the speakers within and finally favoured them in the street with a most unwarranted display of hostility before allowing them to drive away.

It was a hostility given legs by a significant escalation in the WSPU arson campaign - and one of the core perpetrators lived less than an hour away at Whitstone Head, just outside Holsworthy. Olive Wharry, probably one of the few people described as an English artist and arsonist, had recently made national headlines for an act that many found beyond the pale. On Wednesday, 19 February 1913 the tea pavilion at Kew Gardens was being redecorated. As dusk fell, the tea room was closed with the workmen due to return at 6 o'clock the following morning. All was quiet until 3.15am when one of the night attendants noticed a bright light inside the Pavilion and saw two people running away. *The Guardian* takes up the story:

> Police Constable Hill, who was on duty in the vicinity of Kew Gardens at three o'clock yesterday morning, said he observed the reflections of fire, and on climbing the wall from the roadway saw the two prisoners running across the field of the Richmond Cricket Club. He and a colleague followed, and in the course of the pursuit the prisoners each dropped a portmanteau. When the witness caught the prisoner Lenton [Lilian Lenton, well-known for her arson attempts] he said to her, "What are you doing here?' She replied, "I have come to see the fire," and laughed. The witness said, "You will have to come to the station with me," and she replied, "All right; don't touch me." When they got to the gate of the grounds he saw the prisoner Locke [actually Olive Wharry] place a small pocket lamp behind the gate post while they were waiting for the gate to be opened... The police officer produced in court one of the portmanteaux and its contents. There were a large saw, a hammer, a bundle or two, strongly redolent of paraffin, and some pieces of paper.

TEA HOUSE, KEW GARDEN, BURNED BY SUFFRAGETTES

The Morning Post of 8 March reported the trial. 'At the Central Criminal Court, yesterday, before Mr. Justice Bankes and a jury, Olive Wharry, alias Joyce Lock, twenty-seven, student, was placed on trial charged with having set fire to the Tea Pavilion at the Royal Botanic Gardens, Kew. She pleaded not guilty. Mr. Bodkin [prosecuting] said that... the whole of the Tea Pavilion in Kew Gardens and its contents were destroyed and upon the two women who held the refreshment contract from the Crown a very heavy pecuniary loss had fallen. The contents of the building, which were the property of these two women, were worth £900, [around £132,000 today] but were only insured for £500.'

Mr. Justice Bankes, summing up, said that, '...not very long ago it would have been unthinkable that a well-educated, well-brought-up young woman could have committed a crime like this... But, unfortunately - and this was all he wanted to say about it - women as a class had forfeited any presumption in their favour of that kind.'

The jury returned a verdict of guilty. Olive read a long statement denying the jurisdiction of the Court, contending that women should be on the jury, and outlining the case for woman's suffrage. 'Ministers must be warned by the fires in Regent's Park and at Kew lest a worse thing befall them. She was sorry that the two ladies had sustained loss, as she had no grudge against them. At the time she believed that the Pavilion was the property of the Crown, but she wished the two ladies to understand that she was at war, and that in war even non-combatants had to suffer.'

The Judge ordered Olive to pay the costs of the proceedings or be imprisoned in the second division of Holloway for eighteen months and keep the peace for two years. She refused on all counts.

In Holloway, Olive went on hunger strike but attempted to disguise her dramatic weight loss by hiding a hot water bottle under her clothes, a tried and tested strategy to avoid being force fed. In 1911 Vera Holme had received a communication from Holloway regarding prisoner number

11636 - Evelina Haverfield. It read, 'Will you please forward her hot water bottle on at once.' Given this came from the prison authorities it's surprising that it was still a deception going undetected two years later.

Olive was released under the Cat and Mouse Act just over a month later having been on hunger strike for thirty-two days. Her usual weight was 7st 11lbs; when released she weighed 5st 9lbs, a staggering commitment to the cause. She returned home to Whitstone to recuperate with the help of her father, Dr Richard Wharry. Shortly afterwards they were visited by Mr Rowland, a local solicitor's clerk, whose son later recalled:

My father Stanley J. Rowland, a solicitor's clerk aged 19, was sent in 1913 with a fellow junior clerk named Cowling to serve the writ on Olive Wharry at her home... They cycled out to Whitstone from their employer's office in Holsworthy, about 8 miles, and were admitted by her father Dr Wharry. When they explained their business he refused to let them see his daughter and locked them in his study. After a long while they were released and told to leave, taking the writ with them. As they left one of them flung the writ on the doorstep. This was held to be effective service. Dr Wharry flew into a rage and, calling his servants, chased them off the premises.

Dr Wharry was subsequently prosecuted for assaulting a process server acting in the course of his duties and stood trial at the Old Bailey in London, initially pleading Not Guilty. My father and his colleague were ordered to attend as prosecution witnesses. Neither had been East of Exeter before and it was a great adventure. When they arrived in London they were told that the case would start a day late. The only place in London they had heard of was Madam Tussaud's waxworks and so they spent the day there. In the event Dr Wharry changed his plea to Guilty and their evidence was not required. My father had never before then slept a night away from home. The writ to be served on Miss Wharry related to the arson at Kew but I do not know if it was a civil claim for damages or a criminal summons.

James M. Rowland

Olive was arrested and imprisoned a total of eight times up to August 1914, often using the aliases Phyllis North, Joyce Locke or Eileen Ware. Although she became so well known her actual name was often added on the arrest sheet underneath her alias. Her co-conspirator at Kew, Lilian Lenton, later boasted, 'Whenever I was out of prison my object was to burn two buildings a week... The mission was to create an absolutely impossible condition of affairs in the country, to prove it was impossible to govern without the consent of the governed.' It was a stance approved of by Flora Drummond, a prominent figure in the WSPU leadership. Flora, or General Drummond as she was known, had been a key worker with the WSPU since 1906. The success of the numerous processions and demonstrations were down to her organising flair. When interviewed by the press, she stated that incidents such as the burning of Lloyd George's house showed the determination of the women. 'It is an example of how far they will go and we are proud of such women.'

Sylvia Pankhust described this escalation of violence in her *History of the Women's Militant Movement:*

The brief truce before the withdrawal of the Reform [Manhood Suffrage] Bill and its amendments, was followed by destructive militancy on a hitherto unparalleled scale... Boat-houses and sports pavilions in England, Ireland and Scotland, and a grandstand at Ayr race-course were burnt down. Mrs. Cohen... broke the glass of a jewel-case in the Tower of London. Works of art and objects of exceptional value became the target of determined militants. Thirteen pictures were hacked in the Manchester Art Gallery. Refreshment pavilions were burnt down in Regent's Park and Kew Gardens, where the glass in three orchid houses was smashed, and the plants, thus exposed, were broken and torn up by the roots. Empty houses and other unattended buildings were systematically sought out and set on fire, and many were destroyed... Hugh Franklin set fire to an empty railway carriage; he was imprisoned and forcibly fed. An old cannon was fired near Dudley Castle, shattering glass and terrifying the neighbourhood. Bombs were placed near the Bank of England, at

Wheatley Hall, Doncaster, at Oxted Station, and on the steps of a Dublin Insurance Office.

Not only arson, but bombs were now part of the suffragettes arsenal. It was a strategy that brought a deluge of publicity, usually not the kind they hoped for. Undeterred, the Ilfracombe group retaliated with two letters to the *Gazette* simply signed 'Another tax resister,' and 'A tax-paying English woman.' The second is headed:

MILITANT SUFFRAGETTES

Dear Sir - The Press has lately been much concerned with certain attacks on property by certain women. With great unction the papers have gloated over harrowing details of suffrage arsenals, of arson or ruined golf greens and have shed tear after tear of printer's ink in recording the doleful deeds of the "Wild Women". Visions of universal anarchy in which howling female fiends predominate, rise to the minds of the trembling readers as the future probably in store for this unhappy country. Now, sir, we have been so consistently fed with this same highly spiced food, that we are a little satiated with it. What about change? Suppose your interesting paper leads the way, and gives us a weekly diet of some of the reasons and happenings which have gradually driven women into a violence which they hate.

The writer cites the shameful fiasco regarding a women's amendment to the Reform Bill and pours scorn on Cabinet Minister's promises:

Secondly, I suggest that instead of somewhat highly coloured accounts of the "Wild Women's" doings, the press should make a few plain, straight-forward and truthful remarks as to the violent, outrageous and indecent assaults by men on women at various deputations, political and suffrage meetings... These little failings of the male sex, however, the Press usually pass over.

> Now if she's speaking in the street,
> Or any other place,
> Bring up your eggs, or clods of turf,
> And hit her in the face.

> March up, brave boys! By hundreds charge,
> Upset her on the ground!
> Then sit upon her head and twist
> Her elbow gently round.
> March in from all your clubs and pubs
> And toot your motor horn,
> For new sport came to Englishmen
> When Suffragettes were born.

I suggest that when women's attacks upon property receive attention, a little of the limelight should turn on men's attacks on their persons.

Thirdly I suggest that the Press... should endeavour seriously to find the remedy for these distracting events. As it is remarkably simple... it seems extraordinary to us simple-minded women that there should be any difficulty about it. Give us the Vote, that is all... Could anything be more beautifully simple? Why then does the Press not submit that simple remedy to the British public with the same lavish and overflowing generosity with which it submits statements intended to do harm to the women's cause? We cannot admit that the enlightened pressmen of to-day are ignorant; it is unthinkable. We cannot think they are prejudiced: it is unbelievable. We cannot persuade ourselves they are afraid of a few women putting a cross on a ballot paper; it is incredible. The only thing to suppose is that it simply hasn't occurred to them that the thing could be settled so easily. Perhaps, Sir, you will lead the way to the enlightenment of your fellow editors on this point and by so doing earn the gratitude of the women who want freedom, and the men who want peace.

This forthright letter, written by Marie Newby, Annie Ball or Margaret Eldridge - or perhaps composed jointly - oozes with frustration at men's inability to grasp the obvious solution. Give women the vote.

Someone else defending militancy in the press was Edith Clarence, from Axminster. In May she took issue with an article in the *Common*

Cause which stated, 'Militancy has introduced into the Suffrage movement elements of revenge, of contempt for others, of unreason, of deafness to honest and considered criticism, which in a movement which stands for peace and justice and humanity are tragic.' Edith wrote to suggest that, '...if such discordant elements exist in the Suffrage movement to-day, they were not introduced into it by the Militants, but by the Liberal Government...'

The editor posted a rebuttal, claiming that the militants' constant attempts to make others responsible for their actions was lamentable. and, '...the plea that "Men have done these things, Cabinet Ministers have taunted us, politicians have been treacherous first," is a confession of weakness.' Edith responded, clarifying that she hadn't intended to excuse the militants. 'They are quite willing to accept the responsibility of their own actions; it only seemed to me unjust to make them responsible for the errors of the Government as well.' The editor remained unconvinced, but this didn't dent Edith's enthusiasm for the WSPU. She had been a supporter for several years and despite, or perhaps because of, a prison sentence was still active locally and nationally.

The previous year she had taken part in a holiday campaign in Largs, Scotland, and now returned to spend two weeks as a visiting speaker in Glasgow. Then in October she travelled to Southampton where, as the *Suffragette* announced, '...a record Church Congress must mean nothing less than a record WSPU campaign... We urge all members of the WSPU who feel that what the clergy think about Woman Suffrage is a matter of importance to see to it that they take their part in one way or another in the "Church Congress". Edith responded, delivering speeches twice daily from the vantage point of the Clock Tower. It was a demonstration of commitment to the WSPU that she was to continue, both in Devon and further afield.

A SUFFRAGE TUG OF WAR.

A. PATRIOT

Chapter Twenty-Six
Unity and Revival
Spring - Summer 1913

In the spring of 1913, the Ilfracombe suffragettes followed the
example of Exeter, Plymouth and Torquay and rented a shop at 2
High Street. The high ceilinged rooms displayed vibrant banners
declaring 'God defend us for our cause is just', 'Votes for Women'
and 'Great is Truth and will Prevail'. They formed an impressive
backdrop for the fifty or more Ilfracombe residents who took up the
women's invitation to attend three weekly debates.

The usual arguments were aired - that men were superior to
women, women cannot fight and therefore should not have the vote,
that woman's place is in the home. Annie Ball and Margaret Eldridge
fielded most of the objections, including repeated accusations that
militants had set the movement back rather than advancing it. At the

second debate, reported in the *Ilfracombe Gazette,* the antis were
particularly outspoken. 'Women are not physically fitted to sit in the
House of Commons, as it needs a strong physique to stand the
strain... The natives of our Indian possessions would not be loyal if
they knew that England was governed by women... To give votes to
women would mean breaking up home life, which is the greatest asset
this country has ever had... This country must be guided by the
steady hand of man.' Cue loud laughter from the women, possibly
tinged with exasperation. Had they made no inroads into the
entrenched attitudes of the past five decades?

Annie Ball countered. 'An MP was telling his son how he should
deal with correspondents. "Letters from voters should be attended to
at once, and after these the letters from potential voters, but letters
from women could be torn up and thrown in the waste-paper basket."
If the Government had something to get from women in the shape
of the vote, the women would soon have their grievances redressed.'
But the topic of militancy again dominated the second debate. A Mr
Stephens commented, 'Thirty years ago I was in favour of Women
Suffrage, but I had no idea then that women would make such fools
of themselves. If anything has done harm to the movement it is
militancy, which is one of the greatest curses seen in our land. When
women will get the vote now I do not know.'

Well rehearsed arguments ranged back and forth at the final
debate but by the end there was no doubt where some of the women
stood. The heading in the *Ilfracombe Gazette* read:

MILITANTS TACTICS
ILFRACOMBE SUFFRAGETTES ATTITUDE
About a dozen ladies voted in favour of militancy at the third
debate on Woman Suffrage held at the room of the
Ilfracombe Suffrage Society, 2 High St, on Friday evening last.

The women had obviously made an impact, with new members
continuing to join just in time to hear a significant speaker in the
militant campaign. A notice in the *Ilfracombe Gazette* announced, 'This
will be the first time that a representative of one of the men's unions
has spoken in Ilfracombe.' Charles Gray, the pseudonym adopted by
Paul Gliddon to protect his family, was a key member of the Men's

Political Union. It was founded in 1909 as a militant organisation of male suffragists, even adopting the WSPU colours. Henry Harben, the candidate for Barnstaple who had resigned over the force-feeding of women, was a familiar and well-liked face in the Union. He and his wife Agnes had continued to show their support for suffragettes by offering respite at Newland Park, their Buckinghamshire home, for any released under the Cat and Mouse Act. Ilfracombe WSPU had recently sent him a gold-mounted walking stick as a mark of their esteem and gratitude for his principled stand in resigning his candidacy.

They now listened as Charles Gray rose to speak:

Men have no right to deny women the vote. Some women are infinitely superior to some men who exercise the vote. In today's papers there is an account of a woman who has been appointed a Justice of the Peace. Part of her duties will be to certify whether men are sane or insane… It's absurd that she can do this, but is not allowed to vote herself… Instead of trying to crush the movement, the Government should see there is a wrong, and a reason for the discontent. If the Government had been more statesmanlike they would have looked further into the question; they would have seen that militant methods would never have been taken up by women if there had not been real and fundamental reasons beneath.

The *Gazette* continued, '…it may not be generally known that there are several men's societies to which many well-known men who believe in the justice of Votes for Women belong.' One of these was the next society to be represented in Ilfracombe, the Church League for Women's Suffrage. Lieut. John Leonard Cather was the Hon. Secretary and someone who had made his views plain at the time of the census. He refused to complete details of the women in his house while they had no voice. Invitations to the meeting were issued by the Church League organiser who just happened to be - Marie Newby. Like several in the south of the county, she was now actively campaigning in more than one organisation.

Others following a similar path in the spring of 1913 included Marion Phillips, Gwyneth Keys and Edith Fewins. They were still active within the Plymouth NUWSS but entries in the *Suffragette* record them also helping Mary Phillips, the new WSPU organiser, revitalise the campaign there. A programme of events was launched with an 'At Home' at Goodbody's cafe. Further plans included a visit from Mrs Pankhurst on 8 April, an active Self Denial week and more 'At Homes' at the Mikado cafe in Old Town. As it turned out, Emmeline Pankhurst was arrested so was unable to make it to Plymouth. Edith Fewins stepped into the breach, entertaining the audience at the Mikado with her accounts of touring the Midlands with the Suffrage caravan. There was also a special push to increase sales of the *Suffragette*. Marion Phillips was particularly successful, persuading a newsagent to display the paper prominently for two weeks on a sale or return basis. The whole campaign worked; within two weeks they'd sold a hundred copies and more talks were scheduled.

Familiar faces from their NUWSS involvement joined Marion, Edith and Gwyneth in Plymouth. Hatty Baker and Maud Slater were booked as speakers and Frances Latimer agreed to preside at a series of talks. Frances also offered to help Amy Montague at an Exeter WSPU meeting. Miss Tuker from Axminster was to have chaired but she was indisposed - quite possibly because she had again refused to pay her taxes and expected her goods to be seized imminently. They were joined by Mary Phillips, who gave what can only be described as an eye-opening speech condoning a bomb recently placed in St Paul's Cathedral. Her controversial words were reported in the *Western Times*. 'Militancy was intended to awaken people to the justice of the women's cause, and if suffragettes placed a bomb in St Pauls that was a method of getting at the Church people. The Church... had been shamefully inert over this question... although the church was supposed to champion just causes... Even National Treasures like St Pauls must not be allowed to stand before justice to the womanhood of the nation.' It was a disturbing insight into the WSPU reasoning behind the arson and bombing campaigns, views she was soon to expand on in Torquay and Ilfracombe.

Meanwhile it was all hands on deck in Plymouth to welcome Charles Gray, fresh from his meeting in Ilfracombe. He received an enthusiastic reception for his address, interpreted as, '...a clear justification of militancy'. A significant collection was taken, with a very specific purpose in mind. A summer festival was to be held at the Kensington Empress Room in London. West of England groups were stocking the basket stall but Plymouth decided the collection should go towards providing 4lb of Devonshire cream daily!

The next time Marion Phillips addressed the group, at the beginning of June, it was with a heavier heart. Someone who had been in Holloway at the same time as Marie Newby was Emily Wilding Davison. The news they now heard of her, described here by Emmeline Pankhurst, was devastating:

> Emily Wilding Davison, who had been associated with the militant movement since 1906, gave up her life for the women's cause by throwing herself in the path of the thing, next to property, held most sacred to Englishmen - sport. Miss Davison went to the races at Epsom, and breaking through the barriers which separated the vast crowds from the race course, rushed in the path of the galloping horses and caught the bridle of the King's horse, which was leading all the others. The horse fell, throwing his jockey and crushing Miss Davison in such shocking fashion that she was carried from the course in a dying condition.
>
> Emily Wilding Davison was a B. A. of London University, and had taken first class honours at Oxford in English Language and Literature. Yet the women's cause made such an appeal to her reason and her sympathies that she put every intellectual and social appeal aside and devoted herself untiringly and fearlessly to the work of the Union. She had suffered many imprisonments, had been forcibly fed and most brutally treated.
>
> On one occasion when she had barricaded her cell against the prison doctors, a hose pipe was turned on her from the window and she was drenched and all but drowned in the icy water while workmen were breaking down her cell door. Miss Davison, after this experience, expressed to several of her friends the deep conviction that now, as in days called uncivilised, the conscience of the people would awaken only to the sacrifice of a human life.

At one time in prison she tried to kill herself by throwing herself head-long from one of the upper galleries, but she succeeded only in sustaining cruel injuries. Ever after that time she clung to her conviction that one great tragedy, the deliberate throwing into the breach of a human life, would put an end to the intolerable torture of women. And so she threw herself at the King's horse, in full view of the King and Queen and a great multitude of their Majesties subjects, offering up her life as a petition to the King, praying for the release of suffering women throughout England and the world.

Whether Emily 'offered up her life' is still open to question but, whatever the motive, her death rocked and galvanised the movement. Ilfracombe even held a special meeting to welcome the many new members who joined as a result of the news. They sent a cross of flowers in the colours for the funeral while Plymouth opted for a laurel wreath with purple and white ribbons attached, displayed for a while in Messrs Williams' window in Union Street.

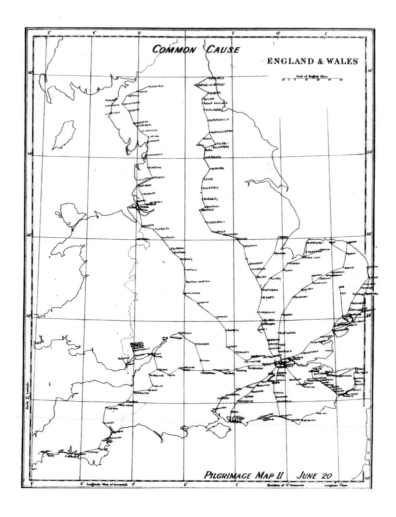

Chapter Twenty-Seven
Devon Pilgrims
Summer 1913

While shocked by the death of Emily Davison, NUWSS members
were intent on continuing to publicise their moderate suffragist cause
step by step, literally, with a Great Pilgrimage. Women were to march
from all parts of England and Wales, including the West Country,
culminating in a mass gathering at Hyde Park in London. Mabel
Ramsay set out their reasoning in the *Common Cause*. 'It is the

conviction of every National Unionist that the Suffrage cause has all to gain and nothing to lose by the education of the public, not only on Suffrage itself, but on all questions of public interest.' But she recognised it would be a long haul. 'It is evidently becoming a question of persistence whether we win the vote at once or not. Politicians always hope they can wear down the patience and enthusiasm of those who clamour for reform... But the least sign of discouragement on our part puts fresh heart into our opponents, and we must see to it that no such encouragement is given.'

Contributions poured in from groups across the country, Barnstaple alone raised £2 9s, [almost £350 today] and on 18 June 1913 preparations were complete. Seven women set out from Land's End attracting curious, and occasionally hostile, crowds as they progressed through Cornwall into Devon. The *Common Cause* reported, '...an extraordinary amount of interest shown by the public... In every important town the audiences can be reckoned in four figures... An enormous amount of propaganda has been accomplished. Eighty dozen *Common Causes* sold so far. The Pilgrims are accompanied by a large covered van with its head-board painted, "Land's End to London" with the red, white and green lettering on its tilt describing the National Union and its methods. Through the length of Cornwall there is a new understanding of the meaning of the suffrage movement...' The colours were displayed on a shoulder sash and marchers were encouraged to wear a raffia cockle shell, the traditional symbol of pilgrimage, pinned to their hats.

After winding their way from Penzance to Camborne, Falmouth. Truro, Bodmin, St Austell and Fowey they arrived to an enormous, and at times unruly, crowd of around 1,500 at Looe, approximately half the town's population. Then it was on to a rousing reception at Plymouth Corn Exchange where they were welcomed by Mabel Ramsay. It was an emotional reunion. Someone who made the entire pilgrimage, part walking, part travelling in the van, was her mother, Annie Ramsay, then in her sixties.

On 1 July the pilgrimage was warmly received at Totnes before moving on, with some trepidation, to Newton Abbot. The *Common Cause* reported, 'Here Mr Murren took the chair and we had a crowded but most orderly meeting of some 3,000 persons. The undisturbed hearing accorded to our speakers was a surprise to everyone for Newton Abbot is notorious for turbulent meetings, and it had been freely professed that we should have disorder.' They were still thinking of the treatment Mrs Pankhurst received in 1908 and the experiences of Mary Mills and Miss Potter later the same year. But apparently the Devon lap saw very little disorder due, according to the *Common Cause*, to the, '...less excitable nature of the people [compared to Cornwall!] Also, the police protected us with special care and have shown admirable firmness in their handling of the crowds.'

On 4 July the Pilgrims left Teignmouth and held meetings at Dawlish and Starcross before crossing by ferry to Exmouth. The following day the *Western Times* covered their progress towards Exeter:

The South West section of the great Suffragist Pilgrimage to London reached Exeter on Saturday. The Pilgrims who have come all the way from Land's End - including Mrs Ramsay (Plymouth) Miss Baly (Exeter) Miss Davis, Miss Misick and Miss Fielder - left Exmouth at about eleven a.m. A large number of sympathisers saw them off, together with many members of the Exmouth society, cycling and on foot, headed by their white banner, appliquéd with red berries and green leaves, and including Miss Joan Retallack (hon. secretary) and Miss Fell (hon. treasurer) who accompanied them all along the road. Rev. Arthur Poulton (Vicar of Kenton) also joined the party, as well as the

Budleigh Salterton group, headed by their handsome banner, and accompanied by Miss Mathieson, who is succeeding Mrs Penry as Hon. secretary of the whole South Western Federation.

'Small meetings were held at Lympstone... and Exton. At Topsham an open air meeting had been arranged by the local branch... Members then joined the Pilgrims for the march to Exeter. They were headed by the large Topsham banner, in the red, white and green colours, carried by Miss Hester Frood and Miss Constance Frood... At Countess Wear Bridge the party was augmented by a Torquay contingent brought by Admiral Sir William Acland in his red, white and green decorated motor car... The Pilgrims, who arrived rather before time, were entertained to tea... joined by representatives from Sidmouth, Teignmouth and Crediton.

Olga Fletcher and others in the Exeter Society had organised a great demonstration. About 300 suffragists marched in procession through the streets, '...providing a most picturesque spectacle with their gallant show of banners. At the end of the procession a monster meeting was held at the bottom of Paris Street, where some six or seven thousand people assembled.' Even at the more conservative end, a crowd of six thousand spectators was impressive.

The following morning the Pilgrimage moved on to Tiverton, Wellington and Taunton. Some spectators confused them with the militants, particularly in Cornwall, but protests were milder by the time they reached Somerset. One man who allowed them to rest in his orchard remarked, 'You may burn the nettles, but please leave me my apple trees.' The ladies continued to attract large crowds, stopping to hold rallies at Bridgwater, Street and in the natural amphitheatre halfway up Cheddar Gorge. They joined pilgrims from Bristol, Bath, Gloucester, Swindon and all places in between until finally massing in Hyde Park, contributing to the estimated crowd of 50,000 finally gathered there.

It was a memorable occasion as recounted in the *Western Times* by 'One of the Pilgrims':

Meet at Warwick Garden, Kensington, at 2.30. So ran the order of the day for the West of England contingent of the great Suffrage Pilgrimage which culminated in Saturday's demonstration in Hyde Park. The large open space encircled by Warwick Garden's two crescents was already thronged with Suffragists when one reached the rendezvous... Banners were being unfurled, and guides, stewards and marshals were arranging the positions of the various sections.

The famous Exeter-built "Land's End to London" van and well-groomed Devon horse... at once attracted the attention of Devonians. Both here, as throughout the pilgrimage, in charge of the trusty driver, Jack Hussey, of Ottery St Mary, who has had the unique experience - for this twentieth century - of making his first journey to London in five weeks by road instead of the more usual five hours by rail.

Four generations of the Bright family took part in the Pilgrimage. John Bright's great-grandsons took a collection of 12s between them. Among those in the picture are Miss Frances Sterling who walked nearly the whole way from Cornwall, and addressed innumerable meetings all the way along the route, and Mrs Ramsay.

Every moment brought fresh arrivals. The veteran Lord Courtney, of Penwith, and Lady Courtney (President of the South-West Federation, N.U.W.S.S.) were present to watch the marshalling of the procession and later followed in their carriage. In the interval one gleaned from the last-named the interesting fact that her honoured husband's first speech in the House of Commons (as of course Mr Leonard Courtney) was made on behalf of Women's Suffrage. 'That was in 1876," Lady

Courtney added, "and if he was not quite howled down, the matter was treated with infinitely less respect than it commands among Parliamentarians today."

...Madame Beatrice Langley, handsome in a navy-blue coat and skirt, and tan Tagel hat with black ostrich plumes, who had made a hurried journey across London on purpose to join the party from her native town, was walking with the Teignmouth banner which Miss Wood carried. Miss Montgomery (Exmouth) was banner bearer for that Society, and Miss Lisle, who joined the Pilgrims on the road at Exeter, carried the Sidmouth banner.

Other Westcountry Suffragists marching included... Miss Dutton and Miss Barney (Sidmouth), Miss Walford, Miss Collier and Miss Edith Splatt (Exeter) [most likely the author of this piece] and Mrs Barton (Newton Abbot)... while many others, unable to reach London in time for the procession, joined the various parties round the South-West and West platforms in the Park.

The place of honour next to the big "Lands End to London" banner was naturally reserved for Mrs Ramsay, mother of Dr Mabel Ramsay, of Plymouth, who has speedily vindicated the Devonshire reputation for courage and endurance by the cheery sangfroid with which, despite her sixty-odd years, she has met the difficulties, and, in some occasions, positive dangers of the Pilgrims Way. Setting out from Land's End, Mrs Ramsay resolved, she confesses, that she would fine herself two-pence for the collecting box for each mile if she failed to walk at least three each day. She merrily boasted at the journey's end that she had only to pay the fine twice in the whole five weeks. Carrying a bouquet of carnations in the colours, which had been presented to her by those who were proud to call themselves her

"Pilgrimage daughters", Mrs Ramsay led the South West Federation's march with a firm and swinging step and made a rousing, humorous speech from her appointed platform at its conclusion. Miss Baly (who carried the Exeter banner), Miss Misick, Miss Chambers, and Miss Helen Fraser were the others in the procession who had shared Mrs Ramsay's enterprise in making the start from Land's End.

The Pilgrimage was hailed as a great success. For once the non-militants were grabbing the headlines, raising awareness of women's campaign for the vote through speeches, sales of the Common Cause and their very presence.

But some, for instance QUISQUIS [literally translated, 'Whoever'] writing in the *Exeter and Plymouth Gazette*, saw it differently:

An "Observant Man" sends me the following notes about the "pilgrims march," which, so far as I have been able to judge, fairly represents the opinion of the majority of the citizens: What funny people these Suffragists - or is it Suffragettes?- are! One party hopes to gain the elusive vote by burning down houses and horse-whipping Cabinet Ministers, and the other by taking a little constitutional from Land's End to London... The word pilgrimage strikes this mere man as something of a misnomer when applied to this country stroll of the ladies... Their progress through the city... was viewed by dense crowds of people, who, although they did not interrupt the triumphal progress of ladies, carts, cars and a motley assortment of banners, looked on with a smile. Of course the ladies regarded the numbers as representing the interest taken in the movement by Exeter. But... the enforced progress of a drunken woman to the police court would have drawn almost as large a crowd. Exeter, it must be remembered, is keen on free amusement, and it was frankly amused by the ladies of the road.

[At the meeting at Gervase Road] The resolution calling upon the government to introduce without delay a Bill for the enfranchisement of women was put. The Chairman said it was undecided whether it was carried or not, but anyone who was without bias would have no hesitation in saying that it was not -

decidedly not… On the whole, I am afraid the ladies must regard their visit to Exeter as something of a "wash out", although the resolution at the second meeting [the triangle at the bottom of Paris Street] was decided as carried… The 'pilgrimage' strikes all sane people as something of a farce.

There were other tensions along the way with hostile crowds in Cornwall taunting the women with cries such as, 'watch out for the bomb in her pocket'. But on the whole they were met with good-natured interest. Whether the pilgrimage had any long-lasting impact across the country is difficult to say but its place in raising morale within the NUWSS was undeniable. Their conviction was growing that 'Votes For Women' was achievable, and through reason not rebellion.

Chapter Twenty-Eight
Militancy Crosses the Border
Summer 1913

Another organisation also planning to make an impact in Devon was the Women's Freedom League [WFL]. Since splitting with the WSPU they had made only a brief appearance in the county, in Torquay for the 1910 election, but they now announced their own Devonshire Holiday Campaign. Constance Andrews, a travelling organiser, took charge from their rented HQ at 5, Wellswood Road, Torquay. The campaign began on 3 July with meetings planned in Exmouth, Exeter, Sidmouth, Teignmouth, Dawlish and Newton Abbot, possibly to raise awareness on the back of the suffragists pilgrimage. They certainly met the pilgrims at Exeter - and worked the crowds there selling *The Vote* - but campaign reports concentrated on work closer to their HQ, with meetings in Torquay, Paignton and Babbacombe. Two weeks in, Constance commented in *The Vote*, 'We have had some opposition, as our movement is practically unknown here, but that only adds zest to our determination to convert this little corner of England to the cause of Women's Suffrage. There's a delightful green at Babbacombe overlooking Torbay where we held our meetings; many of the inhabitants come as well as the visitors. It was been uphill work to make the women understand what we are working for, but once they are convinced we feel sure they will become very staunch supporters.' Perhaps she was unaware of the grudge held locally after the WSPU's opposition to their Liberal candidate.

Feelings had also been stirred up by direct action taken just three weeks earlier, reported in the *Western Morning News*. 'In the pillar letter box at Upton, Torquay, last evening, was found an envelope containing three cartridges, and the wording on the envelope was "To do away with militants give justice to women." In the Castle Circus Street box several letters were found more or less burnt. A similar outrage was committed at the box in Forest Road. The police subsequently watched all the letter-boxes in the town and neighbourhood, but up to a late hour last night no clue had been obtained as to the offenders.' Was it simply chance that these events coincided with the arrival of the WFL, an organisation also committed to militancy?

Early in the campaign, Constance Andrews wrote, 'The crowds at Babbacombe and Torquay have been orderly and attentive, and have given the speakers a fair hearing, though it is evident that we have many "Antis" among the audience.' Although there was respect for the speakers with one anti saying, 'I don't agree with her, but I like the way she puts her subject.' Their mixed reception continued until the crowds grasped the women's cause. Constance commented, rather patronisingly to modern ears, 'We find Devonshire women are willing to acknowledge a fault. Many of them who came to our meetings to jeer have altered their minds on hearing our speeches, and have asked forgiveness for not understanding what we really wanted.' That is, not the vote for all women, as the WSPU were asking after their outrage over the Manhood Suffrage Bill, but simply on the same terms as men.

In July they arranged indoor meetings at Babbacombe and then took a boat to Brixham for their first ever meeting there. 'On landing we came across a statue of William of Orange who landed there in 1688... We excited great curiosity in the town, and found it hard to get away from the children who surrounded us. We had a good meeting and were escorted back to the boat by policemen, who were solicitous that we should not be molested.'

By the middle of August, Constance felt they were making progress. 'Interest has certainly been aroused, and we expect that Devonshire will respond to the call of the Women's Freedom League, and will demand the formation of Branches. Paignton Regatta has been one of the events of the week; we were in despair at finding our pitch occupied by roundabouts and fairs, and had to content ourselves by selling *The Vote*. Sandwiched in between men selling toy bagpipes and tiny balloons, it was amusing to watch the expressions of the Excursionists who gazed upon us sometimes with scorn and sometimes with amusement.' Possibly a disheartening confirmation of a lack of progress.

On 20 August, the *Dartmouth & South Hams Chronicle* reported a WFL meeting. 'On Wednesday of last week the picturesque neighbourhood of Stoke Fleming was invaded by Suffragists. By kind permission of Mrs Barnet a "Votes for Women" meeting was held at Penlee.' This substantial house in a spectacular position on the coast near Stoke Fleming was already a popular high-end holiday destination. According to *The Vote*, '...a Suffrage atmosphere must already have been created as we found our Indian friend and fellow member, Mrs Dubé there.' Despite her earlier comments about the difficulty in getting women to understand what the WFL stood for, she was obviously open to some cooperative working. This meeting was held jointly with Greta Allen, representing the WSPU.

By the end of August, Constance had been won over by Devon's charms. 'Devonshire is a delightful place for a campaign, because when you can snatch a little time away from the incessant meetings you can get away to the moors which are enchanting just now. The gorse is in its full glory, and added to the heather makes a scene of beauty not easily to be described… It has taken a long time to educate people to know that the Suffrage societies have different ways of working and that, though we have a common object, we use different means to attain it… We have one more week in which we hope to put a seal upon the work already accomplished.'

In September, as the campaign came to an end, the most significant accomplishment was the formation of the Torquay and Paignton WFL branch. Mrs Gwynne Dyer was to be honorary secretary, although the wording in *The Vote* was interesting. Constance recorded that Mrs Dyer had *promised* to act as the Secretary - so perhaps not a done deal. Other mainstays of the campaign were Miss Howard, who was thanked for her hospitality and devoting herself to sales of *The Vote,* Miss Woodall, Mrs Hyde and Mrs Pratt, who took collections and rather wonderfully, '… helped to keep noisy sections of the audience in order'. As well as '…another worker whose name may not appear.' Very curious.

For a couple of months Torquay proudly took its place in the list of branches detailed in *The Vote*, giving Gwynne Dyer as the contact. However, by November and through into January 1914 Torquay still had a listing, but without any contact details. It seems that after the enthusiasm of the intensive holiday campaign organised by Constance, the WFL presence in Torquay wasn't self-sustaining.

Meanwhile, the WSPU branch in Ilfracombe, was consolidating its position with an influx of new members in the wake of Emily Wilding Davison's death. The group they joined had fundamentally changed. The recent vote at the open meeting in favour of militancy had forged a new sense of purpose, one that may have consolidated as the controversial tactics of the militant suffragettes crept much closer to home.

Devon residents were unused to reading about militant violence in their home county. There had been reports of pillar boxes attacked and telephone wires cut but nothing like the shocking headlines they woke to on 19 April 1913:

'Plymouth Hoe Bomb', *Teignmouth Post.*
'Plymouth Sensation, Daring attempt to Blow Up Smeaton's
   Tower.' *Western Times.*
'Bomb on the Hoe' *Western Morning News.*

Smeaton's Tower, one of the most prominent landmarks on
Plymouth Hoe, is the old lighthouse that had stood for a century and
a half on the Eddystone Reef. It had been targeted a couple of weeks
earlier to coincide with a visit from Churchill to inspect the
Devonport dockyards. Suffragettes had used white enamel to paint,
'To Mr Churchill. No security till you give women votes, no matter
how big the navy,' and, 'To save the State from shipwreck give women
the vote,' across the Tower.

   Their threat was real. Two weeks later a Mr Chubb was passing
the Tower early on Saturday morning when he noticed a small zinc
container lying against the door. It was cylindrical with a piece of
wick protruding through the cover and printed on it in black letters
were the words, "Votes for Women. Death in ten minutes."
Apparently unfazed, Mr Chubb carried what he believed to be a
bomb to the police. They immediately immersed it in water, before
cutting the top off to reveal a quantity of gunpowder surrounding a
metal tube filled with paraffin that contained the wick. Worryingly the
police could see that the wick had been lit but they believed the wind
had blown it out before it could reach the gunpowder.

   Mabel Ramsay, when approached by the *Western Morning News,*
said she, '...had heard nothing about the bomb... Her own opinion
was that the whole affair was a joke. From the description of the
canister she thought it would appear to be the work of a man, rather
than a woman, and even had it exploded the result would not have
been serious.' She obviously wanted to downplay the whole incident,
possibly because of her ongoing battle to persuade women to support
the moderate's fight for the vote in the face of a tsunami of negative
publicity generated by WSPU militancy.

   But nationally bomb attacks were becoming more frequent.
There were reported at the Bank of England, in the sorting
department of Reading Post Office, on a Waterloo train, in the
Cambridge University football pavilion, in the waiting room at Lime

Street Station, at Aberdeen Railway Station and at a newspaper office in York. There was also a close call with one delivered to Bow Street Magistrates Court. None of these exploded but a bomb thrown from a train crossing the Mersey and another at the Royal Observatory in Edinburgh caused significant damage.

For many WSPU members the suffragettes crossed the line with this spate of bombing, particularly on top of the arson campaign - they had set fire to 14 properties since March, causing thousands of pounds worth of damage. In contrast to the public perception, most of these militant acts weren't carried out by passionate, grass-root supporters of the cause but by travelling militants. They were women such as Olive Wharry, Lilian Lenton and Kitty Marion, all on the payroll of the WSPU and earning salaries anything up to four times the average working wage. It became a full-time occupation for some. Simon Webb, in *The Suffragette Bombers,* theorises that militancy offered the chance for excitement, adventure and travel and that some suffragettes may have become addicted to violence and danger.

It's a perspective that challenges the popular view that they honestly believed violence would force the government to capitulate and grant women the franchise. Had these undoubtedly intelligent women considered that this campaign was becoming increasingly counter-productive? Or were they on a slippery slope into greater acts of destruction to secure the attention they craved? With echoes of the falling out with the WFL, Emmeline and Christabel appeared content to lose a mass membership in favour of a hard core of largely middle and upper class women. Women who were happy to take orders from their charismatic leader and to keep the WSPU afloat with the significant donations that, perhaps surprisingly, increased as militancy intensified.

Whatever the internal dynamics of the WSPU, there was no doubt that Devon was now being targeted. After the bomb at Plymouth, more postboxes were attacked and windows at the back of the Inland Revenue offices in Plymouth were smashed. A notice was found which read, 'Plymouth Suffragists' message to the Government. You have raided our head office but cannot stop militancy except by giving us the vote.' In June an attempt to derail the London to Plymouth Express by placing sleepers on the line was blamed on the Suffragettes but the WSPU issued a denial. 'IMPORTANT. The Women's Social and Political Union are able to state emphatically that the alleged attempt to wreck the London-Plymouth Express is not the work of Suffragettes, as such action would be contrary to the policy of the Union. No interference with the railway system is sanctioned by the WSPU.' Curious given that actions had already taken place involving the railways. But the *Western Evening Herald* supported their denial. 'All the evidence goes to show that the sleepers were placed on the line by mischievous boys, whose monkey tricks are about as rational as those of the mischievous women.'

Then in July 1913 an incident close to the Devon border was announced in the *Langport and Somerton Herald*:

> Attempted Suffragette Outrage at Taunton. A most serious Suffragette outrage was attempted in Taunton during Thursday night of last week when a glass cylindrical bomb was placed inside the palisading around the Lyceum Theatre, which is now fast nearing completion. The bomb comprised a glass cylinder, filled with petrol and fitted with a fuse, connections, and an explosive cartridge... the malicious intent of the perpetrators of the outrage may easily be seen by the fact that the bomb was placed just inside the very high fencing where there are thousands of feet of woodwork of a most combustible character... Attached to the bomb was a piece of stout paper with the following significant sentences clearly written in thick ink - "Votes for Women"; "Judges beware"; "Martyrs of the Law'; and "Release our Sisters."

The presence of the 'stout paper' does beg the question whether the bomb was intended to ignite as the message would have been incinerated if the fuse had been lit, but the messages were certainly prescient for events about to unfold in North Devon.

In July the Ilfracombe group welcomed Mary Phillips to address them on the need for continuing militancy. The *North Devon Herald* reported her claim that, '...the responsibility for it [militancy] lay entirely with the Government, which had turned a deaf ear to argument and reason and had treated the question in Parliament by a series of discreditable tricks and evasions, refusing to give time for suffrage Bills to become law even after they had secured large majorities on their second readings, and had imprisoned and tortured women when they protested, even by the very mild militancy of the early days of the WSPU.' It was a predictable stance from someone who, after a bomb had been placed in St Pauls, commented, '...even national treasures like St Pauls must not be allowed to stand before justice to the woman-hood of the nation.'

As far back as 1909, Mary had pressed Christabel for permission to take part in more militant activity. However organisers were forbidden to risk arrest through direct action, they were simply too valuable in their day to day role. Significantly, Christabel had just decided Mary wasn't effective as an organiser and had dismissed her. Mary had conceded that it had been difficult working up enthusiasm for the WSPU in Plymouth, leaving Christabel to conclude that if an area was reluctant to contribute sufficient finance or volunteers then they couldn't be provided with an organiser. Seemingly the renewed enthusiasm of Marion Phillips and others was insufficient to sustain the branch.

Christabel's claim that she was no longer effective was hard for Mary to hear, especially as she had previously been praised for her work. But she was no longer bound by the restrictions on her role, free to make her own choices about whether or not to take part in militancy. It may not have been a clear decision. According to Emily Blathwayt, Mary was having doubts about WSPU tactics, particularly arson. But she was clearly defending militancy to the substantial audience that gathered to hear her on this July evening in Ilfracombe.

Chapter Twenty-Nine
Flames of Injustice
Summer 1913

The twin towns of Lynton and Lynmouth sit by the coast where
Exmoor meets the sea. The Victorians christened the area 'Little
Switzerland,' reflecting the steep, wooded river valleys that link the
coastline with Exmoor. Visitors arrived by train on the line from
Barnstaple and moved between the two villages on the unique, water-
powered cliff railway, both bequests from the town's most significant
benefactor, Sir George Newnes. In 1890 he bought land above the
town known as Hollerday Hill and commissioned an imposing three-
storied mansion to be built there. No expense was spared. Inside its
stone and mullioned facade it offered twenty-one bedrooms, three
bathrooms, several staircases, a clutch of reception rooms and a
magnificent billiard room.

   Hollerday House became a magnet for some well-known figures
of the day, often connections made through George Newnes's
publishing empire. His runaway successes were *Tit-Bits* and *The Strand
Magazine.* In May 1901 *Tit-Bits* broke the news that, '…presently [Mr
Conan Doyle] will give us an important story to appear in *The Strand*,

in which the great Sherlock Holmes is the principal character.' A few weeks later *The Hound of the Baskervilles* made its debut. Arthur Conan Doyle became a personal friend and was guest of honour when the town unveiled the bust of Sir George at the new town hall. Significantly, Conan Doyle and Sir George had politics in common. Sir George became a Liberal MP in 1885, initially for the constituency of Newmarket then Swansea from 1900, while Conan Doyle stood as a Liberal Unionist in Edinburgh.

One topic Conan Doyle was quite clear on was women's suffrage. The *Times* reported his address to the National League for Opposing Woman Suffrage, given soon after a particularly destructive spate of militancy. 'Mr Conan Doyle said it was necessary to differentiate between the honest Constitutional Suffragist, the female hooligans and the even more contemptible class of people who supplied the latter with money to carry out their malicious monkey tricks… He believed that two years ago they might have had a chance of getting the vote but now they would not get it in a generation.'

Sir George Newnes was known for being a strong, rumbustious man, with a great presence, but during 1909 this began to change. The official line was that it was diabetes; village gossip had it as drink and depression. There was also talk of debts. Some said he was a gambler, others that he'd lost his touch and made bad investments. Whatever the reason, by the end of 1909, with his health failing, he decided to stand down from his Swansea seat. His retirement was planned and anticipated. By contrast, the  defeat of his son, Frank, also a Liberal MP, was a crushing blow, further undermining Sir George's health.

A few months later he was dead. It was a time of mourning in Lynton and Lynmouth. Businesses closed for the day and hundreds lined the route of the funeral procession for Sir George's final journey to the burial plot at the top of the town's graveyard, as close as he could get to his beloved Hollerday estate. Shortly after his death the truth emerged. There was nothing left of the wealth he had so generously shared with Lynton over the years. Frank Newnes had already taken on much of his father's work, becoming President of George Newnes Ltd, but it was an uphill battle saddled with enormous debts. Two years later he tried to sell the Hollerday estate.

By order of the Executors of the late Sir George Newnes, Bart
VERY BEAUTIFUL HOUSE
Commanding views of vast extent and surpassing grandeur
NORTH DEVON - "HOLLERDAY HOUSE", LYNTON,

The contents were auctioned but the house failed to reach the reserve. It was to remain empty for another two years, until one night in August 1913 when its political past caught up with it.

The events that sent shock waves across Devon began late in the evening of Monday 3 August when flames were spotted, as reported in the *North Devon Journal*:

It was 11.10pm to the minute on Monday when the first alarm of the outbreak was given. At that time PC Sparkes [such an appropriate name!] was in the square at Lynton. Hearing a woman shout near by, he looked up and at once saw that

Hollerday House was on fire. The constable sent a man to call ex-constable Bibbings, who promptly summoned the Fire Brigade, and meanwhile hastened up to Hollerday. At first sight it seemed as though a chimney in the tower end was on fire, but closer inspection showed that the staircase under the tower was ablaze. Shortly afterwards PC Sparkes observed another distinct fire on the ground floor in the centre of the mansion so that there were two fires raging separately at the same time in different parts of the house... Whilst inspecting the building and rendering all the help possible, PC Sparkes found the scullery window at the rear of the mansion open and it is supposed that the incendiary entered the building by this window... As time went on, floor after floor collapsed in the mansion, the flames rising to a tremendous height, and the noise at times caused by falling timber and masonry was deafening. The heat was terrific, and at some point the workers could not approach the fire within a distance of fifty feet. Finally the remaining portions of the roof collapsed...

On the hunt for an exclusive, the paper's representative quizzed Mr Slee, the caretaker, over a newspaper report that two ladies had obtained keys to the house on the Monday with a view to watching the sunset from the upper rooms. 'Mr Slee gave this report an emphatic disclaimer, and indirectly suggested an incident that had given rise to this report. On Saturday two American ladies (who had been staying at one of the local hotels) called at the Lodge and asked to be allowed to inspect Hollerday. They were conducted over the mansion by him the next morning. The ladies expressed delight with Hollerday and announced their intention of communicating with the London agents with a view to purchase. The same evening the ladies went up to Hollerday grounds to see the sunset, and he saw them leave by way of the Lodge entrance a little later. He had never allowed the keys out of his possession and the last time the ladies in question were in the house was Sunday morning. He (Mr Slee) had definitely ascertained that these ladies left Lynton for Ilfracombe on Monday morning.' [An interesting direction, possibly making for Marie Newby's home?]

American? Potential purchasers? Perhaps. But there may be another interpretation, particularly given this report in the *North Devon Herald*:

> The vagaries of a lady visitor, who, it is alleged, is a well-known member of the order of militants, have been the sole subject of gossip in the twin villages during the past few days. In the course of her couple of months stay, she has taken apartments in three or four different hotels. On Saturday she was noticed prowling around the stables of a well-known private house in Lynton. This follower of the Order of Militants was ejected without ceremony by the groom. Shortly afterwards a well known Lynton gentleman was standing at the rising ground at the back of the Town Hall when he observed the same lady examining the shaft which leads to the heating apparatus of the town hall. He spoke to her and mumbling some excuse she moved on. It is understood that the police authorities have been communicated with.

The identity of the 'well known member of the order of militants' is not revealed but it was WSPU policy for a small band of trained militants to carry out high profile acts to protect local activists. Two possible candidates for the events about to unfold in Lynton were Olive Wharry from Holsworthy and her partner in crime at Kew, Lilian Lenton. But Olive was in prison and Lilian in hiding, facing re-arrest. This leaves the name immediately beneath Lilian on the list below of Suffragists under the Cat and Mouse Act - Kitty Marion, a known arsonist and likely contender.

Kitty Marion became a militant suffragette as a reaction to the abuse many women endured if they wanted a career in the music hall. Determined to fight back, she enrolled with the 'Young Hot Bloods,' and was often first in line to volunteer for the most daring acts of arson. In the weeks leading up to August 1913, she torched the pavilion at Hurst Park Racecourse, was imprisoned, released under the Cat and Mouse Act, re-arrested on 12 July for breaking Home Office windows and finally released on 17 July. At the beginning of August she was at liberty.

SUFFRAGISTS UNDER THE CAT AND MOUSE ACT

Name.	Sentenced.	Released.	Re-arrested.
Mrs. Pankhurst	April 3	(1) April 12	May 26
		(2) May 30	June 14
		(3) June 16	July 21
Miss Kenney	June 17	(1) June 21	July 2
		(2) July 5	July 14
		(3) July 18	—
Miss Kerr	"	June 25	
Mrs. Sanders	"	(1) June 23	July 9
		(2) July 11	—
Miss Barrett	"	(1) June 21	July 2
		(2) July 5	July 17
		(3) July 21	
Miss Lake	"	June 21	July 2
Miss Lennox	"	(1)	June 29
		(2) July 3	
Mr. Clayton	"	June 23	Missing
Mrs. Shaw	June 21	June 27	"
Mrs. Palmer (Irish)	May 26	June 18	—
Mrs. Ryan	"	"	
Miss Walsh	"	"	
Miss Thomson (Scotch)	May 19	May 23	Missing
Miss A. Scott	"	(1) May 24	June 12
		(2) June 16	Missing
Miss Hudson	"	May 25	"
Mr. Franklin	March 8	April 28	"
Miss Stevenson	March 5	April 29	"
Miss Brady	April 12	"	"
Miss Doan	"	"	"
Mrs. Baines	May 5	(1) May 12	July 10
		(2) July 20	
Miss Lenton	Com. for trial, June 9	June 17	Missing
†Miss Marion	July 3	(1) July 8	July 12
		(2) July 17	
Miss Giveen	"	July 10	Missing
Miss Sylvia Pankhurst	July 8	July 12	—
*Miss Mary Richardson	"	"	July 17
Mrs. Mackworth	July 11	July 16	—
Mrs. Wyan	July 15	July 18	—
Mrs. Rigby	On Remand	(1) July 16	July 17
		(2) July 22	—

'Ready?' the shorter of the two[we will call her Mary] adjusts her hat and drapes her coat over her arm. A little irregular but it is such a fine day.

'Oh, yes.' The taller of the two ladies [we will call her Kitty] has been dozing in the lobby of the Valley of the Rocks Hotel, gathering her strength. Four weeks on hunger strike has left her weak, despite the Blathwayt's ministrations at Batheaston.

'Remember, people can be very curious in the country. They may be suspicious.'

'And all they will find is two ladies in love with this glorious Devon scenery and hoping to spend vast amounts of money on a mansion that has proved unsellable. We'll be welcomed with open arms.'

They step out into the narrow lane. Mary touches Kitty's arm, nodding towards the Stables opposite. 'Marie took a look at those.'

'Too many buildings close by, we can't risk it.'

'The second option is just up here.' Mary walks on.

'Wait, what's that?' Kitty points to their right.

'A funicular. It travels between Lynton and Lynmouth. Another bequest from George Newnes.'

'Is there anything he didn't pay for round here?'

Mary smiles. 'Not a lot! Take the Town Hall.' They pause outside a black and white timbered building towering over the street.

'Look more at home in the Swiss mountains. So another gift of the great and good George Newnes?'

'Yes, to celebrate Frank Newnes coming of age.'

'Now that is interesting.'

'Follow me.' Mary leads the way up the side of the building. 'There.'

'What am I looking at?'

'That shaft,' she points to the back of the building. 'It leads to the heating apparatus.'

Kitty studies the shaft, then turns to scan the neighbouring buildings. 'Still too close.'

'Then on to our third option.' Mary points at the summit of the hill where Hollerday House stands sentinel over the village. 'The currently unoccupied country retreat of Frank Newnes MP.'

Kitty smiles. 'Excellent.'

They stride up the lane beside the town hall to the Lodge. Kitty raps on the door. A man in late middle age opens it, wiping his chin with his hand. 'Mr Slee?' she enquires.

'The very man. Good morning, Ladies. How can I help?'

'I understand you are the caretaker for Hollerday House.'

'Indeed I am. The finest house around these parts, though a little neglected having been empty for some years, since Sir George died. Tragic that, tragic. Such a well-respected gent.'

'A matter of opinion,' Kitty whispers under her breath.

'*Mr Frank has done a fine job but his heart's gone out of Lynton. The house needs some life breathing into it.*'

'*That is why we are here. We have an appointment.*'

'*Yes, of course. I'll be with you by and by.*' Mr Slee disappears inside and returns with his jacket and cap proudly in place ready to escort these genteel ladies over the house and grounds. He'll do his best for Mr Frank, pointing out the charms of the house in its heyday. '*I'll go on ahead and open up. You take your time, it's a bit of a drag.*'

Kitty and Mary stroll up through the cutting towards Hollerday, pausing at the bend to catch their breath and take in the view of Countisbury Hill.

'*Stunning,*' Mary remarks. '*No wonder he chose to build here.*'

'*Little good that it did him,*' Kitty responds.

'*It's this way.*' Mary pulls away and strides up the track.

'*Wait up, Mary.*'

'*I'm sorry. How long on hunger strike this time?*'

'*Four weeks.*'

'*Four! You shouldn't be here. You could wait at the lodge. I can do what needs to be done.*'

'*What! And miss the fun? This is a perfect chance to communicate with our esteemed government. Wouldn't miss it for the world.*'

'*Look, up there.*' Mary points to their right. Just visible is a stone rotunda and a parapet capping the seemingly endless facade of the building. '*I heard it was magnificent but this is...*'

'*Perfect.*'

'*Perfect?*'

'*Cricket pavilions, signal boxes - small fry. But this... this will send a message they can't ignore. That **he** can't ignore.*' There's passion in Kitty's voice.

'*We have to be prepared for a backlash, for harsher sentences. No-one's better placed than Sir Albert De Rutzen for that.*'

'*Let him do his worst. We are equal to it, Mary, you know we are.*'

'*We are, but what about the women here - Marie, Anne, the others?*'

'*Marie has made her position clear. But there won't be any evidence against them will there? And we will be long gone.*'

'*She declared herself a militant ready to do whatever was needed.*'

'*I've no doubt that she will. We have to keep Mrs Newby close to the fold. She will be very useful. But now, we have work to do.*'

Later that night, as the flames took hold, a car was spotted travelling at speed along Lee Road from the direction of the Valley of Rocks, where paths from the Hollerday estate emerged, heading east - remarkable in itself at a time when few could afford such a luxury. In London and elsewhere it was known that militants often used fast cars as getaway vehicles. It would have taken a confident driver to negotiate the dark streets so fast, perhaps a chauffeur? Perhaps someone who could also offer a bolthole close at hand? Peace Cottage, Vera Holme's home with Evelina, at Brendon, was only a few miles away. Evelina was opposed to the WSPU's involvement in arson so it's doubtful she would have agreed to harbour the women. But her mother was critically ill so she may well have been away caring for her, leaving Vera free to make her own decisions.

Lynton and Lynmouth were alive with rumours in the days following the fire, some with more substance than others. In one interview, Sir Thomas Hewitt, from the neighbouring property, had no doubts that the fire was the work of suffragettes. Three of his gardeners distinctly heard a series of explosions, followed in each case by flames. 'This seems clearly the result of the suffrage craze,' said Sir Thomas, 'and everyone in Lynton is of the same opinion.' A credible view, but Sir Thomas may have had a vested interest in blaming the suffragettes. Unknown to the WSPU, just a few weeks before the fire Sir Thomas Hewitt had purchased the freehold of Hollerday House. Frank Newnes was no longer the owner, simply the leaseholder. It was Sir Thomas who sustained the loss not Frank Newnes.

Why should this matter to the Suffragettes? Frank Newnes was an ex-Liberal MP and the man now responsible for the Liberal supporting *Westminster Gazette* founded by his father, a very public association with Liberal policy and politics - reason enough to target Hollerday House. But there was another, even more compelling, reason that settles the matter beyond doubt.

Frank Newnes was soon to marry Emmeline August Louisa, daughter of

Albert Richard Francis Maximilien de Rutzen. The same Sir Albert de Rutzen who, as Chief Magistrate at Bow Street Court, had dismissed Emmeline Pankhurst and Evelina Haverfield's legal challenge and sentenced hundreds of suffragettes to the degradation of the Second Division at Holloway. The consequences of his actions, in condemning these suffragettes to the severest prison conditions, had now been dramatically demonstrated and avenged.

While Lynton absorbed the shock of the destruction of Hollerday House, the conspirators at Peace Cottage may have been looking to maximise their impact. The Devon and Somerset Staghounds were about to hold their opening meet at Cloutsham. It always attracted large crowds - and the women would pass close by on their way back to Bristol. Perhaps it was too good an opportunity to miss, as readers of the local paper were soon to discover:

SOMERSET HILLSIDE ABLAZE
HUGE TONGUES OF FLAME

The opening meet of the Devon and Somerset Staghounds at Cloutsham attracted a large concourse of people and a sensational incident occurred in connection with this meet. Early in the afternoon, smoke was seen rising from the western side of Dunkery, 1,000ft above sea level, and directly facing The Ball at Cloutsham and the woods in which the hounds were at work. In an incredibly short time a large tract was ablaze and, fanned by a stiff breeze, flames swept up the hillside laying waste one side of Joan How, a minor peak, and sweeping then towards the Beacon that marks the summit. Huge tongues of flame swept like waves beneath the dense volume of smoke which arose from the hillside and cast a blur upon an otherwise radiant sky. A big staff endeavoured to cope with the fire but the lurid glare from Dunkery promised a long and difficult task. This outbreak is generally believed to be the work of Suffragettes, the women having been seen through the glasses close to the spot where the fire broke out.

And maybe the women were not done yet:

LARGE RICK FIRE

In consequence of every horse in the neighbourhood having been engaged for the meet (at Cloutsham) the Williton fire brigade were unable to respond to an urgent call to a large rick at Stringston eight miles distant... The burning rick contained quite 100 tons of hay and there was another almost as large close by for which grave fears were entertained.

Stringston is on the road to Bridgwater on the way to Bristol.

Hollerday was just one of many incidents. The following year the *Morning Post* listed all those properties completely or partially destroyed by arson. It demonstrated the scale of the suffragette's campaign over twelve months, an escalation that had a massive financial impact - with losses of £380,000, the equivalent of just under £56 million today.

1913		Locality	House	Est. Loss
Mar.	19	Englefield Green	Lady Whites	£2,300
Apr.	4	Chorley Wood	Roughwood	£2,500
	7	Norwich	The Chase	£2,000
	15	St. Leonards	Loveleigh	£5,000
May.	9	Barrow	Oak Lea	£6,000
	10	Dundee	Faringdon Hall	£10,000
	14	Folkestone	The Highlands	£500
	18	Cambridge	Ridings	£850
June	4	Bradf'd-on-Av'n	Emscross	£7,000
	10	East Lothian	Residence	£2,500
	20	Olton	Residence	£1,000
	30	Balfron	Balikinrain Castle	£25,000
July	4	Sutton Coldfield	Residence	£3,000
	7	Rivington	Bung'low	£20,000
Aug.	**4**	**Lynton**	**Hollerday**	**£9,000**
	22	Edinburgh	Residence	£300
	26	North Finchley	Friern Watch	£500
Sept	12	Sutton	Residence	£500
Oct.	6	Hampton	The Elms	£1,500

	26	Slough	Residence	£1,000
	27	Bramshott	Mill House	£1,000
	28	Bradford	Shirley Manor	£5,000
Nov.	11	Bristol	Begbrook	£4,000
	23	Bath	Bathford	£3,000
Dec.	5	Wemyss Bay	Kelly House	£27,000
	21	Cheltenham	Alstone Lawn	£350
Jan.	24	Lanark	Bonnington	£1,200
Feb.	4	Perthshire	Aberuchill Castle £3,000	
	4	Comrie	House of Ross	£3,000
	4	St. Filans	New Villa	£1,000
	27	Redlynch	Residence	
Mar.	12	Ayrshire	Robertlawn	£15,000
	27	Belfast	Abbeylands	£20,000
Apr.	9	Carrickfergus	Oxlands	£10,000

Numerous other attempts were made to burn dwellings across the country. It's an outrageous, or an impressive, count depending on your point of view. And despite their assertion that they never placed lives in danger there were several close calls. In Lynton, fireman Alfred Berry fell thirty feet off a ladder. He only sustained bruising and a sprained ankle but his injuries could have been much worse.

This may have been the final straw for Evelina Haverfield. Her loyalty to the WSPU had been stretched to breaking point when the Pethick Lawrences were expelled. Having witnessed lives being put at risk on her doorstep, it was time for a complete break. She withdrew entirely from the Paddington branch of the WSPU, removed herself from the speaker's list and followed the Pethick Lawrences to a new organisation, the United Suffragists. This was formed by supporters who remained disillusioned by the lack of success of the NUWSS but who disapproved of the arson campaign of the WSPU. Alongside Emmeline and Frederick Pethick Lawrence Evelina discovered another familiar face, Henry Harben, the previous candidate for the Barnstaple constituency.

However, the Ilfracombe group was unwavering in its loyalty to the WSPU. Just days after the destruction at Lynton they launched their holiday campaign - a brave strategy considering the inevitable local backlash. George Newnes was Lynton's hero. To destroy this important link with him was outrageous. Undeterred, the group entered a parade of pony carriages in the Ilfracombe carnival. One was decorated in the colours of the Tax Resistance League, undoubtedly Annie Ball's work. Another, protesting against the Cat and Mouse Act, attracted large crowds whenever it stopped.

Interest was so great they completely sold out of copies of *The Suffragette,* although the positive interest may have been down to a cunning advertising strategy. An endearing eight-year-old, mostly likely Marie Newby's daughter Kathleen, wove through the crowd selling the newspaper. Marie also had no intention of lying low. She was back in her trademark position by the archway in Ilfracombe High Street, unmissable in her WSPU apron, selling *Votes for Women*, a staggering display of her convictions. Here was a lady of standing in the community - surgeon's wife and pillar of the church - now a common street seller. A courageous and

SUFFRAGETTES AT ILFRACOMBE.

Mrs. du Sautoy Newby selling the paper

very public stand, particularly given the community's reaction to the burning of Hollerday as reported in the *North Devon Herald.* 'For two or three weeks past there has been a good deal of talk about the suffragettes staying in the place but no one thought they would make a serious attempt at Lynton. Now, however, dire vengeance is being vowed upon them, several people stating they would execute all manner of punishment upon the suffragettes if only they could lay hands on them. Revolvers were freely spoken of, and people stated that they would not hesitate to use them whenever the occasion should arise!'

Chapter Thirty
More Fires of Dissent
Autumn - Winter 1913

A few months after the destruction of Hollerday House, Devonians browsing the *Western Evening Herald* could be forgiven for exclaiming, 'not again!' Mrs Pankhurst had evaded prison under the Cat and Mouse Act by sailing to America for a speaking tour. She was now due into Plymouth on the White Star liner, Majestic, and word was out that she would be re-arrested. The paper reported a WSPU meeting in London where the Chair opened, 'If they do arrest Mrs Pankhurst, I am sorry for Plymouth - (cheers). There is a great deal of property in Plymouth - (cheers) - many fine plate-glass windows, and a great opportunity for showing the authorities that if they respect human life so little as to put Mrs Pankhurst in prison, then we shall show no respect on our part for property belonging to the authorities. (cheers)'

This local threat came with a forceful reminder of the lengths to which the WSPU were prepared to go. Sylvia Pankhurst stated, 'We must have an army to muster at the word of command... We are going to learn all the tactics that the police know, and more -(cheers). Let us make the 'people's army' a terror to the Government. Let us make Cabinet Ministers shake in their shoes and be afraid of their lives when they don't give in and give justice.' It was a ringing endorsement of the Pankhurst's dogged determination to continue violent assaults on the government until they caved in and gave women the vote. Still no signs of compromise or reflection, given the negative publicity or ongoing loss of members. Perhaps they subscribed to the maxim that 'no publicity is bad publicity,' with the only true negative being no publicity at all.

The WSPU launched a week long campaign ahead of Mrs Pankhurst's arrival when the 'will she, won't she' debate over whether she would be arrested in Plymouth became a hot topic. The *Suffragette* reported:

> The most wonderful thing about the campaign in Plymouth is the extraordinary feeling of interest that animates the whole town... The organiser and the other speakers confess that never in their lives have they seen such great crowds nor been met with such interest... Friday's meeting in the Market place was a triumph in every way... In less than thirty-six hours we sold over 300 papers, and the people were clamouring for more. We have distributed over 10,000 handbills, and hundreds of people have signed the petition and have written to... the Mayor of Plymouth protesting against the re-arrest of the Women's Leader.
>
> On Sunday on the North Quay there was a crowd of over 2,000 patiently waiting... On the suggestion of a number of the audience the following resolution was put. "That this meeting of working men and women protests against any

attempt being made to rearrest Mrs Pankhurst in Plymouth." This was proposed by the organiser and seconded by the man who made the suggestion and was carried with a perfect forest of hands... the men and women were so delighted at the way the resolution was carried that they threw their caps in the air and cheered again and again and, when invited by the speaker to join the women on Wednesday at the Dock Gates, there was a great response from that great representative gathering of Plymouth, Stonehouse and Devonport citizens.

The whole of this campaign has been one brilliant triumph, not only for Votes for Women, but for the vindication of militancy and the popularity of the Suffragettes... The organiser wishes to thank the various officials of the town, professional men and shopkeepers who have helped in so many ways to make a success of this campaign. She also wishes to thank all those Plymouth members who have helped so splendidly in the very short time at their disposal.

Some of the press were less effusive than the *Suffragette*. The *Western Evening Herald* reported, 'It is some time since that Miss Elizabeth Grew, a London organiser, arrived in the town and opened offices in Drake's Circus. There she was attracting a lot of attention, and at the present is endeavouring to stir up the feeling of the public in favour of her leader... Last night a large crowd listened to the suffragettes in the Market-place... police were present and there was no disorder.'

On the day the Majestic was expected, *The Suffragette* reported that a group of women spent the night in a small open motor launch, drenched to the skin, on the look-out. According to their account, two battleships were sent to intercept their tiny launch to keep them from the Majestic. Meanwhile a large crowd had gathered at Millbay Dock gates expecting to see Mrs Pankhurst. When she failed to arrive there was an appeal to gather again at 11am the next morning. Having got into his stride, the paper's reporter shared that, '...singing was freely indulged in. A section informed all whom it might or might not concern that they had a strong desire to be in Dixieland.'

The next day, 4 December, the Majestic was sighted off Cawsand Bay. Flora Drummond and a core of martial arts trained suffragettes, acting as Mrs Pankhurst's bodyguard, gathered at Ocean Quay, Richmond Walk to prevent her arrest. The quay, a secluded spot close to a rail terminus, was where Chief Constable Sowerby and others had left in a tender to go out to the Majestic so seemed the obvious location for Mrs Pankhurst's landing. A crowd some hundreds strong gathered to witness events. The *Western Morning News* described Miss Gladys Hazel as the heroine of the day. 'From eleven o'clock until after two she kept the crowd outside the gates of the G.W.R. docks interested by her oratory, kept them patient with her cheery good humour, and maintained until the last moment, despite a growing inward conviction that the plans of her friends had gone awry, a pleasant countenance of optimism. This in the face of a bitter wind and frequent showers - a splendid example of courage and endurance.'

Elizabeth Grew then arrived to break the news. Mrs Pankhurst had been arrested aboard the Majestic. Despite the actual arrest being perfectly calm and civilised, in a letter to the *Times* an American passenger wrote, 'It was the most sickening sight that I have ever witnessed. A woman of Mrs Pankhurst's refinement and character being led away as a common criminal!... No one on the steamer who had an opportunity of knowing Mrs Pankhurst saw her go without a feeling of deep disgust for a system of Government that made such a thing possible.'

Emmeline Pankhurst was landed at Bull Point, an obvious choice in retrospect given it was used exclusively by Government vessels and served the Naval Ordnance Depot which was constantly patrolled by police. The crowd that Elizabeth Grew addressed wouldn't have been able to get anywhere near it but she thanked them, '...for the manifestly clear manner they had shown that it was not with their consent that their paid servants, the police, had arrested Mrs Pankhurst... The suffragettes came to Plymouth on a peaceful mission and constitutional agitation, but the government, acting thorough the police, had clearly shown to every man and woman, as well as to herself, that constitutional agitation was not enough. Their peaceful mission was at an end.'

The women also announced that, as Mrs Pankhurst was gone, Plymouth no longer held their interest and they would be leaving at once. But, almost as a throwaway line, the paper concludes, 'It transpires that, in addition to the threat to burn the Argyle ground grandstand, there was another threatening the destruction of the Promenade Pier.' Confirmation that the suffragettes were not yet done with Plymouth was to come very soon.

In Exeter prison, Emmeline Pankhurst immediately went on hunger and thirst strike, prompting a vigil by suffragettes outside. It was a courageous choice. A rowdy crowd physically assaulted them, prompting a rescue by prison warders. Undeterred, they kept up their vigil, whether by the prison walls or in cars close by. Curious crowds gathered from time to time, the perfect opportunity for a speech by Elizabeth Grew. 'We are doing what a member of your cabinet told us to do. Mr Hobhouse said there was no popular demand behind the woman's claim, such as men showed when they burnt down Nottingham Castle and a great part of Bristol to get their vote. If the only popular demand this Government will recognise is that of burning buildings, it's going to get it.'

According to the *Exeter Gazette*, 'The news that the militants had arrived caused some excitement in the city, and anticipating that there would be some stirring events. the police were very much on the alert... close watch was kept at the public buildings of the city and the ordinary staff at the Museums and the Cathedral were warned to keep their eyes open. Several militants stayed at one of the hotels near the Great Western Railway Station. They declined interviews, but one stated they were here to await events.' A deputation of women actually approached the Dean of the Cathedral and asked that Mrs Pankhurst, who was by then in a very serious condition, be mentioned in prayers. He agreed and included her at the morning, afternoon and evening services.

Mrs Pankhurst was released after a few days in a state bordering on collapse, prompting a perceptive reflection from the *Western Times* reporter:

> It is regrettable that a woman who has many admirable qualities and the power of inspiring devotion to a rare degree should deliberately torture herself to no purpose. Mrs Pankhurst began her campaign to hasten the day when the

vote must be conceded to women. At the outset, militancy undoubtedly did advance the cause, but the weakness of a militant policy is that is has to become ever more militant and in due course the borderline between what is legitimate and what is criminal was crossed, and to an unbiassed spectator it seems as if the militants have lost sight of their original quest and are now bent on a personal triumph, at any cost, over the Government... The militant policy, its arsons, its hunger strikes, its wild talk, merely hardens the heart of those who from one cause or another actively resist the vote for women, and leaves the indifferent still indifferent.

These reflections on the weakness of a militant policy certainly chime with earlier comments about the suffragettes becoming addicted to violence and sidetracked by personal agendas.

Exeter NUWSS were at pains to distance themselves from the WSPU. When a representative of the *Western Evening Herald* made contact he was informed, '...that they knew nothing about the matter. A personage of more importance to them was Mrs Fawcett, who is speaking in Exeter tonight in aid of the Women's cause.' The *Exeter Gazette* later reported Mrs Fawcett's address at the Queen's Hall. 'It was a matter of very deep regret [the arrest of Mrs Pankhurst] and she felt bound on an occasion such as this to make once more a public declaration, on her own behalf and on behalf of the National Union of Women's Suffrage Society, of which she had the honour to be President, that they were entirely opposed to the use of violence of any kind as a means of political propaganda... It seemed to her an attempt to overcome evil by evil; an attempt to overcome tyranny by arson.' But arson remained a militant tactic the WSPU were determined to pursue, and in Devon.

On 18 December readers of the *Brixham Guardian* woke to the headline, 'Great Fire At Devonport. Avenging Mrs Pankhurst's Arrest. A disastrous fire occurred early on Monday at Messrs. Fox, Elliott and Co's timber yard at Richmond Walk, Devonport [the site where WSPU leaders waited in vain for Mrs Parkhurst] damage being done to the extent of £10,000. [Almost £1,500,000 today] The *Western Morning News* reported, '...the fire spread with remarkable rapidity; so quickly, in fact, that in a few minutes tongues of flame were shooting into the air, causing a glare in the moisture-laden atmosphere that could be seen for miles away.' *The Western Times* added, 'A fact much commented on is that the fire seemed to be blazing at different parts of the yard at one time, giving ground for suggestion that the work of the alleged incendiaries must have been thoroughly carried out.'

The Suffragette reported, almost too enthusiastically, 'At four o'clock in the morning the fire was still very high and roaring furiously at both ends of the yard. The fire brigades and their hundreds of assistants were fighting with great energy to prevent it spreading. Flames were leaping skyward to a great height, and the lurid glare in the sky was attracting more and more people to the scene from all parts of the Three Towns.'

Suffragette literature and postcards were found at the scene, one reading, 'Votes for Women; Our reply to the torture of Mrs Pankhurst and her cowardly arrest at Plymouth,' and another, 'Revenge on the Government for the arrest of Mrs Pankhurst. Votes for Women.' The wood yard was insured, but not Hancocks Fair just across the road. According to Sophie Hancock the switchback railway, hobbyhorses and roundabouts had been practically destroyed, causing a loss of £2,000 [around £295,000 today], enough to ruin them. Probably collateral damage to the suffragettes but a lack of thought for, or concern about, the consequences of their actions for the general public was in danger of causing even more women to turn their backs on the WSPU.

SANTA CLAUS *Shant we give the Girls some this time?*

Chapter Thirty-One
Growing Chasms
Winter 1913 - Summer 1914

NUWSS groups across Devon capitalised on this backlash. In North Molton, Mrs Clunn declared herself delighted that the first meeting with a suffrage bias ever held there was so crowded. Barnstaple were given a boost by the support of Miss Rosalie Chichester from Arlington Court, who chaired meetings in Barnstaple and Instow during November and in January hosted a non-militant pro-suffrage meeting. Ruth Giles, an organiser with the South West Federation of the NUWSS, was the speaker. She focused on women's growing wish for more responsibility and the need to address wider issues such as their working conditions. She also took up the gauntlet of promoting the NUWSS in Bideford. Despite increasing support for local groups, public meetings there were still a bit of a gamble. As she stood to address an audience of over 700, most seemed eager to listen but a Mr Edes later wrote to the Bideford Gazette to vent his outrage at, '...the senseless and cruel outrages which have been inflicted on all classes by the hysterical hooligans who glory in the debasement of their sex as a means of attaining the vote.' It was one thing for representatives of the NUWSS to say they were non-militants but they still had a way to go to convince some members of the public.

They were trying to do just that across the county, with thriving groups in Tiverton, Sidmouth, Budleigh Salterton, Ottery St Mary, Topsham, Newton Abbot, Torquay, Totnes and Exeter. 1913 had been an exceptional year and for once this group of moderates could revel in the success of their own headline-grabbing event, the Great Pilgrimage. All the groups came together in November for the 'Forest of Christmas Trees' fete held at the Barnfield Hall in Exeter, opened by Lady Lockyer of Sidmouth and chaired by Sir Robert Newman, constant in his support of the NUWSS. Entertainment was provided by Amy Montague, lynchpin of the Exeter WSPU but now also an active member of the NUWSS.

The New Year was a time of ominous foreboding in retrospect, but to the NUWSS in Devon it was simply time to renew their efforts. The Honiton branch, formed the previous November under the presidency of Lady Frances Balfour, held their first public meeting at the Dolphin Hotel at the end of January. A correspondent for *The Exeter Gazette* had only praise for the gathering. 'What a pity those misguided militants who, by burning people's houses and generally making themselves a criminal nuisance, are doing more harm to the woman's cause, than perhaps they are aware, will not take a leaf out of the book of their friends of the NUWSS and strive to gain the sympathy of the public by explaining their cause in a logical and sensible manner. Were they so to do, I am certain that much of the opposition at present existing throughout the country against the extension of the Parliamentary Franchise to women would melt away.'

This was a view gaining increasing support, not only in the sphere of public opinion but in Parliament itself. Even given his personal opposition to granting women the vote, the WSPU's escalation in bombing and arson attacks placed the Prime Minister in an impossible situation. From 1911 the Government had been dealing with domestic riots and significant social unrest focused on demands for improved working conditions. Britain was also engaged in an arms race with Germany, as fears grew about possible conflict, and there was the very real threat of civil war in Ireland as both the Catholics and the Ulster Protestants armed themselves. Given this political background, how could Asquith possibly be seen to surrender to the suffragettes' use of bombs and arson? It would have been a direct encouragement to the paramilitary forces mustering in Ireland.

It feels inescapable that by escalating their violent campaign, the WSPU were fundamentally undermining their chances of success. But the Pankhursts remained committed to militancy, convinced that if they were resolute then the government would have no choice but to bend to their demands. It was an echo of a letter written by Frances Latimer to the *Western Daily Mercury* in 1912. In reply to NUWSS condemnation of militancy she had compared their struggle to that of the striking miners. 'If the Women's Societies stood shoulder-to-shoulder as those of the miners are doing, they would... have the Prime Minister "going cap in hand" to treat with the women as he does with the men. The matter would be settled once and for all in women's favour, and the tragic demands upon the militant section to undertake these misunderstood, self-sacrificing immolations would cease.' It was an argument that possibly rang true on a small scale in Devon where there was already significant cooperation, but of course the women lacked the sanction of being able to withdraw their labour.

In the first few months of 1914 WSPU militancy continued unchecked. The newspapers recorded one incident after another:

- An explosion in St George's Church, Hanover Square
- Arson attack at the Bath Hotel, Felixstowe
- Malicious damage at the British Museum,
- Rokeby Venus slashed at the National Gallery

- Wheat ricks destroyed by fire near Bath
- House destroyed by fire at St Fillian's, Scotland
- Bomb explodes at Glasgow Botanic Gardens
- Ballmenock House almost completely destroyed by fire
- Six Midland Railway carriages destroyed by fire
- Oratory Cricket Pavilion, Birmingham, destroyed by fire
- Attempt to burn down the old parish church at Clevedon
- Watercolour by Exeter artist, John Shapland, damaged
- Carnegie Library in Birmingham destroyed by fire

The public were incredulous at the increasingly random and dangerous nature of the attacks. Targets with a direct connection to the Liberal Government were almost understandable. But churches? Cricket pavilions? Libraries? This last was especially disturbing. A facility donated to the city that was so valuable to ordinary citizens, why on earth would they punish the very women they were trying to win over? But perhaps that was the point. The latest campaign was intended to disrupt the lives of ordinary people so they would put pressure on the government to stop the violence.

The Pankhursts had historically focused on recruiting middle and upper-class, property-owning ladies. Although working class women were part of the WSPU, they tended to be the exception. For them the prospect of arrest and losing their jobs was a significant deterrent to greater involvement. In February 1914 these differences brought conflict between Christabel and Sylvia to crisis point.

Working class women wanted shorter working hours, improved conditions, better wages. As WSPU organiser at Bow in the East End of London, Sylvia embraced this wider agenda and, initially at least, Christabel tacitly sanctioned her work there. But Sylvia increasingly worked with, and supported, men's involvement in the movement. This included speaking alongside Frederick Pethick Lawrence, a step too far for Christabel as she made clear in the *Suffragette*. 'Independence of all men's parties is the basis of the Women's Social and Political Union... so long as men are voters and women are voteless it is dangerous for women to co-operate with men.' It was her opinion that as soon as women gave their time, money and trust to men they abused that trust, possibly the reasoning behind the string of attacks on those quintessentially male bastions - the golf clubs and race courses.

Sylvia issued a statement that she and her East End Federation were independent of any policy Christabel decided in Paris, the first time she had publicly criticised the WSPU. In return, Christabel justified her exclusion of Sylvia from speaking at WSPU meetings. It was a short step from there to Sylvia's perception that she, and her East London Federation, had been expelled. Warnings that Christabel's tactics were undermining the movement were read as evidence that Sylvia and Adela were about to set up a counter organisation. The Pankhurst family splintered, seen by Mrs Pankhurst and Christabel as unavoidable collateral damage.

Christabel's actions have been attributed to paranoia but there were over 50 suffrage societies competing for membership and funds. She firmly believed the WSPU was the most effective and was determined to keep it that way. The split with Sylvia brought fear of the WSPU's impact being diluted close to home, further aggravated by the situation with her other sister, Adela. Disagreements that had been brewing between them for some time came to a head. Emmeline and Christabel feared that the unpredictable and independent-minded Adela, who was also an effective speaker, would join forces with Sylvia and form an alternative organisation. In fact Adela had refused Sylvia's request but, to avoid conflict with her family, she agreed to leave the WSPU - and England. Emmeline enlisted the support of Vida Goldstein, familiar from her visits to the south west, to help Adela make a fresh start in Australia.

While the WSPU fought their internal battles in London and from Paris, the NUWSS continued their recruitment drive in Devon. Sheffield-based suffragist, Mrs Whalley spoke in Dawlish before addressing audiences in Landkey and Bideford, where she took advantage of a crowd gathered on Bideford quay, keen to spot the Bleriot monoplane piloted by French airman Henri Salmet. He was on a promotional tour around the West Country on behalf of his sponsor, the *Daily Mail*. Not one to waste the opportunity of a large gathering, Mrs Whalley's trademark stirring speech provided an interesting diversion as they waited.

Mrs Whalley's appearances were a precursor to an extended caravan tour around the more rural parts of the West Country. The NUWSS had organised an "Active Service League" where each member of the League was invited to give one week's active service during May, June and July. Four ladies, including Mabel Ramsay, came forward to caravan through Cornwall and Devon, breaking entirely new ground and signing up new members. Stops included Holsworthy, Black Torrington, Great Torrington, South Molton, Chulmleigh, Lapford, North Tawton, Okehampton, Bridestowe, Lydford, and Tavistock. As a publicity stunt it was remarkably effective with hundreds of copies of the *Common Cause* sold en-route. Mrs Whalley and Mabel Ramsay were the main speakers, proposing the resolution, 'That this meeting calls on the Government to introduce a measure extending the Parliamentary Franchise to women,' the same resolution it had been putting for so many years. It was carried in every place, except Black Torrington.

The tour was the catalyst for some active canvassing in South Molton by Miss Frost, Mrs Smart and Miss Baly. Like many groups before and since, they took a stall in the market, where the ladies were able to field questions from the general public. A Miss Hedge held an open-air meeting in George Nympton and a week later was back at the Assembly Hall in South Molton with Miss Shapcott of Ashmill in the chair. Talks on 'The History of the Women's Movement' and 'The Vote as a Symbol of Freedom' inspired thirty-one women to join the NUWSS, and there was enthusiasm for forming a group in the town, one more to add to the grand total of 478 active nationwide. Nationally, around 52,000 members were now part of the NUWSS, a stark contrast to the 2,000 signed up to the WSPU.

However, many Devonians still remained confused about who was who in the suffrage movement. Exeter NUWSS hired a market stall to counter ongoing ignorance of the fact that there were two societies, the law abiding NUWSS and the militant WSPU. Two societies with two different leaders, a point completely missed at a meeting of the Exmouth National League for Opposing Women's Suffrage. When the Chairman spoke of Mrs Fawcett as President of the Union of Suffragettes, Joan Retallack, from Exmouth NUWSS, tried to correct him but he wouldn't allow her to speak.

Mabel Ramsay also felt compelled to write to the *Western Morning News* with a correction. 'The society which held a woman's suffrage meeting at Looe last Wednesday was the National Union of Woman's Suffrage Societies (Non-Militant)... Your report states it to be WSPU (Women's Social and Political League)(Non-Militants) There is no non-militant branch of this latter society!... the mistake is made too often to pass un-contradicted.'

Ironically one of the most successful suffrage meetings held for the cause was organised by the anti-suffragists. *Votes for Women*, the paper still published by the Pethick Lawrences, announced in March 1914, 'A recent event of importance at Exeter has been a triumphant Suffrage meeting - arranged by the antis... At meetings held at Exmouth and at Sidmouth, the Suffrage element was so strong in the audience that the organisers did not dare to take a vote, and so put no resolution.' A Mr Samuels had even been engaged to hold a series of meetings in Exeter prior to a public meeting at the Barnfield Hall to drum up anti-suffrage feeling - with mixed results. A working man in the audience at Fountain Square in St Sidwell Street was heard to remark, 'I used to be against the Suffrage for women, "he said, "but I heard you at Gervase Avenue last night, and I've heard you again here tonight, and now I'm *for* votes for women decidedly.'

Nevertheless, after years of renewed suffrage activity it was essentially still the same speeches, the same arguments, the same resolutions, the same confusion amongst the public, the same hopes for fated Suffrage Bills, with very little progress being made. The words of the *Western Times* reporter ring true. 'The militant policy, its arsons, its hunger strikes, its wild talk, merely hardens the heart of those who from one cause or another actively resist the vote for women, and leaves the indifferent still indifferent.'

Undaunted, Marie, Ann, Margaret and other members of the Ilfracombe WSPU forged ahead with their continued support for the Pankhursts. But the chasm between the island of militancy that they had become and other organisations was growing still wider. The Women's Liberal Society [WLA] had consistently passed resolutions for Women's Suffrage but it seemed that they were going backwards in their active support, as reported in the *Gazette*:

SCENE AT WOMEN'S LIBERAL MEETING

At the opening of the annual meeting of the Ilfracombe Women's Liberal Association a painful exhibition was given of the extent to which the Liberal Party Women are still blinded to the vital issues. Mrs Baker, wife of the prospective candidate for the Barnstaple Division was addressing a meeting when a lady who had once been a member of the Association, rose to protest against the treatment of women by the Government. A great uproar followed and the lady who had interrupted was compelled to leave the meeting to which she had not been invited.

These Liberal ladies had apparently forgiven and forgotten the issues which had provoked their earlier spat with Mr Baker, their new and blatantly anti-suffragist candidate. The one exception was Margaret Eldridge. 'I rise to protest against the forcible feeding...' She was drowned out by women shouting, 'Sit down,' 'Go outside,' and 'Put her out.' Having owned up to no longer being a member, she and Annie Ball were ejected. Mr Baker expressed the wish that, '...even if some ladies have grievances he hoped they would be rectified in the equality of Mrs Baker's sharing with him responsibility when the electorate of this Division elected him as their representative in Parliament.' Margaret took to the newspaper to have the last word. 'I fear Mrs Baker, however charming she may be, will not do as a substitute for the vote, which despite the pessimistic views of the President of the Women's Liberal Association, will soon be given to us.'

Margaret Eldridge wasn't the only person losing patience with the WLA. Eleanor Acland had been an enthusiastic advocate for women's suffrage over the years and regularly highlighted the issue through correspondence in the newspapers and with politicians. In the autumn of 1913, when still vice-president of the NUWSS South-Western Federation, she formed the Liberal Women's Suffrage Union (LWSU) with the aim of only supporting Liberal candidates who supported suffragists. In a letter to the Women's Federation News she remarked that the movement's success depended on, '...how much sane, hard-headed sincerity Liberal women can muster.' Eleanor was such a driving force that by the end of the year the LWSU was being described as 'Mrs Acland's Society.' It was ultimately a stance that was incompatible with her role as vice president of the South Western Federation though. In June 1914 her frustration at their non-party, non-political stance, preventing her from supporting Liberal suffragist candidates, caused an irreparable rift and she resigned.

Meanwhile, Ilfracombe WSPU pressed ahead with plans for a major attraction to boost numbers. Flora Drummond had agreed to speak as part of a country-wide tour. She was booked at Oxford Assembly rooms, Brighton Dome and then, on 1 April, at Ilfracombe Town Hall - perhaps an indication of the impact the Ilfracombe group were making at WSPU HQ. Members set about publicising her arrival. A pony-cart was decorated and driven around the town on the Saturday prior to the meeting. Volunteers were recruited to hand out flyers, steward the meeting and sell copies of the *Suffragette*. All was in place. But national events were about to undermine their plans.

Fearing increasing public disorder as a reaction against growing violence, the Government had clamped down on WSPU activities, including a ban on public meetings. But permission had been given for men protesting against Home Rule in Ireland to hold a demonstration in Hyde Park. The *Suffragette* announced, 'This being so, the women applied to the Government to remove the veto on all their meetings. The Government have refused. This unjust refusal the women have declined to accept, and they will hold a Procession on Saturday April 4th at the same time that the Ulster men are holding theirs.' With General Flora Drummond advertised as the principal speaker, and only a few days to organise the event, all other engagements were cancelled.

It was a massive disappointment for the Ilfracombe group. They rarely attracted such a high profile speaker to this rural outpost. But the WSPU was nothing if not resourceful. Within hours another speaker was found. The meeting would go ahead, but with Miss Barbara Wylie. She was a very well-known WSPU activist and close friend of Emmeline Pankhurst who had recently been imprisoned for openly advocating acts of militancy and violence. Now released and actively campaigning again, she was an immediate draw for the crowds in Ilfracombe and, according to Marie Newby '…her splendid speech converted many.' As well as tales of her many exploits that ended in prison sentences, she doubtless had some entertaining anecdotes to share about her times with Emmeline.

But other Devon WSPU groups had grown noticeably quieter in the *Suffragette* and there were fewer reports in the local press. An editor's comment in the *Western Morning News* perhaps explains why. 'In a democratic country the only legitimate way to get reforms is to convert the majority to a belief in the necessity. Arson and violence are not only immoral but bad policy to boot, for they can only delay, instead of accelerating, the reform… No minority, however convinced of the justice of its demand, has either the legal or moral right to attempt to coerce the majority by crime.'

Throughout the spring of 1914 there is little further evidence of militancy in Devon, although suspicions were aroused when two fires broke out within three days of each other. On 17 June Bideford Bowling pavilion was destroyed at a time when there were rumours of suffragettes being seen on Westward Ho! golf course. But no literature was found. The second fire was at Lynton Town Hall, where again there were no clues as to who was responsible. However, the *Suffragette,* when covering fires attributed to suffragettes, included a report from the *Western Daily Mercury* giving Lynton some credibility. The possibility has to be considered, though, that the WSPU might have been taking credit for vandalism even when they were not actually responsible for it

Actions did escalate elsewhere in the country, however. In May, the suffragettes decided to take their appeal to the King at Buckingham Palace. It was an encounter witnessed by suffragette, Kate Parry Frye and recorded in her diary:

Thursday, May 21st 1914… In the afternoon I went to Buckingham Palace to see the Women's deputation – led by Mrs Pankhurst - which went to try and see the King. It was simply awful – oh! those poor pathetic women – dresses half torn off – hair down, hats off, covered with mud and paint and some dragged along looking in the greatest agony… Fancy not arresting them until they got into that state. It is the most wicked and futile persecution because they know we have got to have 'Votes' – and to think they have got us to this state – some women thinking it necessary and right to do the most awful burnings etc in order to bring the question forward. Oh what a pass to come to in a so-called civilised country. I shall never forget those poor dear women.

Kate Fry blamed this government violence for driving women to a point where they felt arson and disruption were the only ways to achieve their aims. But after a time of shock, outrage and sympathy from many at the way the women were treated, there was now a growing shift in public opinion both locally and elsewhere. One of those caught up in the backlash was a familiar Devon face, Mary Fausten. Fellow campaigners and friends in Torquay reading the *Teignmouth Post and Gazette* were probably not surprised to read that she was still active within the WSPU.

WORSHIPPERS ATTACK SUFFRAGETTE BRAWLERS. The rising of popular resentment against militant suffragettes was shown unmistakably in London on Sunday, when the police had to protect the women from rough treatment at the hands of the crowds. Fifteen suffragettes interrupted mass at Brompton Oratory on Sunday morning... A fierce fight between the suffragettes and the congregation, who were fiercely indignant, followed... several of the militants received some hard knocks, and one was seen to be bleeding at the mouth... as one of the arrested women was being placed in a taxicab she was struck across the face by a lady member of the congregation, whose action was loudly cheered by the crowd gathered outside the church.

Mary was surrounded by the crowd in the road outside the church and, while appealing to a policeman for help, was arrested and later charged with obstruction and disorderly behaviour. She was sentenced to fourteen days.

The *Western Times* provided more examples of frustration spilling over into violence against the suffragettes:

A party of militant suffragettes who attempted to hold a meeting on Worthing beach at the Fish Market on Friday, had a hostile reception. The crowd swept the speakers away from their pitch, the suffragettes colours were seized and torn to shreds …

A hostile crowd attacked and demolished the contents of a stall in charge of two members of the Women's Social and Political Union. [In Leicester Market] The stall was laden with confectionary for sale during the self-denial week. Several women in the crowd brought fire lighters threatening to burn the stall.

Suffragettes who at Blackpool sought to press their literature on the girl workers at a local flax factory were severely handled by the girls. Their hats and coats were torn off and personal injury was inflicted in several cases. One suffragette was treated at the infirmary.

A church congregation, market place customers, factory girls - not the police cordons or rowdy troublemakers previously associated with rough treatment of the suffragettes. These were ordinary members of the public roused to very vocal and even violent opposition by the escalation in militancy. The NUWSS and the Conservative and Unionist Women's Franchise Association even united to condemn their actions. The person well qualified to speak for both organisations was Jessie Montgomery. The previous year she had made, '…the greatest sacrifice she had ever made for the cause' when she resigned as Hon. Secretary of Exeter NUWSS to pursue a more political path with the Conservative and Unionist Women's Franchise Association. Olga Fletcher, who became the new Hon. Secretary, generously recognised that Jessie could now influence local politicians in a way the non-party NUWSS could not.

Their joint statement read. 'We the undersigned representatives of law-abiding suffrage societies covering the whole area of Great Britain and Ireland, have often protested against the lawless violence of a small section, and recent events compel us once more to put on record our detestation of methods of arson, destruction and vandalism. We oppose these methods, and always have opposed them… our task of convincing the electorate is rendered infinitely more difficult by such sections.'

As well as the growing chasm between the WSPU and the NUWSS, Christabel was also causing more rifts within the WSPU itself. Meetings were now promoting sales of her recently published book *The Great Scourge and How to End It*. It was a controversial decision. The book concentrated on a subject that was becoming an obsession with Christabel; sexually transmitted diseases and how sexual equality (votes for women) would help the fight against these diseases. It was a justified exposé but came across as a moralising, anti-men stance that proved too much for Charles Gray and other pro-militancy members of the Men's Political Union. The group had been wound up in 1913 when relations with the Pankhursts became 'exceedingly trying.'

It was just another in a long series of splits. The first had resulted in Charlotte Despard and others leaving the WSPU to form the Women's Freedom League in 1907. The next was the fundamental rift with the Pethick Lawrence's in 1912. Then there was the loss of support from the Men's Political Union in 1913 and finally the expulsions of Sylvia and Adela Pankhurst early in 1914.

By contrast, the NUWSS had grown steadily over the years with an occasional parting of the ways but little dissension. Local organisers would come and go but essentially it displayed remarkable unity under the leadership of Millicent Fawcett. She remained firmly convinced that the militants were harming women's chances of gaining the vote by alienating MPs and the public, a view reinforced by the response in much of rural Devon. Several churches were closed in fear of suffragette outrages, with one notice in the *Crediton Gazette* summing up local feeling. 'The following notice has recently appeared at the entrance to a Churchyard in a rural parish in North Devon. "All unauthorised persons trespassing in the Churchyard will be prosecuted with the utmost rigour of the law. Suffragettes will be shot at sight, and other demons dealt with accordingly."'

Whether women would have gone on to achieve the vote through their own actions is a moot point. It's difficult to avoid the conclusion that the suffragette's arson and bombing campaign was sabotaging any chance of this. But Emmeline and Christabel Pankhurst were seemingly indifferent to the loss of public support and dismissive of the impossible position Asquith found himself in. They pressed on with militancy into July 1914, before a far greater crisis was unleashed, war between Great Britain and Germany. On 4 August Winston Churchill described the scene in London:

> It was eleven o'clock at night – twelve by German time – when the ultimatum expired. The windows of the Admiralty were thrown wide open in the warm night air. Under the roof from which Nelson had received his orders were gathered a small group of admirals and captains and a cluster of clerks, pencils in hand, waiting. Along the Mall from the direction of the Palace the sound of an immense concourse singing 'God save the King' floated in. On this deep wave there broke the chimes of Big Ben; and, as the first stroke of the hour boomed out, a rustle of movement swept across the room. The war telegram signalling, 'Commence hostilities against Germany', was flashed to the ships and establishments under the White Ensign all over the world. I walked across the Horse Guards Parade to the Cabinet room and reported to the Prime Minister and the Ministers who were assembled there that the deed was done.

Christabel's reaction was characteristically controversial. 'War is God's vengeance upon the people who have held women in subjection and by so doing destroyed the perfect human balance.' But she quickly declared that the WSPU would abandon its militant campaign and support the British government, a dictate largely obeyed by the WSPU membership. The *Suffragette* was reborn as *Britannia* and adopted an increasingly nationalistic stance.

In January 1915 Annie Kenney was enthusiastically received in Barnstaple to give a talk under the auspices of the WSPU on, 'The War: Why we need more recruits'. The *Barnstaple and Plymouth Gazette* reported her conclusion that, 'They must fight until a lasting and noble peace was secured... she appealed to those of her male listeners who were not wearing khaki to enlist at once.' *The North Devon Journal* covered Alderman Reavell's vote of thanks to Annie. He opened by saying, '...adversity makes strange bed-fellows... if anyone had told him six months ago that Miss Kenney and he were to appear together on the same platform he should have [called him] a perverter of the truth... he had certainly thought some bitter thoughts about Miss Kenney... But this War... had proved one thing... we knew how to sink our differences and stand four square to the enemy. Thus it was that the lion and the lamb were able to sit down together this evening... Miss Kenney being, of course, the lion, and he the lamb.'

While some continued to lobby for the vote throughout the war, Millicent Fawcett recommended the 500 NUWSS branches suspend suffrage propaganda and focus on relief work. 'Let us show ourselves worthy of citizenship, whether our claim to it be recognised or not.' Groups across Devon followed her lead. Exeter, Tiverton, Ottery St Mary and more all announced a cessation of their political work. In September, Mabel Ramsay left for Antwerp to take charge of a hospital for the wounded, one of many suffragists and suffragettes to volunteer in a medical capacity. Evelina Haverfield and Vera Holme both joined the transport wing of the Scottish Women's Hospitals in Serbia.

As the war began to cast a shadow over all their lives, Millicent Fawcett voiced a parallel uncertainty felt by many. 'There is no forecasting what effect the present war may have on the position of the suffrage question... it is also highly probable that the general isolation and status of women in the eyes of the general public will not be improved. At any rate, we should be ready for all emergencies, ready to restart our suffrage campaign at the first opportunity.'

In 'My Own Story,' written at the end of 1914, Emmeline Pankhurst shared her own, possibly more optimistic, thoughts. 'One thing is reasonably certain, and that is that the Cabinet changes which will necessarily result from warfare will make future militancy on the part of women unnecessary. No future Government will repeat the mistakes and the brutality of the Asquith Ministry. None will be willing to undertake the impossible task of crushing or even delaying the march of women towards their rightful heritage of political liberty and social and industrial freedom.'

Four years later they had their answer.

AT LAST!

Reproduced by kind permission of the Proprietors of "PUNCH," from the cartoon of January 23, 1918, and published by the National Union of Women's Suffrage Societies, 62, Oxford Street, W.1.

Chapter Thirty-Two
Votes for Women
1916 - 1928

In February 1918, contrary to Millicent Fawcett's doubts, war seemed to have achieved what years of campaigning had failed to - votes for women. But by no means all women.

It was a potential crisis over male voters that started the ball rolling. Only men resident in the UK for twelve months prior to a general election were eligible to vote. At a stroke, thousands of servicemen risking their lives for their country were disenfranchised, and a large number of men still had no right to vote at all. Something had to be done. In 1916 an inter-party committee was formed to discuss franchise reform. This Speaker's Conference Committee, as it became known, was chaired by the Speaker of the House of Commons, James William Lowther, the same man who, under pressure from Asquith, had ruled against the women in 1913. It didn't bode well.

But in a startling about-turn, Asquith gave a speech to the Commons that implied he was relaxing his opposition to women's suffrage. Why the change of heart? According to Asquith it was to recognise the vital wartime role of women. Over 700,000 were employed in munitions factories. Thousands more worked on farms, in the docks, government departments and other male-dominated industries such as engineering. Not to speak of the huge increase in women in more traditional working roles as typists and secretaries. More than ever, women realised they could function in the work place as well as men. It was something they wouldn't forget once the war was over.

Asquith knew that when the men returned, women would be ousted from roles that had given them confidence, independence, new skills and an income. They would be forced back into domestic work - creating a fertile recruiting ground for the suffragettes. It would be a flashpoint for a return to, as Asquith put it, 'that detestable campaign that disfigured the annals of political agitation in this country'. The escalation of militancy before the war had divided the suffrage movement. Most thought it did more to hinder than advance the cause. But the prospect of a return to that militancy inevitably played a part in Asquith's about-turn. How could he advocate imprisoning and torturing women who had made such a valuable contribution to the war effort? The last thing society needed now was massive social unrest.

On 12 October 1916 the thirty-four members of the Committee began their deliberations. Women across the country held their breath. Under a headline of 'Is It Victory At Last?' *Votes for Women* considered wildly varying rumours that on the one hand claimed woman suffrage would be omitted altogether, and on the other confirmed that the majority of the Committee were in favour.

At least the press had finally made up its mind:

> There will be great disappointment among men of progressive views if the Committee fail to come to any agreement on the question of women's suffrage… This grievous defect will have to be remedied by a courageous government. *Daily Chronicle.*
>
> If it is true that the Speaker's Conference, while dealing with many questions of registration and franchise, has failed to come to an agreement on woman suffrage, that fact is the gravest possible setback to the cause of justice and reform. *The Herald.*
>
> No great measure of electoral reform would be tolerable, or could be tolerated, without it. *Manchester Guardian.*

The days before the report was published were an anxious time for suffrage societies, finally united under the banner of the National Council for Adult Suffrage. In reality, women's suffrage was very much on the Committee's agenda. In a measure of how far attitudes had changed, they considered awarding women an equal franchise with men. But women outnumbered men in the country and to create a female majority was still seen as a step too far. That proposal was narrowly defeated by ten votes to twelve. They compromised with a recommendation that the franchise should be limited to women who were on the Local Government register, or whose husbands were, and over the age of either thirty or thirty-five. This was the proposal presented to Lloyd George, now Prime Minister, in January 1917.

Two months later, twenty-four suffrage societies led by Millicent Fawcett, but without Emmeline and Christabel Pankhurst, met with Government ministers. (The Pankhursts decided to remain detached from the detailed negotiations to make possible post-war militancy more effective.) Discussion ranged back and forth over a proposal that still fell short of their demand for the vote on the same terms as men. It was a double blow given that all men over 21 would now be able to vote and the voting age for servicemen was being reduced, albeit temporarily, to nineteen. But compromise was inevitable. They agreed to support a Bill if the age limit for women was lowered to thirty.

A few weeks later, in a moment of sublime irony, Herbert Asquith stood in the House of Commons to move that a Bill be introduced in accordance with the Speaker's Conference recommendations. The Bill achieved a massive majority at its first reading, 341 votes to 62. Support was undiminished at the second reading and on 19 June 1917 the Commons approved the women's clause by 387 votes to 57.

The *Manchester Guardian* said it all. 'Women, and not a few select women, but women in their millions, will vote at the next election to be held in this country. That is a tremendous event.'

The question has to be asked. Asquith's about-turn was one thing but why did the overwhelming majority of men in the House of Commons rush to support the suffragist cause? The wartime Coalition Government helped. An all-party agreement on women's suffrage removed the fear that one party might benefit from the enfranchisement of women. But many nurtured another agenda, believing a limited franchise would keep the suffragists happy while delaying the more radical reform of full and equal voting rights for men and women for years to come. Conservative Party support for the Bill was rooted in expediency. Their research revealed that 98 out of 142 constituencies supported votes for women. If this was true of the whole country, then the party faced heavy election defeats if it opposed the women.

Whatever their reasoning, the war made it easier for MPs to give ground without losing face. They weren't giving in to violence, but recognising the valiant efforts of women who were helping the nation through a crisis. Over eight million were now on the cusp of achieving what thousands had campaigned long and hard for over the past 60 years.

The Representation of the People Act 1918, given Royal Assent on 6 February, gave the vote to all men over twenty-one, or nineteen if in service in the war, and every woman of thirty or over who was a member or married to a member of the Local Government Register, a property owner, or a graduate voting in a University constituency. The 7.7 million citizens entitled to vote in 1912 leapt to 21.4 million, with women making up about 43% of the electorate.

The majority of women who had contributed so much to the war effort, many risking their lives in munitions factories, were young and single - the very women still denied the vote. Some saw this as a betrayal, treating them as second-class citizens. This political inequality remained the status quo for ten more years until the Equal Franchise Act of 1928 finally gave women the vote on the same terms as men, bringing the number of women eligible to vote up to 15 million. Emmeline Pankhurst died on 14 June 1928, just 18 days before this landmark moment.

Millicent Fawcett declared 1918 was the greatest moment in her life and indeed, for most, it was a watershed. A victory party was held by suffragist societies at the Queen's Hall in March, and November saw the icing on the cake when the Parliament (Qualification of Women) Act 1918 was passed. Women could now not only vote but stand for election as an MP. The following year a woman stepped inside the Houses of Parliament - not to lobby, to plead or to cajole, but to take her place as an equal among men. That woman was Nancy Astor, representing the constituency of Plymouth Sutton, Devon. She was nominated by Mabel Ramsay and owed a great part of her emphatic victory on polling day to the work of the ladies of the NUWSS.

The day Nancy Astor arrived in London to make her way to the Houses of Parliament created quite a stir. The *Western Times* reported, 'Lady Astor, M.P., on arrival at Paddington from Plymouth on Sunday afternoon, had a big reception. Many women wearing the Suffragette colours greeted her ladyship, and so dense was the crowd of cheering men that policemen had to clear a way for the victor of Plymouth.' [Of course, it's probable that suffragists made up the majority of women in the crowd, a distinction that many reporters continued to struggle with.]

Nancy Astor made history as the first woman to take her seat in Parliament and became a powerful role model. At the centenary of her election, there had been a woman MP in at least one of the Plymouth seats for all but six of the previous 100 years. But she wasn't the first to be elected. That honour goes to Countess Markievicz, an aristocrat's daughter from Southern Ireland. But as she stood for Sinn Féin, she never took her seat, leaving Nancy Astor to take that step into history just a year later.

The WSPU disbanded at the end of the war but the Pankhursts were active within a new organisation, the 'Women's Party', launched in November 1917. Two Devon groups remained loyal - Ilfracombe, with Marie Newby still at the helm, and Torquay, with Mrs Greg as the new Hon. Secretary. The Torquay group were particularly active, hosting talks by Miss Bowerman, the south west organiser for the Women's Party, and Christabel Pankhurst. As *Britannia* reported, her '...thrilling speech at the Pavilion... aroused the greatest enthusiasm... It is felt that a tremendous new source of strength for the Women's Party has been found in Torquay.' The power women now held with the vote, Christabel claimed, brought with it increased responsibility to be a balancing force tending to sanity and reason. The focus for this strength and reason was now to be the fight against Bolshevism.

Devon remained a favourite destination with the Pankhursts, a relationship cemented when the WSPU briefly owned Manorville, a Victorian property in Westward Ho! Emmeline Pankhurst stayed there for several months before leaving for America in 1920.

The Representation of the People Bill received Royal Assent on 6 February 1918, a month that also saw the last edition of *Votes for Women,* the journal the Pethick Lawrences had kept going since their split with the Pankhursts. It had chronicled the movement since October 1907 but now was to close, with any regrets '…overwhelmed by the joy and thankfulness we feel at the victory of our cause.' Frederick Pethick Lawrence reflected on the long struggle:

> Ten and a half years ago! Not very long in the life of an individual; still less in the life of a nation. But to women, what a chasm between then and now.
>
> Ten and a half years ago men assumed, and the great mass of women accepted the assumption, that men's point of view was the right point of view, that democracy meant the rule of men, that women were inferior and subject. Into most men's minds today there has come a doubt as to the truth of this assumption, into most women's minds there has come a certainty that it is false.
>
> Ten and a half years ago this paper was founded as the organ of a little body of people who with eyes of faith saw what is seen now by the multitude. Those were days when… merely to believe in votes for women was to be a crank. While for those who went further… and dared to act on this conviction, the penalty was to become the object of general derision.
>
> Different temperaments produce different actions… The conciliatory suffragists placed their entire confidence in argument and persuasion. The militants… flung themselves on the prejudices of the age with the vigour and determination of youth. Many things went under in the struggle - 'ladylike' reserve, old ideas of womanly dutifulness and wifely obedience, implicit confidence in those in high places, respect for the laws of the land. Thousands made the acquaintance of prison cells… they explored the rottenness of the established order and exposed the truthlessness of officialdom alike in the prison and in the highest positions in the State.
>
> This paper supported from the first the militants, and became the recognised organ of one great section [the WSPU]. The years that followed were packed full of incident. Great public meetings, monster demonstrations, 'raids' on Parliament, ejections from Cabinet Minister's audiences, police court proceedings, sentences

in prison, welcomes on release, hunger strikes, forcible feedings, followed one another with startling rapidity. A series of Suffrage Bills were introduced into the House of Commons and suffered their demise. Pledges were given by statesmen and shamelessly broken. Passions rose and methods of violence succeeded mere defiance of the law.

Division and separations came with the suffrage movement... But looking back on the whole story of the agitation one is struck with the value of the contribution supplied by each section of the movement... The war which changed all Europe changed incidentally the character of the struggle for the suffrage... several suffrage societies put up their shutters... This paper, and the organisation to which it had then become attached [United Suffragists] stuck womanly to their purpose.

His final editorial in *Votes for Women* continued:

> We do not know what the future will contain for the new men and women voters... Looking back over the years, seeing the magnificent sacrifices that have been offered up in the cause of women's freedom, we have no fears as to the use that will be made by women of their votes, working side by side with the men whose citizenship they now share. With our faces set to the future, we greet, for the last time through the pages of *VOTES FOR WOMEN*, all those who have travelled with us to the great day which sees the dawn of women's freedom.

This story began with a dedication and now ends with another. To all those women, named or unknown, who played their part in women's fight for the vote in Devon. Women such as Alison Garland, Caroline Brine, Frances Latimer, the Phear and Bragg sisters, Mary Marrack, Amy Montague, Mabel Ramsay, Maud Slater, Jessie Montgomery, Mary Frood, Mary Leigh Browne, Marie Newby, Annie Ball, Margaret Eldridge, Edith Clarence, Mildred Tuker, Marion Phillips, Gwyneth Keyes, Mary Willcocks, Joan Retallack, Olive Wharry and many more. All dedicated West Country women who refused to accept the status quo.

When thinking of the relative effectiveness of the suffragette and suffragist approaches, the fable of the hare and the tortoise comes to mind. While the WSPU were all about swift, incisive, headline-grabbing actions and events, the NUWSS worked in a committed and unceasing way to win hearts and minds in their local communities.

The jury is still out on which approach was ultimately the most effective. Militancy caught the attention of the country in a way that decades of patient lobbying had failed to, but the backlash amongst politicians and the public alike inevitably played a part in delaying progress. So the question remains. What did most to achieve Votes for Women?

Reason, Rebellion… or War?

This is "THE HOUSE" that man built
But oh what a wonderful change inside
The women as well as the men preside
They both hold the reins & no one complains
For the men now admit that the ladies' have brains
And are every bit quite as fitted to sit
As themselves, in this House that man built.

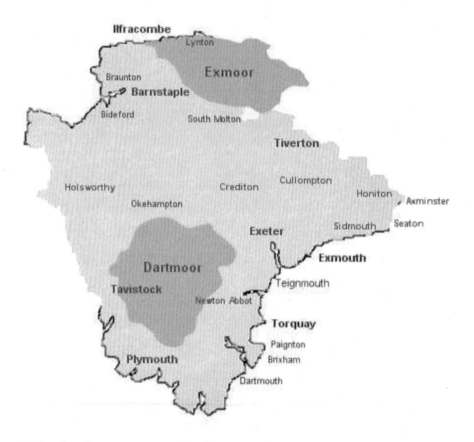

National suffrage groups made a significant investment in Devon, despite its relative distance from the urban centres of activity such as London or Manchester. Why was this?

Devon's population, largely concentrated with the urban areas of Plymouth, Torbay and Exeter, was far larger than any other south western county except the Bristol area of Gloucestershire. A relatively high percentage of the population was made up of middle class women and men, for example in Torbay and East Devon, willing to engage with the suffrage movement whether for or against. Other areas, such as Plymouth, were less prosperous, but with a population of around 230,000 - almost as large as the entire county of Dorset - initially still proved a worthwhile investment of time and effort. The coastal areas were the focus of most campaigning, with some providing surprisingly fertile ground for the militant WSPU.

Map courtesy of:_ ExeterViews.co.uk

Devon Suffrage Timeline

1866: Four Devon women join 1521 others in signing a national petition in support of the vote for women

1870-1908: 253 petitions in favour of Women's suffrage are presented to Parliament from Devon

1871:
- Jane Ronniger speaks at Devonport in favour of the franchise for single and widowed women householders
- Millicent Fawcett tours Tavistock, Plymouth, Devonport & Exeter
- Caroline Brine speaks at Teignmouth

1873:
- Mary Beedy speaks at Plymouth, Exeter, Tavistock, Tiverton & Barnstaple
- Helena Downing speaks at Lynton, Ilfracombe, Teignmouth and Dawlish

1874: Mary Beedy returns accompanied by Lilias Ashworth

1875: Jessie Craigen speaks at Devonport, Exmouth, Exeter & Bideford

1882: Lydia Becker, joined by Caroline Brine, holds a 'Great Demonstration' in Plymouth

1884: Three Towns Women's Liberal Association (WLA) forms in Plymouth with Frances Latimer as President

1889: Mrs Humphrey Ward launches Anti-Suffrage Appeal

1891:
- Women's Suffrage is discussed at WLA conference in Newton Abbot
- Topic is raised in Plymouth, Exeter, Ilfracombe and Barnstaple

1892: Topic of suffrage is kept alive through a growing network of WLAs-inspired by Alison Garland

1896: 17 independent suffrage societies meet to discuss lack of progress

1897: National Union of Women's Suffrage Societies (NUWSS) is formed

1869 -1894: Women win the right to vote in municipal, county and borough council elections

1901-1902: Alison Garland and Mary Marrack lobby within WLAs

1903:
- Phear sisters and Adelaide Montgomery launch Exmouth Women's Suffrage Society
- Anne Martin from Bristol is a speaker at Bideford WLA
- Ethel Phear and Amy Montague hold non-party suffrage meetings in Exmouth and Exeter
- Phear sisters and Adelaide Montgomery launch Exmouth Women's Suffrage Society
- Pankhursts form Women's Social and Political Union (WSPU)

1906: Deputation to Sir Henry Campbell-Bannerman

1907
- Annie Kenney appointed WSPU organiser for the West of England
- Amy Montague organises first WSPU meeting at Exeter, speaker Christabel Pankhurst
- General election - Campaign in Newton Abbot
- WSPU - Emmeline Pankhurst joined by Nellie Martel, Amy Montague, Mary Gawthorpe and others
- NUWSS - Edith Palliser, Selina Cooper, Mrs Tanner

1908:
- Annie and Nell Kenney launch Devon campaign
- Christabel Pankhurst speaks at Plymouth Guildhall
- Annie Kenney and Amy Montague conduct WSPU recruitment tour of Exeter, Torquay, Paignton, Plymouth & Newton Abbot
- Mrs Pethick Lawrence and Annie Kenney at Plymouth Guildhall and in Devonport
- WSPU branch is formed in Plymouth - Gwyneth Keys is secretary
- Devon women attend Hyde Park Rally on Suffrage Sunday
- Anti-Suffrage groups are formed in Exeter, Sidmouth, Torquay & Plymouth
- Autumn WSPU events in Sidmouth, Crediton, Topsham, Appledore, Chulmleigh and Bideford.
- Elsie Howey arrives in November to plan WSPU campaigns in Plymouth, Torquay and Paignton
- Emmeline Pethick Lawrence is a speaker at Plymouth Guildhall
- Sylvia Pankhurst is a speaker at Bath Saloons in Torquay
- NUWSS Organiser Margaret Robertson holds first meetings in Tiverton, Plymouth, Exeter and Sidmouth
- Edith Clarence helps at suffragist shop in Sidmouth

1909:
January
- Men's League for Opposing Women Suffrage is formed
- Adela Pankhurst speaks on Woman's Suffrage at Ilfracombe

February
- Mrs Pankhurst addresses WSPU meetings in Torquay and Plymouth
- NUWSS Exeter branch is launched by organiser Margaret Robertson followed by meetings in Topsham,. Sidmouth, Budleigh Salterton, Newton Abbot, Totnes and Plymouth

March
- Plymouth & Torquay WSPU holding monthly meetings
- Open air meeting in Dartmouth
- WSPU meetings in Paignton
- Growing number of anti-suffrage groups in Honiton, Sidmouth, Budleigh Salterton, Exmouth, Plymouth and Torquay

- Plymouth NUWSS is launched with Clara Daymond as Chair, and Mabel Ramsay as Hon.Sec.

April
- WSPU Shops opened in Plymouth & Torquay
- WSPU organisers: Vera Wentworth in Plymouth. Elsie Howey now Torquay & Paignton
- Weekly WSPU 'At Homes' in Plymouth
- WSPU meetings in Dartmouth, Paignton, Totnes & Teignmouth

May
- Amy Montague of Crediton speaks at Torquay WSPU
- Jessie Kenney, Elsie Howey & Vera Wentworth challenge Prime Minister Asquith at Clovelly Court

July
- Evelina Haverfield and Emmeline Pankhurst in court. Sir Albert De Rutzen refuses their claim to be treated as political prisoners
- Holiday campaign in Ilfracombe
- First WSPU meetings in Tavistock and Torre
- WSPU hold open-air meetings at Devonport Dock Gates, Saltash, Torquay Strand, Plymouth Market Square & St Marychurch
- Exeter WSPU meetings are held daily in anticipation of Earl Carrington's visit
- Mary Phillips, Elsie Howey and Vera Wentworth are arrested in Exeter. They are sentenced to 7 days' imprisonment and become the first hunger strikers in the West Country

August
- WSPU Meetings in Dawlish, Torquay, Paignton and St Marychurch
- Vera Holme makes her first appearance as chauffeur to Mrs Pankhurst

September
- WSPU holiday campaign are conducted in Ilfracombe
- WSPU meeting to hear Exeter hunger strikers
- Reception at Torquay for Miss Elsie Howey after hunger strike

October
- Weekly WSPU 'At Homes' at Barnfield Hall, Exeter

November
- WSPU meetings in Torquay, Exeter, Crediton and Ilfracombe - with Helen Ogston (Lady with the Whip)

December
- Kate James, NUWSS, speaks against militancy in Barnstaple
- Asquith calls general election

1910:
January
- Ex WSPU, now NUWSS, speaker Helen Fraser condemns militancy in speech at Budleigh Salterton

- NUWSS and WSPU conduct election campaigns in Exeter, Plymouth and Paignton
- WSPU Exeter election campaign boosted by Gladice Keevil - they oust the Liberal candidate
- Sir Ernest Soares (Liberal) is returned for Barnstaple
- Annie Kenney draws unprecedented crowds in Bridgwater (Possibly 10,000) - Conservative victory
- Seven Liberals are unseated across the West Country
- Gladice Keevil speaks at Runnacleave Hall, Ilfracombe
- Barnstaple 'At Home' with Helen Ogston

March
- Anti-Suffrage League refuse Exeter NUWSS's challenge to a debate
- Anti-Suffrage League meeting at Killerton House

May
- Death of the King

June
- George Newnes dies at Hollerday House in Lynton. Frank Newnes inherits extensive debts
- Protests at failure of Asquith to progress Conciliation Bill
- Devon suffragettes take part in the Great March in London on June 18th
- Anti-suffrage meetings in Exeter

August
- Ilfracombe launch holiday campaign supported by Helen Craggs - later to be first suffragette imprisoned for arson
- Women's Suffrage meetings held in Barnstaple. Meetings advertised in chalk on pavements. Speakers - Mrs Mackworth & Miss Pridders

September
- Annie Kenney draws crowds at Axminster, Seaton, Lyme Regis, Sidmouth and Ilfracombe
- Edith Clarence hosts Axminster meeting

October
- Ilfracombe WSPU is formed. Meeting addressed by Annie Kenney
- Emmeline Pankhurst visits Exeter. Speaks at the Barnfield Hall and Clarence Hotel
- Juanita Phillips organises meeting at the Dolphin Rooms, Honiton. WSPU branch formed

November
- Lady Isabel Margesson speaks at WSPU meetings in Exeter and Ilfracombe
- Annie Kenney organises series of meetings at Victoria Hall, Exeter
- Lord Lytton speaks at Exeter
- Alice Abadam on tour of South West

- New NUWSS Organiser - Marquerite Norma-Smith begins series of monthly meetings in Plymouth
- NUWSS branches are established in Exeter, Sidmouth, Plymouth, Teignmouth, Ottery St Mary, Topsham and Torquay
- Ada Wright is brutally treated during London protest
- Evelina Haverfield, Elsie Howey, Vera Wentworth, Helen Craggs imprisoned after London protests

December
- WSPU and NUWSS both campaign in Mid Devon as Asquith calls another election
- Women's Freedom League also campaign in Torquay
- WSPU tactics succeed in Torquay, Mid Devon, Tavistock and two Plymouth seats as the Liberals are all ousted

1911:
February
- Letters to North Devon Journal from SUUM CUIQUE - Ilfracombe WSPU
- WSPU meetings at Exeter, Barnstaple and Ilfracombe. Speaker - Frederick Pethick Lawrence
- Torquay WSPU decides on monthly 'At Homes'
- NUWSS Devon Societies now include Exeter, Sidmouth, Teignmouth, Newton Abbot, Three Towns & District and Topsham

April
- Annie Ball in Barnstaple, Mabel Ramsay in Plymouth, Nellie Baker in Torquay and Miss Frood in Topsham host census evaders
- Annie Ball, Nellie Baker, Mildred Tuker and Hope Malleson refuse to pay taxes
- Mrs Kineton Parkes - Women's Tax Resistance League - speaks at Torquay
- Annie Kenney speaks at Ilfracombe, part of a three month campaign including Exeter, South Molton and Dulverton
- By-election in Barnstaple constituency
- Evelina Haverfield purchases Peace Cottage at Brendon
- NUWSS South Western Federation meets in Plymouth

May
- Marie Newby and Evelina Haverfield interview election candidates at Bideford and Appledore
- NUWSS organiser, Marguerite Norma-Smith, visits Lynton, Coombe Martin, Ilfracombe, Bideford, Appledore and Barnstaple as part of the same by-election
- 2nd reading of Women's Suffrage Bill carried with majority of 167
- Anti-Suffrage activity in Plymouth & District

June

- NUWSS forms branches in Barnstaple, Bideford, Instow and Appledore
- Women from Crediton, Exeter, Axminster, Honiton, Ilfracombe, Barnstaple, Plymouth, and Torquay swell estimated 40,000 in the women's Coronation Procession in London.

July
- Ilfracombe WSPU offer 'At Homes' attracting new members
- Marie Newby campaigns with Annie Kenney in the West Somerset by-election
- Marguerite Norma-Smith, NUWSS organiser, also campaigns in West Somerset
- Increasing NUWSS presence in Devon

August
- Annie Ball arranges WSPU stall in Ilfracombe market
- Holiday campaign active throughout Devon
- Edith Clarence particularly active on a 6 week campaign across Devon & Cornwall
- Miss Hatty Baker tours Cornwall and Devon
- Joint NUWSS & WSPU events are planned

September
- Mrs Nash wins a prize in Bideford carnival for her WSPU decorated bicycle
- Annie Kenney leaves as WSPU West Country organiser
- Ilfracombe WSPU organise weekly sewing work-parties

November
- Marie Newby and Evelina Haverfield interview Sir Godfrey Baring at the House of Commons.
- Asquith announces the Manhood Suffrage Bill - women are excluded. Marie Newby joins deputation to Parliament
- NUWSS active in Budleigh Salterton, Ottery St Mary and Plymouth
- Ethel Snowden speaks in Exeter and Plymouth

December
- Miss Davenport is new organiser for SW Federation of NUWSS
- NUWSS numbers increase in response to WSPU militancy
- Launch of Totnes NUWSS Society
- WSPU meeting at Gaiety Hall, Ilfracombe. Speakers - Amy Montague and Jessie Smith

1912:
January
- Mary Willcocks and Miss Davenport speak at NUWSS meetings in Barnstaple, Bideford, Instow, Northam, Appledore

February
- WSPU meetings at Axminster and Torquay
- Other WSPU groups are quieter

- Throughout 1912 some women, such as Marion Phillips, Mary Frood and Mary Willcocks, are involved with both the WSPU and the NUWSS, but are currently more active in the NUWSS
- Ilfracombe most consistently active WSPU group

March
- Marie Newby, Edith Clarence & Olive Wharry are imprisoned in Holloway after taking part in protests in London.
- Marie Newby and Olive Wharry go on hunger strike
- NUWSS Executive member Clara Rackham speaks at Sidmouth, the 8th meeting there that year, Exeter and Plymouth
- Increased anti-suffrage activity in East Devon. Mrs Greatbatch speaks at Ottery St Mary, Exmouth, Sidmouth and Exeter
- Two new branches of the Anti-Suffrage League form in Ottery and Exmouth, adding to Exeter, East Devon, Plymouth and Torquay
- Tax-Resistance sales of goods seized from Annie Ball at Barnstaple. and Ilfracombe
- Christine Wodehouse from Bratton Fleming (cousin of PG Wodehouse) is now Barnstaple NUWSS organiser

June
- Georgina Brackenbury is a speaker at WSPU meetings in Ilfracombe, Axminster & Torquay
- Despite increasing NUWSS numbers, Ilfracombe remains committed to the militant WSPU

July
- Newly appointed prospective Liberal Candidate, Henry Harben, resigns in protest at force-feeding
- Marion Phillips defends WSPU militancy then joins Gwyneth Keys & Mabel Ramsay at NUWSS event
- Successful Torquay WSPU Holiday Campaign
- Edith Clarence supports Glasgow holiday campaign

August
- Ilfracombe WSPU launch holiday campaign
- During spring/summer significant NUWSS activity in Barnstaple, Exeter, Exmouth, Newton Abbot, Tiverton and Plymouth

October
- H.A.Baker adopted as new Liberal candidate in North Devon - confirmed anti-suffragist
- WSPU Barnstaple meeting with Miss Abadam and Rev Hatty Baker
- Pankhursts split with the Pethick Lawrences. Ilfracombe WSPU post regularly in the Pankhurst's new publication *The Suffragette*

1913:
January
- NUWSS are active in Exeter and Sidmouth through the winter

February
- Women's Liberal Association challenge H.A.Baker on his anti-suffrage stance - without success
- Ilfracombe WSPU defend militancy in the local papers
- Olive Wharry, from Whitstone near Holsworthy, is arrested for arson of Kew Gardens tea pavilion. Sentenced to 18 months
- WSPU losing members to NUWSS due to increasing militancy

March
- Olive Wharry is released under Cat and Mouse Act after hunger striking for 32 days
- Marie Newby writes to paper on the need for militancy
- NUWSS Provincial Council meet in Exeter. Concerns over militancy. Fresh commitment made to peaceful campaigning

April
- Suffragettes open a shop at 2 High Street, Ilfracombe
- Ilfracombe WSPU launches weekly debates
- NUWSS stress non-militancy message in Bideford
- Increased WSPU activity in Plymouth with new organiser, Mary Phillips
- Marion Phillips, Gwyneth Keys and Edith Fewins active with Plymouth WSPU again
- WSPU places bomb at Smeaton's Tower in Plymouth
- More militant acts reported in Devon. Telephone wires cut, postboxes are attacked in Plymouth, Exeter and Torquay
- Windows at Plymouth's Inland Revenue Offices smashed

May
- Well attended WSPU meetings at Ilfracombe. A dozen women vote in favour of militancy
- Ilfracombe WSPU explain and justify militancy in the press
- Charles Gray, from the Men's Political Union for Women's Enfranchisement, justifies militancy in Ilfracombe and Plymouth
- Mrs Kineton Parkes, Secretary of the Women's Tax Resistance League, speaks in Torquay and Exeter
- Mary Phillips condones bomb in St Paul's Cathedral

June
- Ilfracombe & Plymouth WSPU send flowers to Emily Davison's funeral
- NUWSS meetings held in Bideford and Barnstaple
- Bideford is labelled an anti-suffrage neighbourhood
- NUWSS Pilgrimage sets out from Land's End
- Mabel Ramsay hosts reception for pilgrims in Plymouth

July
- Pilgrimage visits Totnes, Newton Abbot - a crowd of 3,000 - Teignmouth, Dawlish, Starcross and Exmouth

- At Exeter Pilgrims are joined by contingents from Topsham, Torquay, Sidmouth and Crediton
- 300 suffragists process through Exeter - up to 7,000 spectators
- Place of honour at Hyde Park reserved for Annie Ramsay, Mabel Ramsay's mother, who made the entire distance from Land's End
- Women's Freedom League (WFL) organiser, Constance Andrews, launches Devonshire Holiday Campaign from their HQ in Torquay
- WFL public meetings held in Torquay, Paignton, Babbacombe, and Brixham and an 'At Home' at Stoke Fleming.
- Stoke Fleming meeting jointly organised by WFL and WSPU
- Mary Phillips speaks at Torquay & Ilfracombe on militancy
- Police patrol GWR line from Tiverton Junction to Hele overnight after threatening telegram received from militants
- Suffragette bomb at Taunton theatre

August
- Suffragette arson of Hollerday House, Lynton, North Devon
- Fire on Dunkery Beacon, Exmoor
- Haystacks on fire at Stringston, Somerset
- Reports of further suffragette activity in North Devon
- Chief Constable issues a warning to be vigilant

September
- NUWSS growing in South Devon with regular meetings in Budleigh Salterton, Sidmouth, Newton Abbot, Ottery St Mary, Plymouth, Tiverton, Topsham, Exeter, Torquay and Totnes
- Launch of Torquay and Paignton WFL branch
- Jessie Montgomery resigns as secretary of Exeter NUWSS to join the Conservative and Unionist Women's Franchise Association

November
- Margaret Eldridge is ejected from Ilfracombe WLA meeting
- North Devon NUWSS meetings in North Molton, Instow, Barnstaple and Bideford with organiser, Ruth Giles
- NUWSS 'Forest of Christmas Trees' fete is held in Exeter
- NUWSS Honiton branch launched

December
- WSPU campaign in Plymouth in advance of the arrival of Mrs Pankhurst from America
- Mrs Pankhurst is arrested on board, the authorities thwarting waiting suffragettes, and is taken to Exeter prison
- Suffragettes hold a vigil outside Exeter prison
- Retaliatory WSPU action - fire at a Devonport timber yard and Hancock's Fun Fair
- Significant NUWSS activity in Sidmouth, Tiverton, Topsham, Newton Abbot, Torquay, Totnes and Exeter
- Exeter NUWSS host meeting with Millicent Fawcett

1914:
January-March
- Ilfracombe WSPU meetings continue
- NUWSS at Barnstaple now chaired by Miss Rosalie Chichester
- NUWSS speakers address meetings in Bideford, Instow, Barnstaple and Landkey
- NUWSS caravan tour visits Holsworthy, Black Torrington, Great Torrington, South Molton, Chulmleigh, Lapford, North Tawton, Okehampton, Bridestowe, Lydford, and Tavistock
- NUWSS take a stall in South Molton market
- Anti-Suffrage meetings in Sidmouth, Exmouth and Exeter

April
- Flora Drummond is booked to speak at Ilfracombe
- Flora Drummond arrested so replaced by Barbara Wylie
- NUWSS dominate the Devon suffrage movement with the exception of Ilfracombe, still an island of militancy

May
- Large gathering in South Molton for NUWSS meeting

June
- Lynton Lighthouse closed due to suffragettes
- Fire at Lynton Town Hall attributed to suffragettes
- Churches in North Devon are closed - fear of suffragette outrages
- Bideford Bowling Pavilion destroyed by fire
- Rumours of suffragettes at Westward Ho! golf links

July
- Morning Post includes Hollerday House in list of suffragette arson attacks. Cites loss as £9,000
- NUWSS meetings in George Nympton and South Molton

August
- Exeter, Tiverton, Ottery St Mary and more NUWSS groups across Devon announce a cessation of their political work in favour of support for the war effort
- Mabel Ramsay takes charge of a hospital in Antwerp
- Evelina Haverfield and Vera Holme join transport wing of Scottish Women's Hospitals in Serbia
- Elsie Howey left public life, her health damaged by numerous imprisonments

1915:
- Annie Kenney speaks in Barnstaple in support of the war effort

1916:
- Suffrage Societies unite under banner of the National Council for Adult Suffrage
- October - Speaker's Conference Committee meets to discuss franchise reform

1917

- 17 June - Parliament passes Bill granting the vote to every woman of thirty or over

1918:

- 6 February - Representation of the People Act extends vote to all men over 21, or 19 if in service in the war, and every woman thirty or over who was a member of the Local Government Register, or married to a member, a property owner, or a graduate
- 21.4 million citizens now entitled to vote; women make up 43%
- November - Parliament (Qualification of Women) Act passed allowing women to stand as MPs.
- WSPU disbands
- Ilfracombe and Torquay continue to hold meetings as part of Pankhurst's new Women's Party.

1919:

- Manorville, Westward Ho! bought by the WSPU
- Nancy Astor, supported by Mabel Ramsay and Plymouth NUWSS, is the first woman to take her seat in Parliament, representing Plymouth Sutton constituency

1920:

- Emmeline Pankhurst stays at Manorville before visiting America
- Many Devon suffragists are active in subsequent decades in social and community roles

Illustrations

Selected Bibliography

Atkinson, Diane, *The Suffragettes in Pictures* (The History Press, 2010)

Atkinson, Diane, *Rise Up Women! The Remarkable Lives of the Suffragettes* (Bloomsbury Publishing, 2018)

Bearman C.J., *An Examination of Suffragette Violence* (English Historical Review, April 2005)

Boyce, Lucienne, *The Bristol Suffragettes* (Silverwood, 2013)

Bradley, Katherine, *Friends & Visitors: A First History of the Women's Suffrage Movement in Cornwall 1870-1914* (The Hypatia Trust, 2000)

Bush, Julia, *Women Against the Vote* (Oxford University Press)

Christie, Peter, *A North Devon Chronology. The Heritage Album. 175 years in Devon (1824 -1999)* (Courtesy North Devon Journal)

Colmore, Gertrude, *Suffragette Sally* (Broadview Press, 2008)

Cowman, Krista, *Women of the Right Spirit: Paid Organisers of the Women's Social and Political Union* (Manchester University Press, 2007)

Crawford, Elizabeth, *The Women's Suffrage Movement in Britain and Ireland: A Regional Survey* (Routledge, 2006)

Friederichs, Hulda, *The Life of Sir George Newnes*, (1911)

Glasspool, Tracey, *Struggle and Suffrage in Plymouth* (Pen & Sword History, 2019)

Gray, Todd, *Remarkable Women of Devon* (The Mint Press, 2009)

Harrison, Brian, *Separate Spheres* (Croom Helm Ltd, 1978)

Joannou, Maroula, *The Women's Suffrage Movement: New Feminist Perspectives* (Manchester University Press, 1998)

Kenney, Annie, *Memories of a Militant* (E. Arnold, 1924)

Harrison, Shirley, *Sylvia Pankhurst: A Crusading Life 1882-1960.* (Arum Press)

Heathcote, Sally, *Suffragette* (Jonathan Cape, 2014)

Law, Cheryl, *Suffrage and Power: The Women's Movement 1918-1928* (I.B.Tauris, 2000)

Liddington, Jill, *Vanishing for the Vote: Suffrage, Citizenship and the Battle for the Census* (Manchester University Press, 2014)

Lytton, Constance, *Prisons and Prisoners, The Stirring Testimony of a Suffragette* (Virago, 1988)

Metcalf, A.E. *Women's Effort: A Chronicle of British Women's Fifty Years' Struggle for Citizenship 1865-1914* (Oxford, 1917)

Mackenzie, Midge, *Shoulder to Shoulder.* (Harmondsworth, 1975)

Neville, Julia; Auchterlonie, Mitzi; Auchterlonie, Paul; Roberts, Ann, *Devon Women in Public and Professional life 1900-1950* (University of Exeter Press, 2021)

Pankhurst, Christabel, *Unshackled: The Story of How we Won the Vote.* Ed Lord Pethick Lawrence (London, 1959)

Pankhurst, E. Sylvia: *The Suffragette Movement: An Intimate Account of Persons and Ideals* (Virago, 1977)

Pankhurst, E. Sylvia, *The Suffragette: The History of the Women's Militant Suffrage Movement 1905-1910* (New York, 1911)

Pankhurst, Emmeline, *My Own Story; The Autobiography of Emmeline Pankhurst* (Virago, 1979)

Pugh, Martin, *The Pankhursts*, (Vintage Books, 2008)

Pugh, Martin, *The March of the Women* (Oxford University Press, 2000)

Purvis, June, *Emmeline Pankhurst: A Biography* (Routledge, 2002)

Purvis, June, *Christabel Pankhurst: A Biography* (Routledge, 2018)

Raeburn, Antonia, *The Militant Suffragettes* (Michael Joseph, 1973)

Rendel, Dr Margherita, *The Campaign in Devon for Women's Suffrage, 1866-1908* (Rep.Trans.Devon. Ass.Advmt Sci., 140, 111-151)

Robinson, Jane, *Hearts and Minds* (Doubleday, 2018)

Rosen, Andrew, *Rise up Women! The Militant campaign of the Women's Social and Political Union 1903-1914* (London, 1974)

Rowbotham, Judith, & Stevenson, Kim, *A Point of Justice - Granted or Fought For? Women's Suffrage Campaigns in Plymouth and the South West* (Plymouth Law and Criminal Justice Review, 2016)

Stopes, Charlotte, *The Women's Suffrage Bill in the Queen's Year.* (Report of the Women's Suffrage Societies conference, 1896)

Sykes, Christopher, *Nancy. The Life of Lady Astor* (Granada, 1979)

Tregidga, Gary (Ed) *Killerton, Camborne and Westminster* (Devon & Cornwall Record Society, 2006)

Webb, Simon, *The Suffragette Bombers* (Penn & Sword History, 2014)

Wilson, Gretchen, *With All Her Might* (Holmes & Meier, 1998)

Suffrage Newspapers
Anti-Suffrage Review
Votes for Women (WSPU 1907-12),
Votes for Women (Ed. Pethick Lawrences' 1912-1914)
Votes for Women (United Suffragists 1914-1918)
Suffragette (WSPU 1912-1915)
Britannia (WSPU 1915-1918)
Women's Franchise (NUWSS)
Common Cause (NUWSS)
Free Church Suffrage Times
The Vote (WFL)
Women's Signal
Women's Suffrage Journal
Women's Suffrage Record

National Papers
Bath Chronicle & Weekly Gazette
Birmingham Daily Mail
Daily Chronicle
Daily Herald

Daily Telegraph
Daily Express
Illustrated London News
Langport & Somerton Herald
Liverpool Daily Post & Mercury
Luton Times and Advertiser
Manchester Guardian
Manchester Courier
Morning Post
Newcastle Journal
Pall Mall Gazette
Surrey Herald
The Daily News
The Daily Graphic
The Evening News
The Globe
The Guardian
The Morning Post
The Times
The West Briton
The Yorkshire Post

Local Newspapers
Bath Courier and Weekly Gazette
Bath Chronicle
Bideford Gazette
Brixham Western Guardian
Crediton Gazette
Dartmouth & South Hams Chronicle
Exeter & Plymouth Gazette
Exeter Flying Post
Exmouth Journal
Express & Echo
Ilfracombe Chronicle
Ilfracombe Gazette
North Devon Journal
North Devon Herald
Royal Cornwall Gazette
Sidmouth Herald
Somerset & North Devon Gazette
Tavistock Gazette
Teignmouth Post & Gazette
Torquay Times
The West Briton & Cornwall Advertiser
Western Daily Mercury

West Somerset Free Press
Western Evening Herald
Western Times
Western Morning News

Journals
English Historical Review
History Magazine
Justice
Nineteenth Century
The Englishwoman's Review
Transactions of the Devonshire Association
Women's History Review

Archives
Barnstaple Athenaeum
Bideford & District Community Archive
Braunton Museum
British Library
British Museum
Gloucester Archive
Ilfracombe Museum
London Museum
Sidmouth Museum
The National Archives
Women's Library, LSE
West Country Studies Library

Internet resources
www.britishnewspaperarchive.com
www.nationalarchives.gov.uk/archon
www.thesuffragettes.org
www.lucienneboyce.com
www.womanandhersphere.com
https://www.spartacus-educational.com/women.htm
https://centenaryaction.org.uk/about/our-story/
www.suffragettesandsuffragists.com

The Power of Three
Thomas Fowler, Devon's Forgotten Genius
Winner of the Devon History Society W.G.Hoskins Prize 2017

WOODEN COMPUTER INVENTED IN NORTH DEVON. A striking headline for a provincial newspaper. The article in the *North Devon Journal* continued 'It is fascinating... to know that one of the original pioneers of the computer was a self-taught bookseller and printer of Torrington who was born over 200 years ago. His name was Thomas Fowler.' But surely 'the father of computing' was Charles Babbage? Who was Thomas Fowler?

It was a question that was to take Pamela on an emotional journey, from excitement at this charismatic inventor's early success to despair at his betrayal, from admiration of his ingenuity to the agony of obscurity. Despite an initial reluctance to peer over the precipice into the world of mathematics and the history of computing, she knew this was a story that had to be told.

Thomas Fowler died in 1843 but the final chapter of his story has yet to be written. As twenty-first century scientists rediscover his ground-breaking work, perhaps there is still time for Fowler's dying wish to be fulfilled. 'My greatest wish was to have had a thorough investigation of the whole principle of the Machine and its details as far as I could then explain them, in a way very different from a popular exhibition - this investigation I hope it will still have by some first rate Man of Science before it be laid aside or adopted.'

"Fowler's calculator was in certain respects vastly more promising than Babbage's." Dr Doron Swade MBE, previously Assistant Director and Head of Collections at the Science Museum, London.

"Computers might have changed history and our world almost a century sooner than they did had the ideas of Fowler been understood and adopted by Babbage." Ralph Merkle, Senior Research Fellow at the Institute for Molecular Manufacturing, California, and co-inventor of public key cryptography.

For more information see www.boundstonebooks.co.uk.

Seeds of Doubt

On the evening of 15 August 1952 one of the worst floods ever to hit the west of England destroyed the beautiful coastal village of Lynmouth in North Devon. Newspaper headlines reflected the nation's shock at the scale of this natural disaster. Thirty-four men, women and children lost their lives that night.

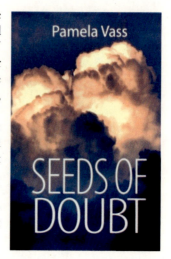

There is no doubt that this was a disaster: but a natural one? There are those who still believe that the events of that night were not so much an Act of God as an Act of Man. This novel blends fact and fiction in a story of one woman's struggle to expose those who contrive to manipulate one of the greatest powers on earth - the weather.

Reader Reviews

"I finished Seeds of Doubt last night. It was a great book… I loved the story, Ingrid's voyage and struggle, and the sense of Devon and history. The research struck me as particularly impressive… thanks for the entertainment of a great book." Simon Hall - Home Affairs correspondent BBC South West.

"…Just had to let you know that I REALLY enjoyed your book – it is well written & constructed, and a very good read."

"…To build a conspiracy thriller on an event as well known as the Lynmouth flood disaster, and to make it both plausible and exciting, is no mean feat. The dialogue is well written and convincing and the plot is unpredictable with enough twists to keep any thriller reader happy."

"…I've just finished Seeds of Doubt; WONDERFUL. I loved it; it has all the right ingredients - drama, tension, intrigue, love, secrets, danger and truth. Looking through the references, why hasn't this made more of a splash (unintended pun) in the national and local press? It's huge. Thank you so much for a thought provoking and thoroughly edge of the seat read."

" … I couldn't put (it) down! It is an amazing story, vividly written… some of your insights and descriptions are so 'word perfect' and then there are the subtle sub plots! The actual theoretical basis is very disturbing - terrifying? - and so it took some hours in the day to shake off from being inside the book. Remarkable. Brilliant! Thrilling. Enthralling…"

Shadow Child
Some Secrets Should Never Be Told.

Nine year old Paul wakes to find his mother standing at his bedroom door. 'I'll just be a minute.' she says. And disappears. He fights against a future decided by others, certain of only one thing - his mother's love.

But why did she leave? Where did she go? He never stops searching. Not as a child. Not as a Man.

Finally he believes he has the answer. But the past casts a long shadow, ensnaring him in a relentless search for the absolute truth - whatever the cost.

Set against the dramatic backdrop of North Devon and the island of Lundy, Shadow Child draws the reader into a world of loss and longing, a world with a deadly secret at its heart.

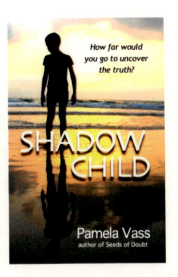

Reader reviews

"Shadow Child is fantastic. You have such a gift for touching people's emotions."

"A very emotive & intriguing subject... Your vast knowledge and experience of the subject really shine through and it is so well written."

"I could not put your book down; a great book."

"I read Shadow Child a little while ago. It was amazing…"

"I have just read Shadow Child. It was a brilliant read …"

"Fantastic book, one you can't put down once you've started. A very gripping story very well portrayed."

"Pamela Vass evokes a good sense of time and place in this dark look at the effects of abandonment. It moves slowly but you are compelled to keep turning the page."

About the Author

Pamela Vass was drawn to England's West Country forty years ago to complete a research degree at Exeter University. It was only afterwards that she discovered a family tree firmly rooted in Devon soil. Since then it has provided much of the inspiration for her writing.

Pamela spent several years as Founder and Director of *The Whodunnit Company*, plotting murder mystery events in the UK and abroad. While directing an event in North Devon, Pamela came across a rumour that outside agencies had played a part in the floods that devastated Lynmouth in 1952. This led her to the National Archive at Kew and previously secret government documents that proved irresistible to a mystery writer. In *Seeds of Doubt*, Pamela blends fact and fiction in a story of one woman's struggle to expose those who contrive to manipulate one of the greatest powers on earth - the weather.

Prior to Whodunnit, Pamela was a social worker with Barnardos and two Social Services Departments, professional experience that provides a strong foundation for *Shadow Child*. This gritty and realistic depiction of the challenges faced by a child abandoned by his mother takes an unexpected turn when his quest for the truth threatens his very future.

Discovering untold stories from the past holds a fascination for Pamela. A scrap of paper about an unknown inventor launched her on a search for the truth about the mathematician and inventor, Thomas Fowler. The result was her prize-winning book, *The Power of Three*. A little later someone asked, 'We all know what happened in London with the suffragettes, but what was the story in Devon?' *Reason or Rebellion? Women's Fight for the Vote in Devon* is her answer. Rumour has it that someone has just asked the same question about Cornwall.

Pamela continues to live and write in the West Country, finding inspiration in its unique landscape and the stories it holds.

For more information see <u>www.boundstonebooks.co.uk</u>